*The Truth
about the Virgin*

I have clung to Thy Truth. (1QH 7:20)

I [thank Thee O Lord], for Thou hast enlightened me through Thy Truth. (1QH 7:26)

. . . instruct them in the mysteries of marvelous Truth that in the midst of the men of the community they may walk perfectly together in all that has been revealed to them. (1QS 9:18–19)

. . . this concerns the men of truth who keep the Law, whose hands shall not slacken in the service of truth. . . . (1QpHab 7:10–13)

When they march out to battle, they shall write on their standards, Truth of God. . . . (1QM 4:6)

SEX AND RITUAL
IN THE DEAD SEA SCROLLS

The Truth
about the Virgin

ITA SHERES AND
ANNE KOHN BLAU

Foreword by
David Noel Freedman

Continuum   New York

For the men of good heart in our lives:

Fred, David, Roger, Emmanuel, Mosche,
Adam, Laurence, Iftach, Douglas, Emil

We also wish to acknowledge the invaluable assistance of David Noel Freedman, who read the manuscript very carefully and made innumerable suggestions, most of which we hope we finally addressed.

3-12-21

1995
The Continuum Publishing Company
370 Lexington Avenue, New York, NY 10017

Printed in the United States of America

ISBN 0-8264-0816-8

Library of Congress Catalog Card Number 95-69621

Contents

Short Historical Chronology
(with a focus on the Judean Second Commonwealth)

334 B.C.E.	Alexander the Great's campaigns in Asia
323–230	The rule of the Ptolemies (Egypt)
305–264	The rule of the Seleucids (Syria)
250	The Septuagint (LXX) translation
197	Judea becomes a province of the Seleucid empire
187–175	Onias III, the Zadokite high priest, resists the influence of Hellenism
175–164	Onias is deposed and replaced by Jason, a Hellenophile; Antiochus IV (Epiphanes) rules the Seleucid empire
172	Jason is expelled in favor of Menelaus, who is a hellenizer
171	Onias III is murdered with Menelaus's initiative; there is forced mass hellenization
169	Antiochus (led by Menelaus) plunders and pollutes the Jerusalem Temple
167	Jerusalem Temple becomes a shrine to Zeus
166	The rise of the Maccabees
164	Cleansing of the Temple
161	Judas Maccabee killed in battle. Jonathan assumes leadership of the rebels
152–145	Jonathan appointed high priest
143–134	Simon is high priest and ethnarch
142	Jonathan executed in prison
140	Foundation of the Maccabean/Hasmonean dynasty
135/134	John Hyrcanus I is high priest and ethnarch; opposed by the Pharisees
135/134–104	John Hyrcanus I is high priest and ethnarch; opposed by the Pharisees

104–103   Aristobulus I is high priest and king
103–76   Alexander Jannaeus is high priest and king. Disliked by Pharisees
76–67   Alexandra (Jannaeus's widow) is queen; she is favored by the Pharisees; Hyrcanus II is high priest
67–63   Aristobulus II is king and high priest; he is taken prisoner by Pompey in 653 after the latter conquers Judea, which then becomes a Roman province
63–40   Hyrcanus II is high priest
37–4   Herod the Great. Hasmonean dynasty comes to an end; Hyrcanus executed in 30
6 (?)   Birth of Jesus
27–30(?) C.E.   Ministry and death of Jesus
66–70   The Great Jewish Rebellion against Rome; destruction of Jerusalem and the Temple by Titus
74   The fall of Masada

DAVID NOEL FREEDMAN

Foreword

In his description of the Essenes, Josephus, the Jewish historian of the first century C.E. (ca. 37–199), states that those initiated into full membership in the community made "tremendous oaths" and, among other solemn commitments, promised to guard the sacred secrets of the group. Now that many of the documents of the Essenes have been discovered, studied, edited, and published, have we learned any of these dark secrets that the members of the community vowed to keep? Although much is known about the underlying principles and basic convictions shared by the sectarians, the organization and operation of their community, and something of the history and expectations of the group, little in the way of supersecret information or arcane knowledge of heavenly mysteries has emerged. There have been hints and allusions to such closely held confidential data, and these clues continue to stir the scholarly pot and challenge researchers in the Dead Sea Scrolls. Perhaps such secret information was reserved for the leadership and kept in memory and transmitted orally, so that no record has survived. In this connection, it is noteworthy that not a single one of the leaders of the community is mentioned or known by a personal name in the Qumran documents; all of them are anonymous and are known only through descriptive titles, as, for example, the most important leader, the Teacher of Righteousness, and others such as the Star, the Wicked Priest, the Angry Lion, and so on. Similarly, the infamous *Copper Scroll,* with its long list of buried treasures, including precious metals and sacred vestments, may reflect an aspect of community life that was intended to be hidden not only from the world but also from all but the leadership, with special care being taken to keep the document itself from prying eyes.

Apart from secrets of a practical nature, designed to protect the personnel and especially the leaders from being identified and attacked by their enemies and to secure the valuable properties of the community from theft or seizure, there are occasional suggestions in the extant literature—particularly in the more recently edited and published documents of the community—about arcane lore and esoteric practices. The authors of the present new book on the Scrolls have made a special study of some of these less well known and much more obscure materials. They have probed more deeply than most into sectarian works of a highly speculative kind, whose complex language and confusing contents are made even more difficult by the fragmentary and dilapidated condition of the manuscripts. At many of the most crucial points, there are gaps in the manuscripts or vital pieces are torn away. Much of the contents of the esoteric texts is more puzzling than clarifying, and, through the accident of wear and tear, unintentionally produces more questions than answers. Nevertheless, these texts offer glimpses and clues, tantalizing hints about secret doctrines and restricted rites of a very startling nature, which were fully worthy of the severe constraints imposed upon the participants and observers. The authors proceed chapter by chapter, step by step, to expose and expound the mysterious rituals of the Essenes until, at the end, the reader will be amazed and astounded. The approach and methodology adopted are entirely rational and logically ordered, and each new stage follows plausibly from the preceding ones. The argument gathers both weight and speed as the narration proceeds from beginning to climax and conclusion. When it is over, the reader will be breathless, if not totally persuaded.

Ultimately, there may not be enough specific data to settle the case conclusively or to prove the case beyond a reasonable doubt, but the main thesis and its argument have great heuristic value and fully deserve an extended hearing on the part of the scholarly community and the reading public. The authors' exploration into the very core of the community's secret doctrines and practices, its existence and eschatological hope, opens up rich veins of precious ore for future mining, centrally important issues for serious discussion and debate. This pioneering work is not for the fainthearted but will light the way for intrepid searchers for the truth, no matter how startling or shocking it may prove to be.

As with any detective story, it would violate literary and critical protocol to describe the results of the authors' labors specifically or in detail. Suffice it to say that the expanded title of the book offers significant clues to the direction of the inquiry and the location of the sacred secrets of the Essenes.

Preface

The Truth about the Virgin is the product of our effort to come to terms with gender issues in the Dead Sea Scrolls. While there is widespread recognition that gender played some kind of role in the Scrolls, there has not been yet any serious scholarly endeavor in that direction. This book is the first one to deal with women and their place in the "camps" of the sectarians. Although some of our conclusions might be considered startling, they are simply the result of our careful reading and analysis of the texts. Other scholars and commentators may wish to pursue this topic further, and still others may read these texts differently. This is the nature of scholarly analysis.

Introduction

And God blessed them and said: "Be fruitful and multiply and fill the earth. . . ." (Genesis 1:28)

The Dead Sea Scrolls, found in hillside caves near Qumran in the Judean desert, are undoubtedly the most important archaeological discovery of our century. Because of what appears to be a close link between the Scrolls and other books from the same period—the turn of the millennium—this critical epoch, the missing link between Judaism and Christianity in this critical epoch is finally becoming decipherable to us. Although those sacred manuscripts were written over a period of time, their unified ideology speaks to their separate, sectarian nature. Whether the distinct group in which this literature arose and its leader, "the Teacher of Righteousness," were Essenes,[1] as was first reported, or Hasideans, or Nazarenes, or People of the Way, or "sons of Zadok" (as they refer to themselves in the Scrolls), their "zeal" for keeping Jewish Law as they understood it, their piety, their holy warrior stance and their proto-Christian beliefs and practices speak for a unique paradox. The most striking, overwhelming sense one gets from reading these texts, besides their poetic pathos in the face of a historic Jewish tragedy, is their uncanny similarity to the New Testament,[2] for example, "For those who are blessed [of him will in]herit the earth . . ." (4QpPs^a 3:9 [quotation of Ps. 37:21–22]) or, "And the humble shall possess the earth and they shall delight in the abundance of peace" (4QpPs^a 2:9 [quotation of Ps 37:11]).[3] Further,

Words of blessing. The Master shall bless them that fear [God and do] His will. . . . May He [favor] you with every [heavenly] blessing; [May He unlock for you the] everlasting [fountain; may He not withhold the waters of life from] them that thirst. (1QSb 1:1–15)[4]

In addition, there are numerous references to an important chosen "son" who will lead the community on the right path.[5] Scholars who are studying these texts have reached differing and sometimes contradictory conclusions about dates and origins of the texts. The most befuddling of interpretations are those just published in a flurry of controversy. This is not helpful to general readers who are interested in the subject and wish to understand the meaning of the Scrolls and their contribution to Western culture.

The messages of the Dead Sea Scrolls are not self-evident; their meaning is hidden beneath layers of symbolic allusions covered over by centuries of silence. Although the ancient public would have understood the symbols and their meaning, we have lost that awareness. Moreover, for the ancients, only some of the special secrets alluded to in these documents would have required privileged knowledge, but to us almost all is esoteric and demands interpretation. Indeed, the whole mind-set of the time, which integrated the natural world with the supernatural, is strange to us. Other texts from that era use the same symbols to describe the same traumatic events in the same hidden way,[6] as do some later religious classics from the rabbinic sages, the church fathers, and later generations of sectarian mystics.

To make the background facts and setting more accessible to our audience, we introduce each chapter in this book with a "brief" about the topic. Throughout the book we include material that will illuminate much of the popular meaning of the ancient symbolic system as well as delve into the deeper, secret symbolic layer. This introduction and chapter 1 will cover the basic mythological and historical references which members of the Qumran community took as common knowledge and on which they built their new interpretations.[7] Although we assume that the Scrolls and other closely associated texts were all written around the turn of the millennium (end of the first century B.C.E. through the first century of the Common Era), coinciding with Roman rule (thus explaining the heightened feelings of tragedy of the Jews in Judea/Palestine), our specialized area of interest in this literature does not depend on fixing precise dates. We focus on the general social context that justified the development of the revolutionary ideology apparent in the texts. We address the legacy of the Scrolls for two thousand years of gender relations in the Western world, especially the promotion of virginity as an ideal. We also share our insights for unlocking the Scrolls' innermost secrets by analyzing two unique rituals performed by the sectarians: the Angelic Sabbath ritual and the rite of Immaculate Conception.

The key texts to which we refer appear to be a relatively unified body of literature—more so even than the books of the Bible.[8] Indeed, we find the traditional classification of some of these ancient texts as apocryphal, pseudepigraphal, Gnostic, and so on to be somewhat arbitrary, because they manifest an extraordinary degree of consistency with the Dead Sea Scrolls. Many of the Scrolls found among the caches in the caves near the Dead Sea, fragmentary though they may be, suggest sectarian authorship, perhaps even multigenerational. As for the Scrolls themselves, it seems that the first account of them, which set them within an obscure Judean sect of "Essene" monks during the Greek-dominated, Maccabean third—first centuries B.C.E., has taken on a life of its own—so much so that people tend to overlook, or conveniently ignore, the fact that there were women's graves found in the cemetery at Qumran.[9] Many still resist the awesome ecumenical conclusion that the Scrolls provide, namely, that there are close links and crossovers between Second Temple Judaism and early Christianity.[10]

We also recognize the partial value of hindsight in particular texts that date a few centuries later. We find that all these writings, the Scrolls and what we call their companion books, are well versed in the same ideology, and all of them rely on similar literary techniques to pass their message on. We will show that the Dead Sea Scrolls now permit access to this imaginative and secret-laden landscape designed to evade censorship and punishment.

How do the Scrolls fit into the larger picture of Israelite history and ideology? We begin by charting a few historical moments that might have contributed to a focused ideology that promoted male exclusivity and female subordination and enabled the Dead Sea sectarians finally to operate the way they did in the desert.

HISTORICAL HIGHLIGHTS

And the clans gathered in the high desert in front of the cave/temple of the holy of holies awaiting the morning star that announces the coming of the sun-deity. The people huddle together; they suffer in their hunger, and all the treasures stored up in the temple/cave, even the secret markings on the precious sunlit metal scroll cannot express their plight. The priestess calls them to the ritual day of atonement for the famine and announces that the goddess invites the chosen patriarch to break bread and drink the holy elixir before undertaking the task of redeeming the land, barren of grain and animal. The ritual procession gets under way; the women lead the group wailing and pounding on their copper pans. The priestess, wearing the ancient crown with its totem horns of mountain goat on her head, and her male cohort will carry out the prescribed ritual so that the sun-deity will send mercy via the son, the rain. (A Re-creation)

Prehistoric, sun-worshiping fertility cults once occupied the same cave sites in which the Dead Sea Scrolls were found. The archaeological remains include a temple, a holy of holies, a necropolis, precious stones, artifacts, a copper scroll, a copper crown, and other copper ritual objects; all of these were found in what archaeologists identify today as the "Cave of the Treasure" from the Chalcolithic period (fourth millennium B.C.E.).[11] "Around 3300 B.C.E. . . . [the sites] were abandoned and they remain unoccupied in subsequent times."[12] Why was the site abandoned? It remains a mystery. But a mystery not as compelling as that of the site's later leaseholder, the millennium brotherhood. How did they get to the desert? Why did the caves become their beds of immortality? Some of the following historical moments shed some light.

But first a digression that will help illuminate an important historical fact as well as a symbol. In the last decade, an astoundingly vast network of caves, connected by tunnels, has been discovered in Israel. They are located in desert valleys of ancient Judea and Galilee (the Shephelah).[13] The artifacts found in the caves suggest that their purpose was for storing ammunition as well as for accommodating humans, who may have lived there for long periods of time. Among the archaeological finds are grain, wine jugs, animal pens, water sources, ventilation, rooms of various sizes indicative of living quarters, assembly halls, and small ritual spaces lighted by candles. Archaeologists relying on coins, pottery, and some correspondence with ancient literary passages identify the so-called hiding places of the Shephelah as being inhabited throughout the first millennium; nevertheless, they tend to emphasize the last attempt against the Romans, namely, the Bar Kochba uprising of 136 C.E. But this narrow slant on the caves fails to recognize a possible earlier significance. We believe that the three groups rebelling against Rome (after 70 C.E.)[14] were connected to the descendants of the militant, puritanical, xenophobic, and secretive social movement commanded by the Dead Sea Scrolls. Further, because we believe that this popular sectarianism was born underground a century before in its homeland of Galilee, we identify this movement's actual withdrawal underground, to the caves and tunnels of the Judean and Galilean Shephelah with Qumran. Appropriately, the Dead Sea is itself the deepest place on earth. Such a conclusion helps to explain why an ancient motif that associates hiding places with religious piety persists in our own times:

books of holy secrets in inaccessible caves, special hidden secret-laden births, devout cowled hermits living in forsaken places, as well as deep catacombs in which forbidden sectarianism was practiced and the dead buried. In fact, we still metaphorically associate radicalism and forbidden opposition with the underground. Bearing this in mind, we now proceed with a more systematic sociohistorical survey.

Whether historically or mythically, one must begin in Canaan (also referred to as Judea, Palestine, or Israel). This area has always been prized, not because of choice fertile land but because of strategic location as a crossroad to international trade. Thus, the history of this valuable but tiny region is one of repeated wars with its neighbors by land and across the sea, which have resulted in periodic displacement through exile. Israelites/Hebrews/Judeans always had a difficult existence in their semi-arid, overpopulated land, but they were sustained by international power games or by commerce in goods and new ideas. A successful ideology maintained their national identity, though many of the ideas that formed the basis of their credo were borrowed from other cultures. For example, from Egypt they borrowed monotheism, circumcision, and the idea of the soul's judgment; from Mesopotamia, the concepts in the Ten Commandments and the notion of writing down rules, or the law for uniformity and conformity. Early Israelite ideology also exhibited a defensive-minded ethos, based on an intense memory of enslavement; this ethos engendered a notion of salvation that informed not only Judaism but Christianity and Islam as well.

From the first agricultural communities and Stone Age populations to the residents of the so-called promised land—Canaanites, "sea peoples" such as the Philistines and Phoenicians, numerous sedentary tribes, and pastoral nomads from the desert and mountain fringes—Canaan was well occupied. Possibly as early as 2000 to 1800 B.C.E., but more likely by 1550–1400 B.C.E., there came to be a group that the Egyptians identified as "Shashu" or "Habiru." Bronze Age records of wild, nomadic clans wandering at the borders of Egyptian territory may point to Hebrews, the followers of a God named Yahweh. Whether Canaanites themselves, as some scholars suggest,[15] or migrants from Mesopotamia as the Abraham–Isaac–Jacob stories in Genesis claim, or both, by 1200 to 1000 B.C.E. Hebrews increasingly came to predominate in Canaan. Ongoing interaction with Egypt, the regional power at that time, was inevitable. According to the Bible, these tribes (identified with the early Iron Age, 1200–1150 B.C.E.) relied on judges to resolve their conflicts and military might to gain territory from their neighbors.[16] Successful alliances among them ultimately resulted in control of valuable overland trade routes, particularly to Arabia, the source of precious incense and silk. The riches associated with trade funded a secure central state, that of the kingdom of David and of his son Solomon, the master-builder. The golden era of 1000–925 B.C.E. became mythologized as the ultimate moment of Jewish nationhood with the grandest Temple built by Solomon. It was memorialized forever and became a mantra at Qumran: "'A staff shall rise from the root of Jesse, [and a Planting from his roots will bear fruit.'] . . . the Branch of David" (4Q285 frag. 7, lines 3–4). The kingdom did not last, partly because of Solomon's taxation system (among other reasons), and in 925 B.C.E. it split into two entities.[17] In 722 B.C.E. much Israelite territory was lost to the Assyrians, who defeated and cut off ten tribes from the northern kingdom of Israel forever.[18] The southern kingdom of Judea with its capital at Jerusalem lived on, interrupted in 586 B.C.E. by another major defeat orchestrated by the Babylonians, who exiled the Jewish elite. When they returned to their homeland some years later, along with their prophets (particularly Second Isaiah),[19] they built the Second Temple at Jerusalem. During the early years of this Second Commonwealth (500–450 B.C.E.), the final priestly compilation of the Hebraic historical tradition began to be assembled as the Bible.

Factions arose during that time too. Nazirites (like Samson) took an oath not to drink liquor, eat meat, or cut their hair. There was a zealous faction who destroyed the horse icons of sun-worshipers in the Temple at Jerusalem and then moved to Egypt in the second century B.C.E., where they built their own temple at Leontopolis. This specific move to Leontopolis was not unusual at that time, because Jews had always migrated in and out of Egypt, sometimes by choice seeking work or pasture during droughts and famines, sometimes by bond. Members of the Jewish community on the Aswan island of Elephantine on the Nile worked as mercenaries for the famed Egyptian cavalry. They too had their own temple, but, as their writings show, they were less strictly devoted to Yahweh and somewhat more liberal toward women in their appeal to the pagan Queen of Heaven.[20]

With the coming of a new empire builder, Alexander the Great (fourth century B.C.E.), the Jews were introduced to Hellenistic/secular ways. Resistance arose to what was foreign, more worldly, and therefore offensive to Jewish noncompromisers. The Maccabean fighters, remembered as heroes by Qumran and Jews everywhere, succeeded in restoring Jewish power for a short while (see the books of Maccabees).

Between the time of the Greeks and that of the Romans who followed them, those who were zealous for the Jewish Law and were committed to the purest priestly way disputed with the compromisers (known at Qumran as "Seekers-after-smooth-things," perhaps the more hellenized Pharisees) about political expediency in desperate times:

> Its interpretation concerns the rule of the Seekers-after-Smooth-Things when there shall not depart from the midst of their congregation the Gentile sword, captivity, and plunder, and heated strife among themselves, and exile from fear of the enemy, and a multitude of guilty corpses shall fall in their days, and there shall be no end to the total of their slain . . . in their body of flesh they shall stumble over their own guilty [ʾašmātām] counsel. (4QpNah 3–4 ii 4b–6)

This sectarian pronouncement is only one example of the bitter division between the desert brothers and the Jerusalem establishment.

The nation was ruled on behalf of Rome by Herodian inbred princes, barely Jewish by blood, and sacrifices in the Temple were conducted by foreigners. Fundamentalist Jews (Zadokites) could see the handwriting on the wall because their resistance movement provoked military retaliation by the Romans; they therefore readied themselves for a holy war and appealed for God's favor by introducing a purer form of worship. This movement is reflected in some of the texts from the Dead Sea that are concerned with mysteries and apocalyptic imagery, which describe a sectarian leadership awaiting the help of the avenging angel of God in the wilderness.[21]

When "revenge" did take place, it was executed ruthlessly as only the Romans knew how:

> Prey departeth not and the sound of the whip and the sound of the rattling of wheels, and galloping horses and bounding chariots, the horseman charging, a blade and flashing spear and a multitude of slain and a great heap of carcasses: and there is no end to the corpses and they shall

stumble over their bodies. (4QpNah 3–4 ii 3–8; quotation of Nah. 3:1b–3; DJD 5:40)

After years of attempted conciliation through puppet rulers, as well as extortion, torture, crucifixion, and enslavement, the whole Jewish state-enterprise, city by city, community by community, was decisively crushed by Roman troops who were intent on a sweeping victory. In 70 C.E. (an important date not only because it was the climactic event of the war against the Jews but also because it is the main event expected in the Scrolls[22]) the last ideological stronghold, the Temple in Jerusalem, was destroyed, along with the Judean popular leadership. Only pockets of resistance remained: Masada's suicidal stand (a stone's throw away from Qumran)—the most dramatic—and the Bar Kochba revolt in 132 C.E.—the last, unsuccessful attempt.[23] After 70 C.E., and even more so after the collapse of the Bar Kochba rebellion, diaspora Jews with their new rabbinic Judaism, rationalists, and mystics alike fled far and wide.

This historical overview opens up a wider ideological window that will now be more explicitly examined to situate the Dead Sea sectarians more precisely within the social panorama of the waning days of the Second Commonwealth.

THE INTERACTION BETWEEN CURRENT EVENTS AND IDEOLOGY

There are roughly three distinct eras in the formation of Israelite society: the eras of fertility, separation, and salvation. In this section we will focus on the poignant circumstances in each that inform the beliefs and values of the sectarians who were responsible for the production of the Dead Sea Scrolls. In addition, we will introduce some specific ideas that will be developed in greater detail in the rest of this book.

First, the concept of fertility in its most primitive manifestation was embodied in a Goddess and a religion associated with temples, lunar holidays, and elaborate rituals. The Goddess religion dominated early societies of the populated centers of western Asia Minor. Archaeology suggests that the Mother Goddess reigned from the Neolithic Age (8500–4300 B.C.E.) into the early agricultural empires of Sumeria, Egypt, India, Assyria, Babylonia, Anatolia, Mycenea/Greece, and Balkan/Etruscan civilizations.[24] As populations multiplied and competition for scarce resources intensified, the Goddess was envisioned as the consort of male war gods, like Astarte and Baal in Canaan. For some Judeans, too, the Goddess was embodied in the Asherah, as a ninth-eighth century B.C.E. inscribed blessing from the northern Negev trade route region reads: "Yahweh of Samaria and his Asherah."[25]

Israelite monotheism struggled throughout its history to override the Goddess religion and its matrilineally based institutions. Particularly troublesome was the popular belief in female spiritual power over the fertility of all living things, including the land and its continuous regeneration. The main ritual of the Goddess religion was the *hieros gamos* (the sacred marriage), held at the winter solstice, which celebrated the mating of the Goddess with the ruler of the land.[26] Yahweh's priesthood promoted instead God's maleness, the rights of patriarchal authority to command, and a patrilineal inheritance system. In Genesis, for example, the patriarchs' power is radicalized to such an extent that they all "begat" their children. Even so, it is quite ironic that the matriarchs name the children and that Judaism, as a religion, recognizes a child's "Jewishness" only if the child is associated with a Jewish mother.[27] A great number of artifacts—"pagan idols" (or *teraphim*), as well as drawings and texts, even the Jewish Bible—attest to the Goddess's continuing popularity; this remained true even to the time of the millennium and the Dead Sea Scrolls.[28] The idea of fertility is important for the present study, where we unravel the meaning and the function of the virgin in a male-oriented society that perceived itself as being under tremendous political and military pressure; it therefore attempted to reinvent Jewish institutions so as to allow for procreation on the one hand and revered virginity on the other.

The second concept—separation—concerns particularly women but also a whole tribe or a people. This idea sheds light on lines of power and prestige as well as gender divisions. Finally, we center on the unique concept of salvation and its narrowly defined possibilities. Not only is salvation related to a select group of people who happen to adopt the tenets of the monotheistic God, but in the literature of the Dead Sea Scrolls, salvation is limited to only those who are "holier" than all other believers and/or those who follow (or join another way to become fruitful) the holy ones. The sectarians who left the presumably corrupt city (for the desert) believed very strongly in a special brand of community which separated from the rest of society for purposes of ritual purity. Because of their strict practices, they believed that they alone would finally reap the fruits of a purer way of life. We will see that even though the Dead Sea brotherhood accepted the main concepts promulgated by the Jews as a people, they nonetheless focused their attention on a way of life that they believed to be superior in purity to the practices of others. Since they were particularly concerned about women's sexuality and its "defiling" impact on the whole human race, they faced a dilemma: procreation was essential, but sexuality was abhorrent. Indeed, the virgin was of immense importance to this brotherhood, because she was the symbol of a kind of perfection that was idealized in that exclusive environment. The sect believed that in order to be worthy of living in the new, perfect world (which would come into being when "the sons of light" [i.e., the sectarians] conquered "the sons of darkness" [i.e., the Romans and their collaborators]) it was necessary to remain inviolate, and virginity was clearly part of that belief.

We will try to show that keeping the virgin intact was a secret activity undertaken by some "most holy" sectarians and that a few selected virgins did remain permanently intact because of ritual and ideological demands made on them by the brotherhood for their highly developed "gnosis" of creation.[29] We will see, however, that virgins in the sect's ideology were as oppressed as other, nonvirgin women, whom they viewed as "vessels." We will thus be better able to understand the role of women in the Dead Sea Scrolls, which has not been examined by any scholar to date but is important as a reflection of a system of thought that has had a significant impact on the West. We will understand their sense of urgency and zeal in the face of a pending catastrophe, with the Romans smashing every Jewish garrison and district. We will realize that they feared the total annihilation of the people and that therefore they imagined and preached that all fleshliness should be sacrificed for the sake of all that seemed left to them: a heavenly salvation.

Sexual desire, transformed into original sin, was the first fleshliness to be condemned.

> And he is limited by the dust and lives by the bread of worms. He, who is saliva which has been emitted, clay which was nipped off and he who *desires* dust. (1QS 11:20–21)

In the landscape of the final years of the Second Commonwealth, which witnessed not only the onslaught of two waves of "Kittiyyim" (first the Greeks and then the Romans) but also the sectarian-led "change of heart," or their realization of a "new heart," an extreme form of virginity finally triumphed. The emphasis on the central *mitzvah* of intergender lovingness and even the valuing of life itself as articulated by the Goddess and her rituals of erotica were becoming irrelevant. With recourse to a new Book, a new supernatural contract (the New Covenant), and a second, penitent Adam (the Son of Man),[30] the sectarian Nazirites stamped society with their peculiar rules of behavior known as the "straight Way." Sex with women was admitted only as a last resort, since they viewed survival as only a temporary matter. They argued that, like their father figure Noah, they withdrew from society to await the final apocalypse, and as their Book records, compulsively washed away their sins.

We will maintain that the sectarians' Book, known today as the Dead Sea Scrolls, became no less than the founding document of Western civilization. With the exception of a patronizing bent for charity to the poor, its message tainted the wells of Western history for two thousand years. Its ideology celebrated chosenness in death and, hypocritically, suggested the enduring of poverty as a temporary condition. Without giving up competitiveness and aggression, or the "sin" of reproduction of the species, the Word and the Way became reified in the three salvation religions. The only positive trace left of the Goddess in the context of these religions was the a-sexual Mother, who remained in her niche essentially silent. Sexual pleasure was totally abandoned or relegated to sinners, and the virgin was adopted as the idealized woman who was closest to God; in fact, the virgin man was also believed to be the exemplary male.

But one of the most pressing questions that the sectarians attempted to answer while waiting for "the end" had to do with the status of the holiest of men in relation to the virgin woman: How do both of them maintain their perfection? That is the riddle that we will attempt to unravel. That was the "truth" that the sectarians articulated as a "mystery," which was known only to the most "righteous." That "truth" is tied in with major tenets of the ideology of the Dead Sea sectarians, and it particularly elucidates the "marvels" beheld by the sectarian and his ability to "pierce the mystery to come" (1QS 11:3–4).

But, in an ironic twist, the sectarians, who preached strict monotheism, still echoed some of the more mysterious, secretive aspects of the Goddess religion, which still appealed to a broad spectrum of people. The sectarian initiates were forbidden to reveal community secrets as well, but all that secrecy contributed to a further clouding of major beliefs and practices of their religion. Indeed, there are still heavy clouds covering the horizons of the sectarian movement in Judea during the Second Commonwealth.

Despite the success of patriarchy, Goddess practices and rituals were popularly accepted throughout the region. The appealing part of the sectarian movement must thus be seen within a context that the sectarians, on the surface, totally rejected. But the various texts that originated in that period and express the longings, hopes, and dreams as well as the cold realities of the day, retrieve and leverage that feminine principle that Yahwism denied and repressed.

Since our main concern in this book is the role of women in the Scrolls and particularly the role of the virgin, we will try to understand more fully what is meant by "virginal conception" and thus to offer another approach to a basic question of religion and faith as well as of history. We will draw examples and analogies from various Qumran-related texts so as to paint a clearer ritualistic picture of a setting in which fertility and human processes associated with it were at the top of people's agenda, but also a setting in which that agenda was faltering because of the preoccupation of men with "the assembly of flesh" and "the Sons of Heaven" (1QS 11:7–8).

THE LITERARY RECORD

The Garden of Eden and Fruitfulness

In many ways, the biblical concept of monogenesis (creation and procreation by *one* pair) is a reflection of an old clannish ideology that did not necessarily emphasize the importance and power of a sole creator, but rather the value of the maxim "to be fruitful and multiply." The societies that could be recognized as fostering this postulate were composed of small numbers of people, were less complex (in their modes of labor), less diverse ethnically, and less stratified.

Since they were not engaged in agricultural projects, they were more able to focus on basic celebrations of life and love. Furthermore, they promoted cooperation for the difficult task of obtaining and storing food as well as avoiding natural disasters. The story of the "society" of the Garden of Eden is indeed one that seems to appreciate these ideas even though the way the myth has been edited forewarns about harsher, less tolerant circumstances. The first man and woman (Adam and Eve) are described in fairly egalitarian terms. They seem to be free of complex social structures, and they are specifically told by the God of the garden to "be fruitful and multiply." Life was an important value in that society (so much so that it was primarily vegetarian), and its main symbols were the Tree of Life and the Tree of Knowledge: one representing immortality, and the other its opposite. Although knowledge as such is not automatically associated with death and destruction, it acquired that connotation when placed "in the midst of the garden" and when delineated by the powerful God of the garden (via the biased political voice of the editor)[31] as bearing "death" (you will surely die!).

When the serpent in the garden offers the woman its "commentary" on the command of God, it clearly contradicts God and draws the woman's attention to the "desirability" and "beauty" of the Tree of Knowledge. When the woman tastes of the fruit, she gives it to her man, who is also enchanted. The myth thus explains how people "learned" about sexuality, placing it, properly, within the context of the clan. The negative connotations that were superimposed on the written narrative were introduced by the biblical author who wrote the story down, after it had been circulating orally in exile and from the perspective of political defeat.[32] Hence, throughout the ages, the emphasis on disobedience was stronger than the accent on the more "mellow" account about humans in paradise who tried to establish a small framework of operation which allowed them to survive holistically.

It is therefore no accident that as soon as the first couple leaves the Garden of Eden they begin the process of propagation, reinforcing the idea that the basic act of eating of the fruit of the Tree of Knowledge was ultimately their introduction to the world of sex. Significantly, we find that it was the alluring serpent who proposed to the couple the enchantments of sex and the promise of immortality, thus embodying the pledges of the Goddess and her priests and priestesses.[33] In contrast, the male God warned about the consequences of disobedience, thus playing the role of the future, stern, tribal deity who will demand discipline and exclusive loyalty. Moreover, that God will ultimately place a wedge between the genders and will firmly insist that the man become the master and the woman his subject. The egalitarian garden was quickly fading into the past; the lush environment and the lax, forgiving serpent became a hazy memory.

The biblical author who wrote the story of the garden undercut the Goddess by insinuating that she and those who worshiped her were responsible for misery and pain and that the all-powerful male God who created Adam was indeed a creator of life—which suggests that the role of the woman as life-giver was at best only secondary. There is additionally an emphasis in the story on disobedience which leads to exile and loss and which fits the mentality of an exilic author who attempts to comprehend his own (and his people's) condition in a foreign, Babylonian world.

Genesis/Exodus and Separateness

The first birth by a woman recorded in Genesis is the birth of a child/man, Cain, who is said to have been conceived by Eve with God as her counterpart (Gen. 4:1). Cain can accordingly be seen as the first son to be "immaculately" conceived and therefore to have a special relationship with the deity (his Father?), who does not ultimately dispose of him after he (Cain) kills his younger brother, Abel.[34] Cain goes on to multiply by "begetting" Enoch and by establishing a separate city (civilization?) named for his son. Enoch would later play a significant part for the community of the Dead Sea Scrolls, where he is rewritten as a mystic-seer-wise man. Enoch is accorded immortality and has access to historical and metaphysical knowledge that ultimately is transmitted only to those who could actually absorb and were ready to accept it.[35] From the sectarians' point of view, Enoch represented an ancient and stable female line associated with the principle of wisdom.[36] Additionally, the sectarians fashioned for themselves their own genealogies, back to this earliest source, in order to prove that their line was purer and more reliable. Cain "begets" Enoch, who "begets" Lamech, who "begets" Noah. And Noah is the honorary covenantal father of the Qumran lineage. In fact, the sectarian authors of the Dead Sea Scrolls identify themselves with these characters on a very real level to the point of actually borrowing their names, perhaps using them as titles.[37]

The various genealogies that are carefully recorded in Genesis and further underline the importance of fertility and regeneration emphasize the eminent role of men in the regeneration process. In the genealogical recounting, it is not the woman who is giving birth; rather, it is the man who becomes responsible for his own progeny. The Qumran sectarians appreciated that particular aspect of the Genesis tradition and ultimately focused on it in a novel and radical way. For the sectarians, the issue of genealogies, progeny, and "seed" was of utmost importance, as we will see when we discuss their attitude to women as a whole and to virgins in particular. Even in the narration of genealogies in Genesis, where only the male line is mentioned, the women are almost completely missing; and since they are the ones who actually give birth, their role is irrationally objectified. In the sectarian literature, whatever is left of the woman serves as propaganda, as allegory, and as a tool for the correct process of immaculate conception.

When the clan metamorphoses into the larger unit of the tribe, the intimate surroundings associated with the family of Adam and Eve give place to a harsher, starker, more active landscape. The consequence of the clan's early fertility promotions—more people—led to tribalism and a different emphasis and ideology: one that promoted separateness, not harmony. In the context of Genesis, when the family of the patriarch Jacob goes "down" to Egypt to find respite from famine, the Israelite familial saga comes to a close and the tribe pushes to the forefront. Jacob and the rest of the family, with the help of Joseph, who is already married to the daughter of the priest of On (Leontopolis), Aseneth, settles in Egypt, providing the reader with a contextual excuse for the presence of future Hebrews in that country.

We thus find that in the more distinctly Israelite story of origins that places a band of disorganized slaves in the desert pushing hard to enter into Canaan, the roots of the Genesis chronology are fairly strongly felt. Though this story, on the face of it, is the exact opposite of the story of the garden, it has similar ingredients—namely, a preconfederate group, clannish in nature, hard pressed in difficult circumstances (the desert) where basic survival is the crucial motivation. The group stresses togetherness, sharing, and continuity through common worship—here of a Goddess of fertility (e.g., the golden calf, the "son" of the cow [Exodus 32], or the god and goddess at Baal Peor; see Deut. 4:3; Num. 23:28; Ps. 106:28). Wandering in the desert is the Hebraic metaphor for the group's togetherness, and when they are poised to enter the Land of Canaan they are also ready to be transformed from their seminomadic, clannish makeup to a more stable tribe with land rights. The tribal mentality was more narrowly focused, exalting the use of power for the sake of survival. Concomitantly, the emergence of a Hebrew tribe of people in the vicinity of the hotly disputed fertile crescent necessitated a new approach to religious ideology—one that ultimately led to the elevation of Yahweh, a more warlike and commanding God, and to his exclusivity.[38]

Because the many tribes of Canaan lived at the margins of rich, alluvial agricultural empires built on war and slavery, there was increased competition for scarce resources.[39] The Hebrew tribes, too, developed a warrior ethos and elevated a separate caste to leadership. The practice of survival of the fittest in war promoted hypermasculinity and aggressiveness. While fertility remained a strong directive (with women viewed increasingly as chattel) for enhancing the group's numbers and force, the way of separateness, symbolized by the sacrifice of the foreskin (Genesis 17), simultaneously deemphasized lovingness and the once-powerful influence of the Goddess of fertility. Thus, the principle of the Yahwistic covenant, which is based on the bonding of males with each other and their God, was further enhanced. The impact of this covenant on women was tantamount to a serious erosion in their political and social power. It is particularly instructive to follow the early stories in Genesis about women and their function in the text; they have a voice and seem to be determined to pursue their agenda, but the male voice is dominant and issues of raw power, competition for land, and legitimacy overshadow all the stories.

The more the Hebrews focused on their national aspirations and put their sights on Canaan as the ultimate farming locale where their survival could be assured, the more favored was Yahweh's male priesthood in all its zeal.[40] Because of the makeup of that priesthood, combined with traditional tribal rivalries, it was becoming more and more expensive to afford a society-wide emphasis on the softer, sharing side of human nature associated with femininity. That more ancient way of the Goddess was marginalized along with women. Nonetheless, there was an enduring Goddess presence throughout the ancient world and beyond mainly because of its overt message of immortality. Even when the male God finally triumphed, there were pockets of Goddess followers who insisted on worshiping the old way. Key symbols related to the Goddess were reinterpreted and thus preserved even under the most difficult circumstances.

The marginalizing of women was accompanied by their demonization because of their association with menstrual blood and the sexual promiscuity practiced at times by the adherents of the Goddess religion.[41] Because sexually communicable diseases (syphilis and leprosy, in particular) were widespread in the ancient world, there was a visible reason (in addition to the apparent desire of men for power) for the biblical association of sacramental sex with impurity. The solution to the various "unclean" problems of infection and illness offered by the Hebrew priests was a very severe form of cleansing; first, for the real purpose of staying healthy, and, second, for purposes of separation. The priests insisted on the tribe's need to be as holy as God even at the very high price of some individuals' isolation and segregation from the group. The practice of special rituals and the exhortation to obey certain taboos were only two of the ways the priests/physicians/healers/magicians maintained their authority. Thus it was that a healthy person became holier than one who was sick. Thus also began the ideological separation between the genders, with the women increasingly relegated to the camp of pollution and defilement.[42]

TOWARD CHOSENNESS AND SALVATIONISM

After the early period of increasing numbers and "fertility" and after the era of separateness characterized by a desire to stay within Canaan[43] came the period of the ideology of "chosenness" and even more constriction of women's rights.[44] Survival was still the primary value, and fertility was controlled by men. Yet this male control was still resisted by women through rituals[45] and symbols related to the biblically infamous Asherah.[46] To better understand this concept of "chosenness," it is important to fill in some historical circumstances that provided the fertile ground for it.

There are two major traumatic events in Jewish history that become lessons for later direction. The Assyrian invasion and conquest of the northern Israelite kingdom (722 B.C.E.) are the first such trauma; this conquest contributed to the rise of the classical prophets (e.g., Hosea, Amos, Isaiah[47]), who depicted the social fabric of Israel in a radically new light. They were strong opponents of the priests, and, although emphasizing the centrality of the kingship, they slowly moved toward recognizing the house of David as the clear choice of God particularly "in the end of days" (Isa. 11:1). It is interesting that even at the end of the First Commonwealth, in another major setback for the Goddess adherents, the prophetic "reformers" were busy destroying the Asherah worship that was performed by the people in the midst of the Temple in Jerusalem (2 Kings 23). But the prophets' main agenda was social and religious; they were horrified by the possibility of utter political destruction and felt that the nation ought to be prepared for the worst in more than just a political way. The prophets were Yahwists who, when the final and most calamitous destruction occurred, felt that Yahweh (and particularly they as his messengers) was vindicated and that the people from that point on (586 B.C.E., the Babylonian defeat of Judah) would seriously undertake worshiping him. That prophetic missive was coupled with a strongly articulated anti-Goddess harangue professing that there was a direct connection between political defeat and loss and worshiping "the Queen of Heaven" (see especially Jeremiah 44). And so it was that as a result of multiple defeats (by the Assyrians in 722 B.C.E. and the Babylonians in 587/6 B.C.E.), a history of being overrun by empires on both sides, an elite being dragged into captivity (see Jeremiah 39–41; 2 Kings 25; and Daniel 1), the Hebrew tribes finally coalesced into a confederate national identity.

The Second Jewish Commonwealth came into being as a result of the Persian emperor Cyrus's decree in 538 B.C.E., but Jewish autonomy in the wake of the "return to Zion" was unstable and became increasingly defensive. The idea of "chosenness," elaborated and commented on by the great prophet Deutero-Isaiah, demanded that as a people, Jews should hold fast to the precepts of Yahweh, particularly truth and righteousness (ʾĕmet wĕṣedeq). In return, Yahweh will create for them a special role in history, a role that was embodied in the persona of the Servant of Yahweh.[48] Hand in hand with that ideology and social perception, the priests introduced the priestly book, which ensured that the Law would be kept in the most exacting fashion.

Thus, at the millennium, as the Second Commonwealth was drawing to a close, the dominant Yahwistic ideology demanded yet a cleaner separation of the nation's seed from any others, because the people of Yahweh were to be tested once more. Those in power advocated a more tightly knit chosenness. As it is stated by the sectarians at Qumran:

> No [stranger shall approach] the well-spring of life or drink the water of holiness with the everlasting trees, or bear fruit with [the Plant] of heaven, who seeing has not discerned, and considering has not believed in the fountain of life, who has turned [his hand against] the everlasting [bud]. (1QH 8:12c–14)

Will they prove worthy? Will they finally enter a new phase of metahistory which will accommodate those who indeed believe in and accept the One God? The kings having been overturned by external powers,[49] only priests and prophets, or extreme sectarians, were left to lead the many to these more cosmic objectives.

The term "zealots" (*qannaim*) may be the most suitable to describe generally the men who were ready to defend their God to the bitter end.

> A deep religious driving force lies behind this name, which can best be expressed as "zeal for God and his law." This zeal was in turn expressed in a rigorous refusal to compromise in carrying out God's commandments and in the use of violence against all who did not obey those commandments, which were interpreted in the most radical way.[50]

Trying to get it right—trying to assuage the apparent wrath of God and return to a kingdom, or nationhood status—the Zealot leadership toyed with martyrdom and, as described by Josephus (the most important Jewish historian from the first century C.E.), they got their wish. "They endured quite unusual forms of death and disregarded the death penalty in the case of relatives and friends, if only they needed to call no man Lord . . . the words of this account may be too weak to describe their disregard of the excess of suffering that they have accepted" (*Antiquities* 18.23). It seems that the blood of these martyrs finally mingled with the "seed" of the approaching new world.[51]

That "saved" world and the salvationism perceived by the sectarians rested on another biblical concept, Naziritism (ritual dedication to Yahweh), transformed into a new ideology that envisioned Wisdom, a female essence,[52] resting on an elect warrior-priest-hero, supported by a penitent, purified brotherhood. The sectarians most revered hero is described from the moment of his birth:

> He is born in the night and he comes out Perfect. . . . His birth and the spirit of his breath . . . his [p]lans will endure forever. (4Q534–536)

CHAPTER ONE

"Pagan" World Surroundings

But we will do everything that we have vowed, burn incense to the Queen of Heaven and pour out libations to her, as we did, both we and our fathers, our kings and our princes, in the cities of Judah and in the streets of Jerusalem. (Jeremiah 44:17)

BRIEF: OVERVIEW

Before we explain the rise of Naziritism, we must digress briefly to elaborate on the pagan culture of the time. The ancient Goddess religion (8500–4300 B.C.E.) had long been in decline, but the mixed-gender pantheon instituted by empire builders was on the way out too.[1] The masses about whom the Qumran community was concerned—"the poor who [shall possess] the whole world as an inheritance" (4QpPs[a] frag. 3, line 29)—had given up the Goddess refrains and stubbornly clung to their form of monotheism.

The fertility Goddess herself, although prohibited by powerful male clerics, was never too far from women in their everyday moments of need, whether in the marriage bed or at the birthing stool. Peasants too, so dependent on the fertility of crops and always mindful of what had worked well before, were not so easily persuaded to give up customs of beseeching the Goddess. Surely those at the precipice of illness or death would have appealed to her, even if only for double measure. Indeed, Goddess images and icons have been found in great numbers in Judea from temple floor mosaics to nude *teraphim* tucked into grain bins and full-bodied *asherot* lost for centuries in the ground.[2] The ancient holidays of the Goddess marking the agricultural cycles remained.[3] Her symbols, now pilfered, cued the populace into different priestly rules; and her rituals of worship, even her places of worship, although taken over for the male God, still evoked the ancient meanings for many worshipers.

Monotheistic Judaism, with its Temple and harsh rules and taboos, was surrounded by the "pagan" as the norm. Judaism had therefore an ongoing struggle with its populace to overcome the stubborn influence of the Goddess and the pleasurable world she recalled. Artifacts and writings show that much of the pagan culture coexisted quite well with Temple Judaism. The monotheists took over and incorporated much of the pagan culture, but the "harlot" side of these things remained silent or hidden. Standard practices included magical incantations; the laying on of hands for healing; the power of naming (a deity or a person); pilgrimages to sacred trees or places; astrological charts and forecasts; amulets; fertility potions from mandrakes, pomegranates, and other drugs; special purifications in the Temple itself (such as the ashes of the sacrificed red heifer sprinkled in holy water); initiations with honey; and the sweet odors of expensive frankincense and myrrh (also used, respectively, as medicine for female disorders and to mask the smell of cremations),[4] to banish evil (perhaps oversexed satyrlike) spirits. At Qumran too we find the red heifer ablutions, exorcisms, divinations, and magical amulets:

> [(I adjure) by the Name of He who for]gives sin and transgression, O fever and chills and heartburn [. . . and forbidden to disturb by night in dreams or by day] in sleep, the male PRK-demon and the female PRK-demon, those who breach(?). . . . (4Q560 1 i 4–5)[5]

The priesthood's main preoccupation, in fact, the sacrifice of animals on an altar facing toward Yahweh's particular mountain, is the most blatant fingerprint of pagan co-option. But all Jews were not orthodox in practice. Those large populations living outside Judea[6] did not necessarily succeed in synchronizing their rituals and beliefs with those of the Temple in Jerusalem. And none, even in Judea, lived in a vacuum. They existed in and traded with a profoundly pagan world.

In this chapter, we touch on some key insights into the popular understanding of the Goddess that became the heritage of paganism at the turn of the millennium. The whole hellenized secular environment must be accounted for as well because of the deep impact of this culture on the Jews in Judea and beyond. We also call attention to Goddess incarnations from three regions of historical contact: Mesopotamia, where the Hebrew patriarchs claim their origin and where later in Babylonian captivity they were exposed to the Goddess once again; Judea itself with its indigenous Canaanite and Philistine sources; and the high culture of Egypt, where some kind of exodus as well as continuous neighborly intercourse took place.[7]

The name and function of the Goddess were arbitrary from place to place and could be changed to fit social circumstances; however, her most primitive symbols, such as the regenerating snake, the blood of women, the veil of the hymen ("the gate to heaven"), the honey substance of reproduction and sexual initiation, her tree of knowledge and its messenger birds, and the heavenly bodies of the night sky, remain constant.[8] Notably, we see there the moon with its quarter phase (like bull horns), the morning star of Venus, and the starry clusters, especially the ubiquitous Seven Sisters (seven being the Goddess's holy number), the Pleiades constellation in Taurus the bull.

In the broadest sense, new wisdom rarely usurps first concepts; the older is just overlaid, recycled, and remodeled. Even today, the progress of modern science with its theory of evolution, its laws of physics, and its developments in biochemistry has not sealed the fate of the salvation religions—this, despite the difficulty in reconciling their often-conflicting versions of "truth." Even today, "be fruitful and multiply" holds sway against all rational odds.

Because we assert throughout the book that the ancient language of the Goddess was both adapted and repressed in favor of the ways of Yahweh, we point to the threads of pagan influence that are resurrected in the Dead Sea Scrolls and which undeniably reinstate the Goddess's legacy. We dare not suggest any intention on the part of the sectarians to celebrate the Goddess; like the priests of the establishment before them, their writings show an attempt to drown out her sensuous voice by raising theirs to a fever pitch. But the Goddess's presence has been so prolific, so deep, so appealing to the "many" that it was impossible to erase. Moreover, if one wished to depart from any "normative" tradition (including establishment Judaism of the Second Temple period) and still be popular, one indeed had to echo the language and traditions of the Goddess. Even the minimalist, cavelike retreats of the sectarian colonies suggest a "new" Garden of Eden, but in the desert—and, we think, an attempt to capture something of a lost past image of her simple-tented holy of holies.

THE GRECO-ROMAN MILIEU: WORLDLINESS

Whatever her avocation, be it hunter, artist, farmer, mother, nurse, miner, fisher, dreamer/witch/sibyl/prophet, or victorious warrior, the Goddess indulges in sexual pleasure and excess. Her sexual activity is not restricted to the other deities; she sometimes takes license with human beings or some animals. The Goddess is more earthly, more like a rich human patroness who could be temperamental and subject to a bribe or gift, usually the sacrifice of food (especially a cornucopia of fruit, wine, and honey). She is excited by singing of psalms announcing her praise, by clapping, loud music, and ecstatic dancing. Musical instruments such as the harp, timbrel, cymbal, strings, and pipe get her attention. This music-making motif has been transferred to the biblical tradition and can be found frequently in the Psalms. Significantly, in Psalm 151 of Qumran's *Psalms Scroll,* David is described as a royal musician: "My hands have made an instrument and my fingers a lyre" (11QPs^a 28:2). In Greek mythology, Orpheus, who is the original shepherd musician (before David), is also thus described. In the same *Psalms Scroll,* there is a list of various musical instruments: "Praise him with timbrel and dance; praise him with strings and pipe . . . with sounding cymbals . . . with loud clashing cymbals."[9] While the praise and the singing remain within a monotheistic frame, the ecstatic spirit and the desire to thus praise God echo the rituals and ceremonies of the Goddess.[10]

Feasting and indulgences (often on occasions such as marriage and death) on behalf of the various deities coexisted in the high cultures of ancient Greece and Rome along with piety.[11] According to those individuals who left us their commentaries, the common people tended, naïvely, to take the symbol of the supernatural at face value, whereas the more sophisticated understood its metaphoric and philosophical meaning. Outside of militant fundamentalist circles such as those in Judea, religion and cultic expression were essentially a free choice, something like political parties today. For the majority of "pagans" (excluding, perhaps, warrior cults like the bloody bull-sacrificing Mithras, which was very concerned with death and the hope for redemption),[12] there was little need perceived for a threatening or rewarding afterlife.

Moral behavior, which was insisted upon, engendered the satisfaction that comes from fulfilling ideals of personal obligations as appropriate to one's position in the community.[13] Sexual ethics was a matter of private conscience, but conduct was kept more or less in line by the various cult "philosophies."[14]

The gender attributes of the ancient Goddess are not limited to either her fecundity (like Aphrodite or Isis)[15] or her sexuality, as the Bible would have us believe. The prophets and the authors of the Bible repeatedly depict Asherah (or Ashtoreth of Canaan) or the strong "pillar"/foundations of the Philistines in purely sexual terms (cf. the story of Samson's fall in Judges 16). The biblical authors never recognize that the pillar figure, like the Asherah of Judea, *hold up,* as well as *build up* their respective communities. Sophia or Wisdom in the Gnostic texts, the Shekinah of Jewish lore[16] (whose authority on earthly matters is passed through the male judges, e.g., Samuel, to David), and the Holy Spirit of the Dead Sea Scrolls are traditionally female essences. But by the time of the sectarians the female essence is completely disembodied,[17] and her authority seems to be identified with the male psyche. Prophecy, however, the wisdom to read the future on earth, did not fully disappear from the realm of women, particularly elderly women. Some think that the whole realm of prophecy originated with "the Sibyls, ten female visionaries of venerable age who were presumed to have lived in various places throughout the Mediterranean."[18] The sibyllines' words of prophecy were treasured and recorded in a number of messianic and apocalyptic texts coinciding with sectarian activities.[19]

The Holy Spirit, though genderless in accepted church liturgy, remains essentially female in the early Gnostic years (despite attempts to wipe her out) and is closely allied with Mary. In the Gnostic texts, not always kind to women, we read the following: "Some said, 'Mary conceived by the holy spirit.' They are in error. They do not know what they are saying. When did a woman ever conceive by a woman?" (*Gospel of Philip* 55:23–26)[20] In another Gnostic book, there is a description of the divine Mother: "(She is) . . . the image of the invisible, virginal, perfect spirit. . . . She became the Mother of everything, for she existed before them, the mother-father" (*Apocryphon of John* 4.34–5.7).[21]

In the Qumran writings, a fragment (4Q185) alludes to a female Wisdom essence which the speaker urges to follow in order to *do* the right thing, to be obedient to God: "And now listen to me, my people, . . . become wise [through the might of God?]. Remember His miracles which He did in Egypt" (1:8b–15a). Further, "Happy is the man who does it and is not willing [. . .] . . . as *she* is given to his fathers, so shall he inherit *her* [. . .] . . . and he shall give *her* as an inheritance to his offspring" (2:13b–15).[22] The sectarians seem thus to preserve the tradition that links Wisdom with a female principle, though the message is ultimately about God and his deliverance.

Even Justice, or the harmonious Egyptian Maat of truth and justice with her still-famous scales, the blind judge, or seer of hidden just things, is still seen in our court statuary as a female goddess figure. At Qumran too they value the "scales of Righteousness" (4Q416, 418 frag. 6, line 6).

THE SIGNIFICANCE OF EGYPT: IMMORTALITY

While the Goddess religion with its specific symbolic vernacular, fine-tuned to local conditions and local names, washed over the trade routes of Judea time and time again, the sequential waves of Egyptian spiritual ways were most appealing for Qumran. For it is in this proximate, literate, and scientific land of Egypt, a place of frequent Jewish sojourn,[23] that we find the most compatible male and female deities, brother-sister models that allowed for the inspired compromise that could convince "the many" as well as the "princes" among men. However, in its practical reinterpretation at Qumran, the sister/mother bends her knees to the will of the brother/son.

Unlike the ways of Mesopotamia, so influential in early Canaan and Israel, what was distinctive about Egypt was its elaborate afterlife (at least for the elite), beginning in the tomb with the ceremony of "the opening of the mouth,"[24] which was located in the heavens and not in the ordinary underworld (the *Sheol* of Judaic lore), where the dead just slept away. While the older perspective was agricultural and focused on the annual recycling of earth matter, the new view of gazing at the limitless stars made for divining grander schemes: "To divine by constellations and to be gazers by the stars."[25] Spiritual essences, something quite unlike the body that decays with the worms, became possible with these ideas: an individual soul that can be judged; a hovering spirit of knowledge to guide it rightly; and the powerful determinant spirit of a creator.[26] Because of this expansive view, it was also possible to imagine the ruling and priestly hierarchy (the pharaoh and his ruling sister/wife as well as the privileged princes assigned to territories and functions) as predestined positions, mirrored in the heavens. In the case of the Egyptians, a divinely ordained pharaoh could, narcissistically, conceive of himself as "the son of the sun," superior in rank even after death to the other sainted stars; he was launched from the highest point of the pyramid and ferried to the sun in his golden barge.[27]

As this astrological lore developed, the solar disk (within the realm of the sky Goddess Nut) was seen to rule over everything else, from the deeps of the cosmic primordial ocean (characterized by the bisexual Nnun)[28]—the source of the vital waters of the Nile—to their human-occupied shores. The effeminate Pharaoh Akhenaton (Amenhotep IV, 1375–1358 B.C.E.)[29] is credited with inventing monotheism.

However, before this phenomenon, Atum, the one who comes from the mystery of the creation at Heliopolis, and who gave birth to himself through masturbation,[30] coexisted with the sun-god, along with other gods and goddesses (often of uncertain or mixed gender) with their particular animal totems and their various mystery rites. Of utmost importance, as elsewhere in the ancient world, was the goddess of fertility and sometimes her daughter (later on, transformed into her son), and her often more human spouse (like the Sumerian Goddess Inanna and her shepherd Dummuzi and the Canaanite Goddess Ishtar and her shepherd Tammuz[31]), who required an annual rescue from the underworld—indeed, a resurrection. But it was the Goddess, above all, who in her mercy initiated this act of redemption and granted renewed life. The Egyptian belief in Isis, "the Queen of Heaven," and her son Horus, conceived with the crucial part of her mate Osiris after his death, epitomized this scenario.[32] The resurrection of Osiris was a public holiday celebrated at the winter solstice, a *hieros gamos*.[33] Isis's credo was, thereafter, symbolized by the ankh;[34] as many have pointed out, this was not so unlike the Christian version of sacrifice and metamorphism.

In an extraordinary literary expression, Isis (during the Greco-Egyptian, or Hellenistic period) is portrayed as a goddess who "seeks and discovers."[35] Her most overwhelming "discovery" is that of life itself:

> O wealth-giver, Queen of the gods, Hermouthis [goddess of the cereal grain], Lady . . . greatly renowned Isis, Deo, highest Discoverer of all life, manifold miracles were Your care that You might bring livelihood to mankind and morality to all . . . Because of You heaven and the whole earth have their being . . . All mortals who live on the boundless earth . . . Express your fair Name, a Name greatly honoured among all, . . . Each (speaks) in his own language, in his own land. The Syrians call you: Astarte, Artemis, Nanaia . . . And the Greeks (call you) Hera of the Great Throne, Aphrodite . . . Mighty One, I shall not cease to sing of Your great power . . . (Hymn I [Plate VI], lines 1–25)

The most outstanding attribute of Isis, according to this ardent worshiper, is her universality; she is identified by the whole world and she is venerated by "all mortals." The journey she undertakes seems to be her most astounding accomplishment because she thus gives birth to the very concept "life." In a more typical vein, Isis is also projected as the goddess of cereal and grain, a more traditional goddess role. In fact, the priestesses of the ancient world were, by and large, the guardians of the temples' storehouses where the grain was kept (a bank, if you will) for the benefit of the whole populace.

Hathor (sometimes called Neith-Hathor) the yoke-headdressed or necklaced cow goddess dripping with the milk of humanity, recalls more earthy, ancient ways from the time of the once-great serpent[36]— days of a herding and plowing community where the deities, the animals, and the seasonal living floods were one. She is also conceived of as the goddess of precious copper metal. Eventually, as the empire's focus became heaven-bound, she became known as the "Lady of Heaven" at the temple of Dendera.[37] Thus, Hathor's special stones were the turquoise and opal so reflective of the sky:

> All hail, jubilation to you, O Golden One . . .
> Sole ruler . . .
> Mysterious one, who gives birth to the divine entities,
> forms the animals, models them as she pleases, fashions men . . .
> O Mother! . . . Luminous One who thrusts back the darkness,
> who illuminates every human creature with her rays,
> Hail Great One of many names . . .
> It is the Golden One . . . the lady of drunkenness, of music, of dance, of
> frankincense, of the crown of young women, whom men acclaim
> because they love her![38]

Hathor was herself "Gold of the Gods" and (at Dendera) "She of the Pillar" and associated with the "sacred tree" all of which connote the secrets of immortality.[39] Hathor was thus the erotic great mother whose "birth has not been revealed."[40]

> I am the male of masculinity
> I slid forth from the outflow between her thighs
> in this my name of Jackal of the Light.
> I broke forth from the egg, I oozed out of her essence,
> I escaped in her blood. I am the master of the redness.
> I am the bull of the Confusion, my mother Isis generated me
> though she was ignorant of herself
> beneath the fingers of the Lord of the gods . . .
> I took shape, I grew, I crawled about, I crept around, I grew big,
> I became tall like my father when he rose to his full height . . .
> My mother Isis suckled me, I tasted of her sweetness . . .
> I am the babe in the Primeval waters . . . .[41]

The outspoken independence of the female is the outstanding element of the poem, as is the close relationship with Isis, here mother and daughter.

By the end of the millennium, if not earlier, Hathor and Isis had become interchangeable in the people's mind. She was the divine yet earthly, sexy feminine, and the supernatural aspects of the masculine became unified too, as men reached for greater heights. This consolidation and greater distancing of the deities from the populace take place throughout the Mediterranean at about this time.[42] Nevertheless, in Egypt the remnant devotees of the fertility goddess (as in Judea) still held her close in the many temples that dotted the landscape of the Nile River valley. The fading pharaonic empire's international commercial network and its religious authority reached even into Judea itself, as the Temple of Hathor in the Sinai bears witness.[43] What was practiced in these "houses" in their inner cavelike holy of holies and the secrets that the priestly professionals kept, particularly the mysteries of existence in the House of Life,[44] were of great interest to our sectarian leadership and to their brethren all the way from Egypt to Judea.

To Celebrate: Racial Purity

What was once a female-dominated image of birth and regeneration somehow became its opposite by the millennium, when cultic worship and ecstatic celebration became mostly dour, guilt-ridden brotherhoods. Yet the symbols of the old, based on convictions related to basic human necessities, were very resistant to change.

The first sacramental sign of life, suckling, was understood to be related to rejuvenation. The baby suckling on the knees and at his mother's breast (like Isis and Horus) was a key sacred image for the Egyptians. The religious holiday in conjunction with that image was the festival of the Sed, a five-day festival of renewal to celebrate the renewed power of the king.[45]

At the center was the cow goddess, Sekhat-Hor ("She who remembers Horus") "the divine nurse who suckled the god-king and who is . . . the protectress of cattle."[46] Once again there is a tight link between the rejuvenation and regeneration of people and that of their source of livelihood. The cow Goddess, Hathor, blended in with Isis (the mother of Horus), presents the people and their kings and officials with a compelling symbol of the present and the future tied together. The appeal of the symbol is elemental, and its simplicity is further underlined by the people's realization of a divine right to rule, that their kings, priests, gods, and goddesses are driven by exactly the same forces. Simultaneously, the mystery of the birth of Horus is still maintained and further contributes to the heightened sense of awe and respect.

But suckling goddesses (like Hathor) were also symbols of protection and nurture, and because of that the role of the wife was very important in ancient Egypt. The wife was in charge of the future of the house of the pharaohs, and she was the transporter of "racial" purity, which was important for the dynastic succession.[47]

The Yahwistic morality articulated by the Hebrew prophets was in direct contradiction to the messages of fertility offered by the Goddess religion. While adhering to a dictum about fruitfulness and "multiplying," the Hebrew moralists attempted to divorce it from the realm of women and focus on that of men and the purity of their "seed." Thus, women's birthing—with all of their bodily emissions (blood, embryonic fluids, and placenta) and appeals in their travail for succor from the Mother Goddess—was set apart and made taboo. In fact, the biblical editors state time and again that the "seed" of the patriarch will indeed be blessed, thus pushing the woman away from the center of fertility. Even in the realm of ritual and ceremony woman did not play a significant role, except for her apparent "right" to name her children and assure their inheritance.[48] This latter practice, combined with the still-current halakah (oral legal tradition) about the mother determining her child's Jewishness, precisely suggest that the populace as a whole never fully bought into the ceremonial male takeover of fertility magic.

Interior of Cave 11, Qumran. *Photo by David Harris, Jerusalem.*

General view of the Qumran area and the Dead Sea.
Photo by David Harris, Jerusalem.

The jars in which
the scrolls of Cave 1
were found.
*Photo by David
Harris, Jerusalem.*

Portion of the commentary on Habakkuk found among the Dead
Sea Scrolls. *Photo by David Harris, Jerusalem.*

CHAPTER TWO

Of Woman Born

The man said, "The woman whom thou gavest to be with me, she gave me fruit of the tree, and I ate." (Genesis 3:12)

To the woman he said, "I will greatly multiply your pain in child-bearing; in pain you shall bring forth children, yet your desire shall be for your husband, and he shall rule over you." (Genesis 3:16)

BRIEF: SECTARIAN MISOGYNISM?

Even though there are echoes of misogynism in the Hebrew classical prophets, the doctrine of original sin slowly developed and reached a certain climax during the Middle Ages.[1] Qumran sectarians had already used the basic concept, which was familiar to other authors and intellectuals of the time. The sectarians' strong involvement with issues of sin and redemption, coupled with a forceful realization that the world was about to come to an end, led them to articulate an extremist position about "iniquity" and "guilt." Nevertheless, everything they said was consistent with the spirit of the time. The sectarian concept of "the first sin" (*pešaᶜ riʾšôn*) was the first in a series of reinterpretations that ultimately led the Qumran community to drastic actions aimed at erasing sexual sin.

FULL OF GUILT

We are encompassed by iniquity since (from) the womb, and since (from) the breasts by gui[lt]. (4Q507 frag. 1, line 1)[2]

At the point when people began to interpret the myth of the Garden of Eden, its two people and the accompanying serpent, the seeds of the metaphor of original sin had already been sown. However one interprets original sin, one must admit to the extremism of it. To appraise this radical explication of the story we first have to recall that the practice of writing was confined to the domain of educated men in authority; thus, they were able to control all book knowledge and to put their mark on the correct reading. By tightening that rein and by insisting on their hold on "truth," a few powerful men managed consistently to determine what was culturally coherent and valuable.

Guilt in the Apocrypha and Pseudepigrapha

Although it is not possible to point accurately to an exact moment in time when the notion of "original sin" (so integral to Christianity) came into being,[3] we can examine some apocryphal books, written between the murky, seminal time of priestly Judaism and formal Christianity, which already maintain that there is an elemental "pollution" associated with sexuality, women, and nakedness. That condition is described by authors in terms that point to the sorry state of sexual union, but the writings suggest some possible "solutions" to overcoming it.

4 Ezra.   The apocryphal book 4 Ezra is quite explicit in its pronouncement about the nature of human existence: "For *all* who have been born are involved in iniquities, and are *full of sins* and burdened with transgressions" (7:68). Evil, sin, and iniquity, all of which are associated with social and sexual mores, are related in this book to "all who have been born." This echoes the idea that there is an essential human fault associated with the eating of the fruit (which, incidentally, is the standard offering to the Goddess) in the Garden of Eden and its effect on the rest of humankind. 4 Ezra goes on to describe the body as "mortal" and even more pointedly as "the corruptible vessel" (7:88). The author of 4 Ezra claims that the origins of evil and discord can be traced directly to Adam, the decision maker: "O Adam, what have you done? For though it was you who sinned, the fall was not yours alone, but ours also who are your descendants" (7:118). The author describes his apocalyptic vision in terms of two distinct worlds: he associates the "present world" with a lack of "full glory" and anticipates another world, where "corruption has passed away, sinful indulgence has come to an end . . . and righteousness has increased" (7:112–115). It is significant that the vision of the new world is exclusive: "The Most High made this world for the sake of many, but the world to come for the sake of few" (8:1), and "many have been created, but few will be saved" (v. 3). 4 Ezra uses agricultural images to make this point:

> For just as the farmer sows many seeds upon the ground and plants a multitude of seedlings, and yet not all that have been sown will come up in due season, and not all that were planted will take root; so all those who have been sown in the world will not be saved. (4 Ezra 8:41)

What is implied here is altogether radical because the passage insinuates that there is something so fundamentally wrong with the process of planting, "seeds, and growth" of people that no one who is associated with it will or can survive. The ramifications are extraordinary: among other things, the new world envisioned by 4 Ezra will perhaps bring about a new birth, which will result in a different, more positive growth. Certainly the text suggests that the new world will be inhabited by a different kind of person: "And they shall see the men who were taken up, who from their birth have not tasted death; and the heart of the earth's inhabitants shall be changed and converted to a different spirit" (6:26). The author speaks of the eminence of the new world and associates the corruption of the present world with the sin of Adam; he alludes to a different birth, which did "not taste death." Indeed, as most commentators point out, what we have here is an elaborate description of a "new world order"; but we cannot ignore the concept of "a different birth" as well. We will see later that the sectarians took this notion of a "new birth" in a fairly spectacular direction.

4 Ezra's vision of the barren woman who finally had a son whom she cherished and raised is emotionally charged. The woman is described as being of "low estate" and refers to herself as "handmaid"; she has "lived with her husband thirty years . . . and after thirty years God heard . . . and looked upon . . . and considered my distress, and gave me a son" (9:44–45). Like some of the barren biblical matriarchs (e.g., Sarah and Rachel) who ultimately conceive and attribute their conception to God, the lowly woman of this vision is also beholden to

God for his response to her. The woman continues with her story, telling of the elaborate marriage ceremony. Unexpectedly for her, on that day she loses her son: he *died* as soon as he "entered his wedding chamber" (10:1).

This "vision" reflects an important postbiblical Jewish view—a concern about corruption related to the most human of activities, sexuality and birth. Further, the symbols used in the vision of the woman in mourning disguise the reality behind them. For example, we read elsewhere that the "wedding chamber" is the one place where sexual ecstasy normally takes place; it is a place of happiness and union between two people; it brings continuity and regeneration. Most important, the image of the wedding chamber is derived from the world of the Goddess and rituals of rejoicing. Here in 4 Ezra, the exact opposite of joy and ecstasy takes place; the supposed life-giving chamber becomes a mausoleum, and the young groom dies—and "then we all put out the lamps" (10:2). The author proclaims here that the Goddess is dead! In an extraordinary statement that both echoes the Goddess's memory and rejects it, the author maintains that, just like the mourning, grieving woman,

> we, the whole world, [are sorrowing] for our mother. Now ask the earth, and she will tell you that it is she who ought to mourn over so many who have come into being upon her. And from the beginning all have been born of her, and others will come. (10:9–10)

Then, comparing the woman with the earth, the author of 4 Ezra says: "As you brought forth in sorrow, so the earth also has from the beginning given her fruit, that is, man, to him who made her" (10:14). In a subtle manner, death, the taste of ashes, is equated with sexual union, especially by emphasizing the role of the earth-woman-Goddess in that process. The author's conclusion is therefore that the woman has acknowledged "the decree of God," who will send the son back to her "in due time" (10:16c). And in an obvious concluding remark, Ezra tells the woman: "Therefore go into the city to your husband," or submit to him (10:17). 4 Ezra's solution to the problem of corruption and political destruction is the rejection of the Goddess and a woman-oriented culture and the acceptance of a male God and a husband who will assure the race's continuity. Oddly enough, the woman refuses to listen to Ezra and would rather die in the field than go back into the city. The vision of 4 Ezra ends on a typically dominating male note: "And I looked, and behold, the woman was *no longer visible to me,* but there was an established city, and a place of huge foundations showed itself" (10:27). The woman is totally objectified: not only does she become invisible and silent; she is replaced by "an established city," Zion, which signifies the triumph of God and his agenda for the people. Even so, there is irony in the use of the term "foundations," which brings to mind the symbolic "pillars" of the Asherah and her fertility.[4]

Note, too, that there is a dichotomy in this vision between the "field" and the "city": "Therefore I told you to go into the field where there was no foundation of any building" (10:55). 4 Ezra envisions the future in its relationship to the past in the field; there he also has the chance to meet with an angel (Uriel), who finally explains to him what he finds hard to comprehend. The field fits into the author's dislike for the present; he escapes there in order to avoid the corruption of the city and thus conforms into a classical Israelite pattern of escaping to fields, deserts, and mountains during difficult moments in history.[5] The Dead Sea community's act of retreating from Zion/Jerusalem fits this format. The sectarians refer over and over again to the unforgiving, bare desert as an oasis, a new "paradise." Qumran writings repeatedly depersonalize women as cities or regions or other objects, thus almost ignoring female existence.

Within the Hebraic metaphorical landscape, a luscious garden of the kind described in Genesis 2 had to give way to a harsher, more condemning configuration. The disobedience that occurred in the Garden of Eden was slowly transformed not only to the "first sin" but to an overall indictment against human weakness and its tendency to commit that sin repeatedly. Above all, that "sin" became a hallmark and a flag for those who maintained that to overcome sin and weakness, to be worthy again of an association with the divine and good fortune, it was important to minimize contacts with the flesh and its trappings. The various "fences" that believers, religious scholars, and others began to "build" in order to assure themselves that the covenant between God and the "God-fearers" would be preserved were finally expressed as an assault against the Goddess religion and its adherents. The male God could reign supreme only if the Goddess were conquered—indeed, only if people left Eden, whose symbols and images were too obviously sensual, sexual, and hence "fleshly."[6]

1 Enoch. In the apocryphal book *1 Enoch,* a book that seems to have been very popular at Qumran,[7] the concepts of sexuality and defilement go hand in hand: "and they lay together with them—with those women—and defiled themselves, and revealed to them every (kind of) sin" (9:8). In Enoch's vision, "defilement" is equated with "blood" in an attempt to explain to the reader why it will be ultimately necessary to destroy this world "and the many" and bring about a new one. *1 Enoch,* unlike 4 Ezra, is using the story of the approaching flood in an apocalyptic setting. The author elaborates quite extensively on the cryptic story of the *běnê ʾělōhîm* ("sons of God"), who had intercourse with "the daughters of men" (Gen. 6:1) and who presumably led the world into utter degradation—so much so that God decided to destroy it. Enoch makes the clear connection, which is not in the original story of Genesis, between that intercourse and ensuing human corruption. Moreover, since the images that are in the center of *1 Enoch's* narrative are sexually driven, the narrator emphasizes sexual "sin" and harks back to the story of the garden and the transgression of the woman. The main themes distinguish between the good and evil angels as well as point to a war in heaven (maybe mirroring the war on earth) between those servants and messengers loyal to God and those who are not. Enoch's vision maintains that distinction and elaborates on the rebelliousness of *běnê ʾělōhîm* and their link with human corruption. But, in the process of condemning the "sons of God" who descended to the earth, the author focuses on their main activity, which happened to be sexual intercourse, alluding to the glaring connection between evil acts and sexuality.

When the *běnê ʾělōhîm* fall and become *něphîlîm* ("fallen giants"),[8] we learn of the utter corruption of the universe, which leads God to destroy it as well as to preserve one "righteous man," Noah. This story was revered at Qumran, where they too emphasized concepts of corruption related to sexuality and other so-called impurities and iniquities. For the sectarians, it was as if two incompatible species had been joined together; in a way, what happened between the "evil angels" and the daughters of men was a mixing of seed, which was abhorrent to Jews and particularly to the sectarians. The fault, though, was finally Eve's, a "daughter" of man (Adam's rib), her sexual attraction and deceptive proclivity the obstacle to a more perfect universe.

The Wisdom of Ben Sira. It is left to the apocryphal book the Wisdom of Ben Sira (significant Hebrew portions of which were found in the Qumran caves)[9] to articulate fully the "wisdom" of "original sin." In a series of statements about women, wicked and virtuous (mainly wicked!), Yeshua (Jesus) Ben Sira gives voice to misogyny that distinguishes between men and women in a divisive, insulting manner. The author's major message is political and social: "Give no woman power over you to trample upon your dignity" (Ben Sira 9:2).[10] It is a classical statement about power and male chauvinism. "Dignity" is purely external in the context of this passage, and, while trying to allude to a higher instinct, the author urges men to maintain their social and political superiority over women at all costs. Ben Sira then goes on literally to rail against women: "No poison worse than that of a serpent,/no venom greater than that of a woman" (25:15). Or: "There is scarce any evil like that in a woman;/may she fall to the lot of the sinner!" (25:19).[11] The conclusion to Ben Sira's tirade against women can be found in his flat assertion that "in a woman was sin's beginning:/on her account we all die" (25:24).[12] Ben Sira, however, is only one of the authors who clearly details the corruption of women and their very existence as a danger to men.[13] In a way, Ben Sira in his time can be seen as opening the floodgates for others who would focus even more closely on the connection between Eve, the first woman, and the "original sin."[14]

Jubilees. The book of *Jubilees,* fragments of which (in Hebrew) were found both at Qumran and Masada, is directly related to the sectarians perception of original sin.[15] There the "sin" of the first couple is articulated as shameful: "they should cover their shame and they should not be uncovered as the gentiles are" (3:31).[16] Further, in line with this period's emphasis on the woman's culpability (more than the man's), *Jubilees* claims that God was angry ("forever") and cursed the serpent: "And he was angry with the woman also" (3:23). The woman seems to be only a little less "bad" than the serpent, because God does not seem to be angry with her "forever." The word "anger" is not used in the description of God's attitude toward the man. In fact, when Adam left the garden, he offered a "sweet-smelling" sacrifice, which presumably pacified the angry God.

"Destroy the Works of Femaleness"

How evil and wily are women in the Dead Sea Scrolls? They
hardly appear at all, and when they do, they are usually referred to as
cities, trade routes, harlots, and wilers, as well as Sheol (hell) itself
with its wide gullet that swallows up men: "Her gates are the gates of
death, in the opening of her house it stalks. To Sheol a[l]l [. . .] will
return, and all who possess her will go down to the Pit" (4Q184 lines
10b–11). Most often woman represents evil, particularly of the sexual
kind; she is a harlot who lifts her skirts and shows her nakedness or
practices her wiles on unsuspecting men. But she is almost always
nameless. Women are finally reduced to lingering spiritual, abstract
essences, for example, the spirit of wisdom—always referred to as a
female; the red heifer, a sacrificial female (reminiscent of Hathor, the
cow goddess) that exorcises sin. The sectarians portrayed women as
silent and invisible; they ultimately succeeded in wiping women out
of their historical record, perhaps because of their obsessive fear of
defiling that record. As we will try to show, at Qumran, women were
essentially nothing but functional wombs, not deserving of being
named.[17] Whereas Qumran literature converts male biblical names to
its own use in an attempt to disguise living persons, the writings do
the same thing for only one woman, Sarai (Sarah).

We can clearly identify some women of power during the Second
Commonwealth,[18] but there is no one like them in the Dead Sea
Scrolls. Sarai (Sarah) is named in the *Genesis Apocryphon,* and, curiously enough, she functions there as a virgin. The "sectarian" Sarai
(the "princess"\matriarch from Genesis) plays the part of the foundation virgin mother. Apart from her, all individual female names have
been blotted out from these sacred texts. Even women like Eve and
the Hebrew biblical matriarchs (Rachel[19] and Rebekah) as well as
Miriam, the celebrated sister of Moses and Aaron and the woman
most associated with personal and communal redemption in the
desert, are missing.[20] What we find as substitutes for women in the
Scrolls are allegories and moral lessons. Thus, it is no wonder that the
Esther story, bits of which were found in the caves, took on a quality
more surreal than that of the original.[21] The biblical story itself does
not come through too clearly in the Qumran fragments, but it is obvious that the role of Esther is reduced to a stereotypical, subservient
one: "*whatever you desire, command me*" (4QprotEstherd 1 iv 6). More

than that, Qumran's Esther is a flat portrait, used more as a fable.[22] Not only is she marginalized (there is hardly a reference to her), but she seems to be used as a fable about Jewish women caught in a foreign net of mischief and corruption. Her behavior under these circumstances is held up as exemplary, thus serving as a moral lesson for other women who might find themselves in similar circumstances. In many ways, Esther is treated by the sectarians as another Judith, who confronted the foreign enemy, risked her life, used her sexual powers to subdue him (like a modern Matahari), but did not abandon her essential Jewishness.

The other positive reference to the feminine in Qumran is the mother of Noah, Bathenosh, though her name and function indicate metaphor and allegory too. She is "the daughter of mankind" (*bat ʾĕnôš*), who gave birth to Noah under extraordinary circumstances. When Lamech, her husband, confronts her about the "strange" birth in his confusion and fear, she responds that she has been "true" to him. The dialogue between the two is basically about the woman's loyalty and is an attempt on the part of Bathenosh to allay her husband's fears. In fact, even after she vehemently defends herself and conclusively maintains her innocence, he still rushes to his father, Enoch, to double-check her claim.[23] We will see that the center of the encounter between Bathenosh and Lamech is the quasi-miraculous birth of Noah, a biblical figure associated with rain, covenant, and the sun. He is one of the most popular forefathers (if not the most popular one) of the sectarians.

The only real women mentioned in the fragments of the Dead Sea Scrolls (in addition to Sarah) are the "daughters of truth" (described as an order of women at Qumran) in the Marriage Ritual (see 4Q502 frags. 1, 2, line 6); typically, they are not named. In addition, certain women (maybe the same "daughters of truth") were entrusted with other women's "calendars," or with calculating menstrual cycles[24]—a position that, by and large, furthered the agenda of the men and signifies women's obedience.

The most extensive discussion of women in the Qumran writings is in the *Temple Scroll*, where the authors' main concern is with women's bodies, sexual purity, and cleanness, including their blood and nakedness. Menstruating women and those who just completed their confinement are not allowed in the city of the Temple; neither are they allowed to enter the battle camps, which are regarded as being visited by "holy angels . . . in communion with their hosts" (11QTemple 7:5–6). The woman with a dead fetus is treated as a symbol of utter uncleanness: "If a woman is pregnant, and her child dies in her womb, all the days which it is dead inside her, she is unclean like the grave, and every house she comes into is unclean" (11QTemple 50:20–21). We should note that the talmudic rabbis, who are stringent about purity laws, do not go as far as the sectarians.[25] The sectarians consider this woman "a grave"—indeed an ominous image![26]

It is therefore plain that if there was a role for women to play at Qumran, it was secondary, subservient, and oppressive. What we find at Qumran agrees with the spirit of the times. To be truly virginal was most desirable and holiest; therefore, God conversed only with those who were designated "virgin." All nonvirginal conditions were by definition "degenerate" and "polluted."[27]

The Qumranites created their own unique solution to the "problem" of "the first sin," which provided for both the man and the woman to play crucial roles in a very significant drama that would lead the world to redemption. Some sectarians gave up sexual life altogether and were fully dedicated to "holiness"; but followers had more choices. As opposed to the "congregation of perverse men," the sectarians saw themselves as "penitents," "saints," "the perfect," "men of perfect holiness," who took on the sins of "the many" in the wilderness. These adjectives pertain to every aspect of these people's lives but also hint at a hierarchical order of "holiness" which recognizes that some people are "holier" than others either because of their birth prerogatives (priests and the vowed *nĕzîrîm* [Nazirites]) or because of their life accomplishments. In that sense, the Qumran sectarians were not different from the earlier Israelites, who recognized too that priests and Levites, both inherited positions, were of different hierarchical orders. Even among the separate orders they clearly established the high priest as the most accomplished and therefore the holiest.

But the central role of the priests was not sufficient for the sectarians. Their obsession with the concept of holiness and separation is coupled with their grasp of the doctrine of the "chosen," and it reflects the mentality of the survivor who is constantly on the defensive, always running for cover and desperately trying to hold on to what may be slipping away. Their beliefs notwithstanding, the histori-

cal moment was just as crucial. The "end" was coming, politically per-haps; the millennium, from the time of David, was creeping to a close and they had to be prepared. "Pollution" had to be combatted and a new breed of people had to be nurtured. At Qumran they proclaimed:

> they shall separate from the habitation of ungodly men and shall go into the wilderness to prepare the way of Him; as it is written, "Prepare in the wilderness the way of . . . make straight in the desert a path for our God" (Isa. 40:3). . . . And no man among the members of the Covenant of the Community (*yaḥad*) who deliberately, on any point whatever, turns aside from all that is commanded shall touch the pure meal of the men of holiness or know anything of their counsel until his deeds are puri-fied from all falsehoods and he walks in perfection of way. (1QS 8:12–20)

"Purity," "cleanness," "straightness (wholeness) of way" (*těmîm derek*), and the "purification of the men of holiness," coupled with clean, rit-ual food, are symptomatic of the new way of the community in the wilderness. "Pure deeds" are juxtaposed with the "evil deeds" of those who "fornicate" and engage in perverted sexual practices and all other "falsehoods." The sectarians stressed the responsibility (and guilt) of men in an age of uncertainty and corruption. They viewed women as essentially corrupt; and, if not for the state of virginity, women would be beyond redemption. But men are different, and because they realize that the social fabric is tearing at the seams and the whole world is about to explode, they must react. Those in the wilderness declare their readiness; they have undertaken an extreme kind of discipline and recognize that they have some responsibility for the imperfection. In fact, since men are superior in more than just one way, it is their duty and obligation to follow the Teacher who will teach them great secrets that will ultimately erase original sin and lit-erally create a new man.

A CREATURE OF CLAY

There are numerous references in the Dead Sea Scrolls to the inferiority of the body and the essential corruption and uncleanness of people. In the *Hodayot* (*Thanksgiving Scroll*, 1QH), where the speaker seems to attempt to communicate with his God, the principal stance is one of total inferiority: "Before Thee no man is just . . . /[that he may] understand all Thy mysteries/or give answer [to Thy rebuke"

(1QH 12:19–20). The speaker, of some stature, articulates an ideology and a worldview that are consistent with the other writings just examined. In an attempt to denigrate totally the function of the body within the sectarian environment of Qumran, the speaker maintains:

> And [I was taken] from dust [and] fashioned [out of clay]
> as a source of uncleanness (*niddâ*) and a shameful nakedness,
> a heap of dust (*miqwēh ʿāphār*), and a kneading [with water][28]
> . . .
> and a house of darkness,
> a creature of clay returning to dust,
> returning [at the appointed time
> to dwell] in the dust whence it was taken. (1QH 12:24b–27)

"Uncleanness related to blood," "dust," "shameful nakedness," "clay"— all are images harking back to the original Adamic story of the Fall. By invoking words such as "nakedness" and "clay" in particular, the speaker compels the audience to revisit the "scene of the accident" and to force the notion that indeed there is something sinister in a body's nakedness; that people are in their very essence "unclean," spiritually weak, and in need of constant vigilance; and that the main signal of their weakness indeed is their "returning to dust," albeit "at the appointed time."[29] The focus of the hymn is God's greatness and charity as well as his unique ability to establish a relationship with people. While the speaker of the hymn is astonished at this phenomenon, he nonetheless asserts humbly:

> And how shall I speak unless Thou open my mouth;
> how understand unless Thou teach me?
> How shall I seek Thee unless Thou uncover my heart,
> and how follow the way that is straight
> unless [Thou guide me?] (1QH 10:3–7)

The speaker declares his dependence on God, but at the same time he perceives of himself as "righteous" because God chose him as a servant. It is God who prefers him over others; it is the same God who "opens his mouth," that is, gives him human life typified by speech; and it is God who affords him knowledge and wisdom. The speaker is both overwhelmed and feels privileged and unique. Typically, the sectarians see themselves as singularly positioned to both decry the pollution and corruption of the Jerusalem priesthood and kingship and to present their community as true, clean, pure, and holy, newly chosen by God to fulfill his covenant with Israel.

Whether or not the hymns actually reveal some of the historical circumstances related to the Teacher of Righteousness and his adversaries, they do reflect a mentality that draws clear distinctions between "us" and "them," or "the sons of light" versus "the sons of darkness." Dark, hellish imagery is used to connote human corruption and worthlessness, whereas light refers to God's choice of his servant (the speaker), whose "heart" is "uncovered" only because God is his teacher. This unique communication with God means that the power of speech is to be used appropriately to "fall and a[sk for me]rcy for his transgression (*pešaᶜ*) and to ask for the spirit (*rûaḥ*)" (1QH 16:6). Both *pešaᶜ* and *rûaḥ* are used frequently throughout the Scrolls to contrast the condition of "pollution" related to physical corruption with the purer, more spiritual condition of the chosen sectarian community, whose attempts at cleansing the flesh were aimed at achieving the "spirit." In a climactic expression that can be found in one of Qumran's hymns, the hymnist asserts:

> [I will bow down] and implore Thy mercy on (for) the sins of the first (or, my first sins) [and wicked] deeds, and on (for) the perversity of [my heart], for I have wallowed in uncleanness (*nida*) and [was created] from the secret (*sod*) of [nakedness], and have not refrained from asking for your mercies . . . . (1QH 17:19–20)

The poet is conscious of the original sin and its attendant *niddâ* (related to blood) and ᶜ*erwâ* (related to nakedness); with the help of God and his own human will power, the speaker hopes to overcome those "fleshly" weaknesses. In fact, in one of the *Testaments of the Twelve Patriarchs,* another apocryphal book (pieces of which were found at Qumran), the patriarch Jacob commands:

> So guard yourself against sexual promiscuity, and if you want to remain pure in your mind, protect your senses from women. And tell them not to consort with men, so that they too might be pure in their minds. For even recurrent chance meetings—although the impious act itself is not committed—are for these women an incurable disease, but for us they are the plague of Beliar and an eternal disgrace. (*Testament of Reuben* 6:13)

In Qumran's *Damascus Document* (CD) there are numerous references to the body's weakness and therefore the necessity of depending on God, in language reminiscent of classical biblical prophets (who also warned about social and political corruption in the context of religious/cultic and sexual misbehavior). There is a regular warning about "not straying after thoughts of guilty lust or after whoring eyes" (CD 2:16). The sectarians' comment on chapter 24 of Isaiah suggests "three nets" or vices of Belial: "the first is prostitution (*zĕnût*); the second is riches; (and) the third is defilement of the Sanctuary" (CD 4:15–17).[30] To start living a life of holiness, they had to be fully cleansed of the "filth" which was brought into the world first of all by sexual intercourse.

It should come as no surprise that in addition to the "bad karma" emanating from women in the Dead Sea Scrolls, they are also directly attacked as a "species." This attack serves the "holy" design of the sectarians and places them within the more general framework of misogynism as their enduring legacy even today.[31] For example, the most appalling aspect of women is their "wiles," their attempt to snare the righteous:

> [Such women] seek out a righteous man and lead him astray, and a perfect man to make him stumble; upright men to divert (their) path, and those chosen for righteousness from keeping (*nṣr*) the commandments. (4Q184 lines 14–15)[32]

The last line of the document continues: "to make the humble rebel from God, and to turn their steps from the ways of righteousness" (line 16). The very sharp depiction of the corrupting power of women's sexuality is particularly disturbing to the author when confronted with God's "chosen for righteousness."[33]

The function of "the elect" is diametrically opposed to the function of the wayward woman. The gaping dissimilarity between the world of the "righteous" and that of the woman is illustrated by presenting women as prone to evil, seductive, and betraying: they are one-dimensional, flat beings. Words and phrases such as "skirts," "garments," "adornments," beds as "couches of corruption" (line 5c)[34] are associated with negative images of women and sexuality as opposites of more positive sexual associations in other texts of the same period. Splendid garments and jewels can usually be found in descriptions of a bride on the day of her wedding. Whereas the "secret places" where the woman described in this text can be found (4Q184 line 11) are echoes of hell and paths that lead to death, in a more positive environment such paths could lead to a world of beauty and perfection. The "couch" of the wayward woman could be transformed into a bridal bed, where the virgin is getting ready for a special ritual which will enrich her, her counterpart, and the community around them. But, ironically, it is because of this negative perception of sexual involvement that the sectarians were searching for a "new" way to be released from sexual desires.

The sectarians believed that their New Covenant was based on the old covenant, which had been "desecrated" by the people and their leaders. The New Covenant was tightly controlled and articulated, and its rituals signified "apartness" and "exactness." The signs that accompanied the New Covenant included the desert wilderness,[35] a new circumcision, new vows, a new Sabbath, new manner of dress, and a new calendar with new holidays.

Noah's covenant after the flood signified the beginning of a new age, a quasi millennium that followed the escalating corruption of people after their "fall" from the Garden of Eden. Noah was the recognized "righteous" man whose life and acts were to bring peace and security in the newly washed world, signified by the rainbow. The covenant with Abraham under the sign of circumcision moved in the direction of "consecration and dedication from the womb" to ward off the taint of earlier original sin.

Signs of the covenant are both physical and abstract; they signify intimate commitment to the God of the covenant and they carry a promise of spiritual regeneration. From the rainbow to circumcision to strict keeping of the Sabbath and dietary laws, covenants and their signs were meant to erase basic flaws in individualistic behavior and increase group power. The Qumran covenanters added another sign, the vow. Their vows included consecration in the womb, celibacy for certain periods of time or certain persons, periods of silence, and sex without sex—connoted, curiously, by the Goddess's number seven. As stated by Philo, a hellenized Jewish philosopher, in the spirit of the times: he "sees the number seven as being most closely related to the monad, the beginning of all things."[36] It is thus interesting to note some of the epithets he applies to this number. Seven is "the virgin among the numbers," the essentially "motherless," "begotten by the father of the universe alone," "the ideal form of the male sex *with nothing of the female*," "the manliest and bravest of the numbers," "well-gifted by nature for sovereignty and leadership," "the opportune moment," "the symbol of knowledge and perfection of mind."[37]

From the classical prophets of the Hebrew Bible to the more mystical, esoteric works of later writers who commented (directly or indirectly) on the events of the garden and its inhabitants, there was a steady escalation of rhetoric against sexuality. The environment was ripe for a "new way" out of this morass; writers, philosophers, and mystics considered issues of sexual corruption in more and more detail. The preoccupation with these questions was so profound and disturbing that some sects that flourished at the end of the Second Commonwealth and later undertook a monastic life-style. In this context it is not surprising that the Qumranites were initially taken to be celibates.[38]

In line with this attitude toward women, we can now decipher better the Gnostics' indebtedness to the Dead Sea Scrolls. The *Dialogue of the Savior* states: "Pray in the place where there is no woman . . . 'Destroy the works of femaleness' not because there is another [manner of birth], but so that they (the works) will cease [from you]" (144.15–20). Interestingly, Mariam (Mary, the mother of Jesus), who is present when this exchange takes place, disagrees: "Will they never be destroyed?" (144.20). Mary seems to take the Goddess's position and affirms her legacy, saying that it is quite impossible ever to "destroy" these "works." Though Mariam is ultimately turned down by the males, her response reverberates in the *Dialogue.*

The sectarians indeed embarked on a path to "destroy the works of femaleness." A similar motif is expressed in one of the *Testaments of the Twelve Patriarchs*, which decries being "enslaved by sexual impulses" (*Testament of Judah* 15:2b). Virginity was seen more and more as a way out from evil and toward the good. Although the sectarians at Qumran reflected the ideas and practices of their age, their unique political and social circumstances led them to search for (and find) a more decisive resolution to the predicament of original sin in their new model for the female, the perfect, radiant, white virgin. She is described in the *Genesis Apocryphon* under the name of Sarai (Sarah), who performs a *hieros gamos* in which she is cured of original sin by the laying on of hands by Abram (Abraham) the physician:

> How beautiful (is) the look of her face . . .
> and how . . . fi]ne is the hair of her head! How
> fair are her eyes and how pleasing is her nose

and all the radiance of her face . . . .
How beautiful her breast and how lovely all her whiteness!
Her arms goodly to look upon and her hands, how perfect . . . .
How fair are her palms, how long and slender are
the fingers of her hands! Her feet how beautiful they are,
and how perfect are her legs! No virgin, no bride
that enters into the marriage chamber will ever be
more beautiful than she. And above all women is she full
of beauty and her beauty prevails over the beauty
of all women. And with all this beauty there is
much wisdom in her. And the tip of her hands
is so fair. (1QapGen 20:2–8a)

Sarah's idealized portrayal as the most perfect of virgins fits the allegorical mode set aside for Qumran's women, as we suggested earlier. The meaning of her "virginity" and "perfection" in relation to the "bridal chamber" will be more fully discussed in the next two chapters.

CHAPTER THREE

Birth Narratives—
A Forgotten Ritual

BRIEF: THE NAZIRITE VOW AND TRADITION

When either a man or a woman makes a special vow, the vow of a Nazirite, to separate himself to the Lord [Yahweh], he shall separate himself from wine and strong drink; he shall drink no vinegar made from wine or strong drink, and shall not drink any juice of grapes or eat grapes, fresh or dried. All the days of his separation he shall eat nothing that is produced by the grapevine, not even the seeds or the skins. All the days of his vow of separation no razor shall come upon his head; until the time is completed for which he separates himself to the Lord, he shall be holy; he shall let the locks of hair of his head grow long. (Numbers 6:2–5 RSV)

The Nazirite dedication is unique in Israel, and references to the Nazirite vows in the Torah are very explicit. There are very few *nĕzîrîm* (Nazirites) in the biblical tradition.

Naziritism resurfaces in intertestamental literature, and *nĕzîrîm* play an important role in the literature of the Dead Sea Scrolls. There they are associated with the holy brotherhood and see themselves as performing a crucial role in either furthering or bringing to fruition the plan of God for the Jews and the world. They are, in other words, the "saviors" of their environment, as Samson, the first Nazirite, was the redeemer of his. Even more specifically, the "Teacher of Righteousness," to whom the New Covenant is given (by God) is spiritually linked to Samson and his "head of hair." In the *Rule of the Blessings* (1QSb) there are a few references to the "head" and the *nēzer* (crown) as important attributes of the holy, chosen man:

May he [lift] his countenance towards all your congregation; may he place upon your head [and glorify your name . . .] in everlasting [glory]; and may he sanctify your seed in eternal glory. (lines 32–34)

In another part of the *Blessings* we read: "may everlasting blessings be the crown (ʿăṭārâ) upon your head" (line 55). Also:

> May he designate you as holy amongst his people and a big light of knowledge to the whole world, and to enlighten the faces of many [with the wisdom of life and place on you] a crown (*nēzer*) of the holy of holies. (lines 66–67)[1]

Holiness, wisdom, knowledge, and authority are related to the "head" or the "crown" in its various associations and are crucial to the members of the community and particularly to its real "head," the Teacher. Even while participating in the present and ongoing activities of their community, the Dead Sea Scrolls discuss the uniqueness of the *nôzrê habbĕrît* ("keepers of the covenant") as opposed to those who violate the covenant.[2] These *nôzĕrîm* are identified by specific acts that point to their status and differentiate them from those who lay claim to the mainstream priesthood and Torah but whose actions are contrary to the intentions of the Law.[3] Thus, Qumran adds to the Nazirite format including not only the person who withdraws from certain foods and drinks but also one who rejects the life of imperfection and "pollution." In this elaboration, they attest to the direct princely genealogy of their leadership, similar to the claim of establishment priests.

In the first wave of scholarly studies of the Dead Sea Scrolls, there was a discussion of "the connection between the requirements of the Nazirite . . . and the priesthood." When the sectarian "priests" "seceded from Jerusalem and the service of the altar, they became virtually and in practice Nazirites." More than that, Qumran was not the only Nazirite-type center: "a related group had established itself . . . in Egypt—the Therapeutae," who, according to Philo, were involved in healing via ritual baths (the network of basins still remain today). There may have been other fundamentalist, Nazirite-type sects as well.[4]

The sectarian frame of mind can be discovered by examining their reinterpretation of biblical stories. In this chapter we will look closely at the birth stories of Samson, Samuel, and Noah as well as the Davidic Psalms. The "root" (*šōreš*) and the "earth" (*ʾădāmâ*) combine to create the special birth of a special person whose task is to improve and change the nation and its environment. Verses from the Torah quoted in Qumran literature indicate the Qumranites' interest in the topic of special births: "I will raise up for them a prophet like you [Moses] from among their brethren" (Deut. 18:18; quoted in 4Q175 frag. 1, DJD 5:57); "A star shall come out of Jacob and a scepter shall rise out of Israel" (Num. 24:16; quoted in 4Q175). In an early fragment, we read of a special person thus: "[Thou didst raise up] for them a faithful shepherd . . . ." In the final hymn of the *Community Rule* (1QS), the speaker discusses the "elect of mankind" and prays to God that he will "grant that the son of thy handmaid may stand before thee forever." The "son of a handmaid" (like the sons of Sarah's and Rachel's and Leah's handmaids) has proved before to be quite special and he is presented as such here as well.[5]

The concept *nāzîr* (Nazirite) is related to *nēṣer* ("sprout," "shoot"), that is, linked with a family or the seed of a family. These two concepts are combined in the biblical utterance about David's future descendants as "David's righteous seed" (Jer. 23:5); in Proverbs we read that "the fruit of the righteous is the tree of life" (11:30). Both the "righteous seed" and "the tree of life" reverberate with extraordinary, metanatural ideas. The phrases celebrate the power of men in the procreational process without any allusions to sexual activities in the normal, intergender sense of the term. For the Dead Sea community, the importance of the heroic, royal Davidic line, in conjunction with the pure, priestly, righteous line of Zadok (the high priest of the house of Aaron, appointed by Zadok), which they traced back one thousand years, was crucial and fundamentally salvationist.[6]

The Scrolls refer to the millennium and to a count of one thousand years between the reign of David and the end of the Second Commonwealth. The sectarians used a solar-based calendar, which set them apart from the Jerusalem establishment and the traditional lunar calendar of the Jewish festival schedule. Thus, everything in the Qumran community became "new" and numerically neat.[7] Moreover, it was their sense of the "end" (*qēṣ*) and the approaching catastrophe embodied in the Kittiyyim (Romans) that lent urgency to the various sectarian writings of that milieu. At the time of Samson (and the other judges) God appointed a savior as the leader of the oppressed Israelites; now too the "new priests" or *nôzrê habbĕrît* ("keepers of the covenant") at Qumran tell us about their appointed leader/s:

> And in all of them (at all times) He has
> raised up for Himself duly designated men,
> so that He might provide a remnant for the earth
> and fill the face of the world with their seed.
> And to these has He revealed His holy spirit
> at the hands of His anointed (*mĕšîḥô*)
> and [disclosed] the truth;
> and He has clearly specified who they were;
> and those He hated, He led astray. (CD 2:11–13)

The "chosen/designated" men are "the sons of Zadok . . . who stand in the end of days" (CD 4:3b–4). The brotherhood of Nazirite origins divorced itself from the corrupt "vineyard" at Jerusalem, with all its soured fruit.[8] The sectarians withdrew both physically, to the wilderness, and bodily, by not imbibing or eating that particular produce which had been traditionally (along with honey) the nectar of the gods and goddesses. Instead, as their own words proclaim, the sectarians' intention was to establish a new "root" from the pure "branch" of David. In this tight metaphor, the fruit of the new vine would be tended by the Elect Ones and nourished and purified by "living water" and by the glowing red sun. The Teacher of Righteousness would reveal exactly how. We should not overlook the fact that the planting of vineyards and the use of wine metaphors[9] are related to Noah's possible sexual activity after the flood. The planting of the vineyard here is a re-sowing, and its new fruit (celebrated in the ritual of the Pure Meal)[10] will erase the old wine that soured because of Noah's quasi-incestuous encounter with his younger son.[11]

Turning to the miraculous birth narratives, we must remember that their meaning for the sectarians was quite different from the original; indeed, the Qumranites modified the biblical forefathers to fit their own perspective. These narratives were vehicles to express and report the brotherhood's worldview. The tales were accommodated to the society of the Qumran community and included new names (where the originals were lacking names) that probably signified living people. By the time of the Dead Sea Scrolls, hundreds of years had elapsed since some of the books of the Bible were written down (between the sixth and the second century B.C.E.). Social and political changes of tremendous proportions had enabled the new priests of Qumran and their cadres to solidify an ideology of exclusive male power that placed women more on the margins of society than the biblical authors had ever dared. The only positive mentions of the feminine in Qumran and its companion literature are the mothers of the Nazirite heroes, who do have a voice—even a prophetic one. This "prophetic" voice indicates that they knew the importance of the children they carried in their wombs.

The brothers in the desert rejected both the priestly and the kingly power bases in the "harlot" city of Jerusalem; they perceived themselves to be the true heirs of Zadok, King David's high priest. They described themselves thus:

> The penitents of the desert who will live a thousand generations in uprightness; and to them will be all man's [Adam's?] inheritance, and to their seed forever. (4QpPs[a] 3:1–2)[12]

SAMSON AND HIS BEAUTIFUL HAIR

The most intriguing biblical birth narrative is that of Samson in Judges 13. From his name (*šemeš*, "sun") to his major accomplishments, Samson's story is filled with images of miracles, food and drink (wine and honey), a curious wedding, and ritual dedication to Yahweh. This first explicitly Nazirite story in the Bible begins with the description of his mother as Manoah's "barren wife" (13:2b), which immediately places her within the tradition of Sarah, Rebekah, and Rachel, who were also described as "barren." Moreover, when the "angel of Yahweh appears to the woman" (Judg. 13:3a), he tells her, as the "angels" did in the story of Sarah, that she will bear a son who will be dedicated to Yahweh as a *nāzîr* and a "savior." When the woman recounts the story to her husband, Manoah, she describes the "angel" as "a man of God (*ʾîš ʾĕlōhîm*) . . . who looked like an angel of God, very awesome; and I did not ask him from where he was; neither did he tell me his name" (13:6). The nameless man/angel is certainly significant in any attempt to understand the relationship between the barren woman and the son whom she will bear. Manoah seems to be perturbed about this "man," and he wishes to meet with him in order to further understand "what to do to the born youth" (v. 8b).[13] Was Manoah concerned about his paternity? And what precisely does he mean when he refers to the unborn baby as a "youth"? This reference seems to echo the term used in the birth of Cain, who was called by Eve "man" (*ʾîš*) as soon as he was born "with God." The narrative seems to suggest that the special characteristics of these redeemers, while noticeable in their early years (especially in the way they look), are much more pronounced when they become youths capable of knowledge (the tradition in Judaism assigns a man communal responsibilities at the age of thirteen).

The focus of the Judges narrative is the "angelic" revelation to Manoah's wife. The woman tells of the "awesomeness" (*nôrâ*) of the man.[14] The issue of name is brought up again by Manoah (v. 17), who is pressing the man/angel; Manoah wishes to maintain some control over the events that, up to that point, were running away from him. In those days it was believed that naming (a child or a deity) was indeed a powerful tool which gave a person control over who or what was named—it stamped their traits.[15] But Manoah does not have control even when he learns that the angel's name is "wondrous" (*pel[ʾ]î*); nor does he control the conception and birthing process. One of the most glaring absences in the narrative is the phrase "and he knew his wife" before the actual pregnancy and birth occur. Manoah does not "know" his wife; she gives birth after assuring her worrying mate, strangely, that God has no intention of killing them (v. 23).

Manoah's wife is at the center of the Bible story, and it is her voice that we hear, not only because she is the woman who is about to give birth to a "savior" but because she is sensible about becoming a mother after being "barren," or possibly a "virgin."[16] Under these circumstances, when Manoah "appeals" to Yahweh for a repeat performance, God "listens to Manoah's voice" (v. 9). But, more appropriately, "the angel of God came again to the woman while she was sitting in the field and Manoah her husband was not with her" (v. 9b). The setting is one of fertility ("the field"), where her husband is poignantly absent. A woman who is not in the house (or in the tent) but rather outside of it is noticeable in any biblical narrative (or compared with some purdah customs today). In the book of Judges, "going out" of the house is tantamount to a death sentence.[17] Unlike Rebekah and Rachel (as well as Hannah in the Samuel story), Manoah's wife seems to be content with her nameless lot, and the close correlation between her "barrenness" and the angel's appearance to her suggests a certain spirituality which is, by comparison, lacking on the surface of the Genesis matriarchs' stories.[18] Notably, the woman is told by the angel to abstain from wine and liquor as well as to stay away from "everything that is polluted" (v. 4b). From the various hints in the story, Manoah's wife appears to be in charge of the events (these are her vows), and her husband's role is to "get up and follow after [her]" (v. 11).

In one of the most important parts of the story, when Manoah suggests preparing a meal for the angel of Yahweh, he is rejected rather sternly: "And the angel of Yahweh said to Manoah 'if you detain me I shall not eat of your bread and if you make an offering, offer it to Yahweh'; because Manoah did not know that it was the angel of Yahweh" (v. 16). Manoah is almost rebuked by the angel, who reminds him that his status (as angel) does not afford him the possibility of eating and drinking and that indeed all offerings in a Yahwistic context are made directly to God. In addition, the angel insists that his mission is urgent and must be fully accomplished; everything else is of marginal importance. Though we will see that ritualized meals are significant in birth narratives, the angel's reaction to Manoah suggests that he does not trust him to do the right thing; it is the woman's duty to act correctly. Moreover, there is some confusion in the text about the origin of the angel. Although he is depicted as a "man/angel," it seems that at various points in the narrative Manoah is not sure who this messenger is and how to approach him.

The final comment about the angel is the most puzzling: "And the angel of Yahweh did not appear again to Manoah and his wife; then Manoah knew that it was the angel of Yahweh" (v. 21). Manoah seems to "recognize" the angel in his absence and to realize that his only course of action is acceptance. Thus, he is concerned for his (and his wife's) life ("we shall surely die because we have seen God," v. 22).

The birth of the child is described thus: "the woman bore a son and she named him Samson; and the lad (youth) grew up and Yahweh blessed him" (v. 24). Samson is named by his mother; she does not seem to be obligated to Yahweh or any other named deity—as if this pregnancy is her right or even her destiny. Neither does Manoah's wife make an early commitment of her son (as Hannah does in the case of Samuel) to God.

The woman of this Bible story remains independent, but her role is still basically biological and after she gives birth to Samson she virtually disappears from the text. Manoah's role is still of some significance; the author's intent was to place him in the center of events. His name faintly echoes that of Noah, a real heroic figure in the tradition and someone who was "righteous" and "walked with God." Manoah's spirituality and his relationship to God are somewhat undefined, but the correlation with the name of Noah places Manoah within the realm of "peace," "tranquillity," and "rest." All of the latter metaphors allude to a "stormy" reality that must first be overcome before the final "rest" can be accomplished. Noah is the savior of mankind; Manoah's son is the savior of Israel. In the story of Noah we are told that the world was corrupted by both sexual perversion and other "polluting" matters; Samson "saves" the Israelites from the unclean hands of the Philistines, who worship a fertility god, Dagon.

Manoah is of the tribe of Dan (which seems to hold some significance for sectarian origins[19]), from a place called "Zor'ah" ("bee"). Not coincidentally, when Samson, whose name is associated with the sun,[20] operates in Israel, he is associated with bees and stings and honey (symbols of the Goddess that erupt from even the most male-centered narratives). The honey episode, particularly in the form of a riddle, is narrated as a part of the hero's wedding celebration, even though, surprisingly, that marriage was not officially consummated. It is the wiles of a woman (with her compatriots) that make Samson lose the bet he devises.[21] Later, Samson is completely betrayed again by another woman, Delilah, a Philistine, who emasculates him by cutting his hair and thus exposing his weakness; or, more poignantly, she strips him of the shelter of the principle of wisdom, Sophia, that kept his strength and maintained his credibility as a spiritual hero. With his hair gone, the "king"/holy warrior is naked.

Samson's redemption comes when he takes his final revenge, in the temple of Dagon (an agricultural, Philistine god associated with corn and growth). He leans against its "pillars" and tears them down. The imagery of the "pillars" is not only phallic but, more graphically, demonstrates male anxiety in a goddess-oriented culture.[22] The Goddess and women's positive surroundings are absent from all of Samson's life; all of the women with whom he consorts are treacherous or completely evil.[23] Thus, what Samson is pulling down is the Goddess herself.

Samson's adventures are unique in the Bible and he is a much more colorful character than the other judges in the book. Yet there are no other (biblical) references to his heroics; he has no progeny and seems to act as a lone individual who has just one purpose in life, which, once consummated, leaves him with nothing else to do. No other son born in a miraculous birth went down to such biblical obscurity. But later Jewish texts as well as the talmudic rabbis indulged in various stories about Samson—particularly about his birth, which was of tremendous importance during the Second Commonwealth and beyond.[24]

SAMSON'S STORY AT THE MILLENNIUM

A well-known version of Samson's miraculous birth is found in the *Antiquities* of Josephus, the Roman Jewish historian. He portrays Manoah as "a person of such great virtue that he had few men his equals and without dispute the principal person of his country" (5.8.2–3). Contrast this to the biblical narrative, where Manoah is almost a nonentity. The author carefully charts out a tale that has hidden meanings and possibly a hidden agenda to evade the censors of the powerful elite in Jerusalem or in Rome. In a way, Josephus places Manoah within the heroic tradition of Noah by claiming that he was a man of "great virtue" and that "he had few equals"; Noah was just that type of person. Josephus describes Noah as "a man of righteousness" who was "loved" by God (*Antiquities* 1.3) and who offered sacrifices to the deity for fear of further destruction. Pointedly,

Josephus uses the term "pollution" to describe the original fallen world and to justify God's extreme actions in destroying it. Manoah's "principal" position in the "country," which is not part of the original biblical story is quite curious and might serve as a commentary on another "country"/community, more familiar to Josephus himself. We will see that the Qumran sectarians functioned as a "new country" within a country; their "New Covenant," based on Noachic authority, was their road to redemption and a more perfect life; their leader(s) were clearly special and specially born.

Josephus was enchanted with the life of sectarianism, and, while he does not describe in detail any of the Dead Sea communities, he does mention the Essenes (who may have been a specific celibate order within the larger Dead Sea community) at some length. In his *Vita*, Josephus describes his pursuit of practical knowledge (fairly widespread among the elites at the time) and discusses someone named Bannous:

> At about the age of sixteen I determined to gain personal experience of the several sects into which our nation is divided . . . Pharisees . . . Sadducees . . . Essenes. I thought that after a thorough investigation, I should be in a position to select the best. So I submitted myself to hard training and laborious exercises and passed through the three courses. Not content, however, with the experience thus gained, on hearing of one named Bannous, who dwelt in the wilderness, wearing only such clothing as trees provided, feeding on such things as grew of themselves, and using frequent ablutions of cold water, by day and night, for purity's sake, I became a devoted disciple. (2.7–11)

There is no scholarly consensus yet about the identity of "Bannous," though it is interesting to point to a few distinct images associated with him: he was in the wilderness (Dead Sea?); he wore clothes that were provided by trees (the flax plant, or linen); and he used frequent "ablutions of cold water."[25] Such ablutions were a central part of the ideology and practice of the sectarians. The remains of many ritual immersion facilities have been found at Qumran.[26] Although the Essenes were known to use water for cleansing purposes, Josephus does not speak about Bannous as being an Essene. But it is reasonable to assume that Josephus would at some point have found out about the sectarians in the wilderness. We think it credible that the movement was well known and quite popular.[27]

In the landscape of "Bannous" and the sectarian wilderness, it is plausible that Manoah's "principal" position in the country is a crucial role appropriate to a founding father, maybe among newly chosen disciples. Significantly, Josephus does not necessarily mention Dan as the locality under consideration. By comparison and very pointedly, when Josephus's Samson is formulating for the Philistines his famous honey riddle, he promises that whoever decodes the mystery will be given "a linen shirt." The linen shirt may indicate an initiate's outfit at Qumran. More poignantly, though Manoah is married, he has no children and he is saddened by it: "being uneasy at his want of posterity, he entreated God to give them seed of their own bodies to succeed them." In a curious shift of positions from the older story, Manoah, not the woman, appeals to God for children. He is the one who is concerned about "posterity" and his own immortality; he is specifically looking for "seed" of his very own. In other words, in the biblical tradition (male-begetting wishful thinking aside), it was the role of the woman to cry and beseech and appeal to the deity for posterity in order to build up her foundation, her house, and her family rather than that of her husband.[28]

Josephus focuses and embellishes his male hero, though he ultimately must recognize the presence of the female too because populating the "new world" is a necessity. The woman is described as exceedingly beautiful, "excelling her contemporaries." Perhaps her "beauty," like Manoah's "principalness," was a signal of her "chosenness" and/or preparedness for a fertility rite, because indeed this is what happens next.

Josephus emphasizes the passionate love of Manoah for his wife and his jealousy, hinting at what various commentators before and after him suggested, namely, that he was not comfortable with the ultimate product of his wife's womb, that he was dubious about his link with this son; and that maybe the angel/young man himself was the source of the woman's impregnation. Although the surface text (even in the Hebrew Bible) is very suggestive, Josephus's version is radically different from the original. Josephus is careful to characterize each of the participants, including the formula angel. We know more about Manoah's emotions, and we have a clearer picture of his wife—even though, again, she is not named. Josephus seems to connect Manoah and Noah as if they are equals; hence, the son that will ultimately be born to Manoah should be seen as a very special one.

In line with the biblical text, Josephus stresses that the angel appeared to the woman when she was alone; "it was an angel of God, and resembled a young man, beautiful and tall" (*Antiquities* 5.8.2).

The author describes an annunciation scene with the annunciator/ angel portrayed in sexually attractive terms. Nowhere in the Hebrew Bible do we come across that kind of description related to angels, who mostly are either cryptic or simply convey messages. In another strange deviation from the original, Josephus goes on to say that the child to be born should avoid all kinds of drinks "and be entirely contented with water." Once again, while water appears throughout the Hebrew text (and particularly in the Noah story in Genesis), it is not as strongly associated with the Samson or Samuel stories. By contrast, the sectarian writers were preoccupied with water because of their practices of cleansing and "planting."

The jealous Manoah, who suspects his wife's story, is ultimately pacified by the reappearance of the angel, even though he (the angel) does not accept the sacrificial lamb that the couple offer him as a token of their appreciation. Instead, the angel performs a miracle:

> When all was ready, the angel enjoined them to set the loaves and the flesh, but without the vessels, upon the rock; . . . he touched the flesh with the rod which he had in his hand, which upon the breaking out of a flame, was consumed, together with the loaves. And the angel ascended openly, in their sight, up to heaven, by means of the smoke, as by a vehicle. (*Antiquities* 5.8.3)

Echoes of other miracle stories and motifs, such as the story of Abraham and Sarah, that of Moses' recognition of Yahweh in the desert, and the motif of the prophet Elijah ascending to the heavens in a chariot, are abundant here. This is high ritual, a sacrificial scene. The use of "loaves," in particular, is culturally charged (all the way back to the Goddess) because of the association of loaves with the angelic announcement to Sarah and Abraham about the future birth of Isaac (Gen. 18:4–6). The "fire" is equally potent because of its ongoing connection with sacrificial rituals, punishments, and cleansing. (Fire is also the vehicle used by the Romans to destroy Judean cities and the Temple in Jerusalem in 70 C.E.; this image appears in the sectarian writings connected with apocalyptic, millenarian expectations.[29]) Finally, Josephus tells us that the fall of Samson was because of his falling "in love with a woman that was a harlot, among the Philistines" (5.8.11). Delilah was a "harlot," not a virgin.[30] Moreover, Delilah was a "Philistine," a foreigner. Therefore, the great judge should not have had intercourse with her because he should not have mixed his "seed" within her.[31]

PSEUDO-PHILO'S SAMSON

The anonymous work known as Pseudo-Philo's *Liber Antiqui-tatum Biblicarum* (*LAB*), written before 70 C.E.,[32] assigns a name to Manoah's wife, Eluma. This name may be related to the Hebrew phrase "the god of a nation" (El Umah); it is also suggestive of something hidden.[33] But, what is more important, Pseudo-Philo allots to Manoah a very elaborate genealogy that is directly traced to the biblical Dan, one of the original sons of Jacob and Bilhah. We may recall that Bilhah, the maidservant, gave birth to Dan in a surrogacy arrangement with Rachel, the "barren," beloved wife, her "maid-servant." In fact, Dan is recognized by Rachel as her son even though he was carried in Bilhah's womb: "And Rachel said: 'God (*ʾĕlōhîm*) judged (*dān*) me and he also listened to my voice and he gave me a son'; that is why she named (called) him Dan" (Gen. 30:6).[34] Pseudo-Philo goes even further, describing the constant arguments between Samson's parents before his birth and Manoah's conviction that their lack of children was not "his fault."[35] Indeed, when the angel appears to Eluma, he confirms Manoah's position. More important, Pseudo-Philo puts words of prayer in Eluma's mouth as well as a vow of silence. The prayer is narrowly focused: "reveal to me whether it has not been granted to my husband or to me to produce children" (*LAB* 42:2b). Eluma tries to throw some light on the controversy of the time about who the parent is—mother or father. The ensuing silence is a sign of submission and obedience on the part of Eluma: "I am placing my hand upon my mouth, and I will be silent before you all the days because I have boasted in vain and have not believed your words" (42:4). In this particular version, it is now the angel who has the power to name and who announces to the mother the name of her future son:

> You are the sterile one who does not bring forth
> and you are the womb that is forbidden so as not to
> bear fruit. But now the Lord has heard your voice
> and paid attention to your tears and opened your
> womb. And behold you will conceive and bear a son
> and you will call his name Samson. For this one will
> be dedicated to your Lord. (*LAB* 42:3)

These various additions, missing in the original biblical text, have strong parallels in the announcements of the births of John the Baptist and Jesus (Luke 1:5–38). It is interesting to note the reference to

Eluma's barrenness as a "forbidden womb"; this places her, like so many others in the same predicament, within a more priestly framework. The picture that emerges is of a woman who is surrounded by a certain amount of holiness, and in that sense it is "forbidden" to tamper with her. But once the "ban" on her womb is removed, she is told that she will bear a son who will be dedicated to God, which reinforces the priestly flavor of the story. Curiously, in a Dead Sea Scrolls fragment, there are similar expressions dealing with a "fruitful womb": ". . . a reward is the fruit of the womb. Its interpretation: 'the fruit' [. . . . . the Te]acher of Righteous[ness . . ." (4Q173 frag. 2, line 1).[36]

In the later rabbinic tradition, Samson is upheld as a Nazirite for life who is clearly different from other Nazirites: "What is the difference between a life-long Nazirite and a Nazirite in the status of Samson?" (*Women, Nazir* 1:2). Those who are lifelong Nazirites who become contaminated are obliged either to cut their hair or to make an offering "on account of uncleanness." Samson is special and does not have to abide by these rules. Nonetheless, the rabbis, who are puritanical in their sexual mores, condemn Samson, who followed his eyes (that is, courted various women) and therefore "the Philistines put out his eyes . . . ."[37]

A final word about Manoah's wife in the rabbinic tradition may clarify events of the millennium. The rabbis speak of the stature of Samson's mother, here named Hazzelelponi, who (in line with the mother's genealogy as the determining factor), they claim, came from the Davidic, messianic line (*Genesis Rabbah* 98.13; *Numbers Rabbah* 10.5).[38]

Samson, the Nazirite warrior named for the sun, as both wise man and holy warrior was an evocative model of behavior for the "Sons of Light" at Qumran. He had been memorialized and followed in later traditions. The memory of Samson's connection with Essenes living "by the eastern shores of the Dead Sea" is even noted three centuries later by Epiphanius, a Christian writer, who talks about a sect called "Sampseans," whom he designates as unorthodox Christians.[39]

THE BIBLICAL SAMUEL—"BORROWED FROM YAHWEH"

The motif of the warrior Nazirite newly transformed into a priest is further narrated in the biblical story of Hannah and another hero, her son Samuel. Like Manoah's wife, Hannah is barren; like Rebekah and Rachel, she desires to become pregnant. She appeals to God in her yearly visits to the Temple and utters an extraordinary request: "If you [Yahweh] remember me and do not forget your servant (*ᵓāmâ*) and will give your servant a man's seed and I will give him to Yahweh for the rest of his life and no razor will touch his head" (1 Sam. 1:11).[40] The Septuagint, the earliest Greek version of the Bible, has a fuller version: "Then I shall set him before you as a Nazirite . . . and wine and strong drink he will not drink." Since there is a linguistic connection between the word *ᵓāmâ* ("servant") and *ᵓēm* ("mother"), it seems that the narrator places Hannah in a familiar context of special holy women with special pregnancies. At only one obscure point in the story are we told about a sexual encounter between Hannah and her husband: "And they got up in the morning and they bowed down before Yahweh and they returned and came to their home in Ramah; and Elkanah knew Hannah, his wife, and Yahweh remembered her" (1 Sam. 1:19). Elkanah "knows" Hannah, but Yahweh "remembers": the latter is of greater significance and puts Hannah in the company of Sarah, who was also "remembered" by God, as well as Rachel. In Sarah's story, "Yahweh did to her as he spoke" (Gen. 21:1b), and in the case of Rachel "Elohim remembered Rachel and he, God, heard her and opened her womb" (Gen. 30:22). For Sarah and Rachel there is some divine intervention that is solely responsible for the pregnancy; this is also the case with Hannah, though here her husband, Elkanah, seems to be marginally involved as well. Samuel is then removed from his family background and is accorded surrogate parents (particularly a father), presumably to be schooled in the temple in Shiloh, thus losing his mother.[41] Similarly, the sons of the Genesis matriarchs become the sons of the fathers and heirs to the Yahwistic covenant even before they are born.

In both these stories the role of the mother after the actual birth is fairly limited. In the story about Samuel, he initially remains the son of Hannah, who is in control of his early life and who alone dedicated him before his birth to the life of a priest.[42] The Qumran Samuel fragments (4QSam) mention the Nazirite functions of Samuel, who refers to himself as leader of the people and as judge, and who is memorialized as "a rock for a headstone" (4Q160 frag. 2).[43]

LATER SAMUEL STORIES: THE LIGHT OF THE PEOPLE

The rendition of the Samuel story in the *Antiquities* of Josephus is quite instructive in its manipulation of all of the themes that we have discussed so far. As with the story of Samson, Josephus finds it important to emphasize the role and status of the father of the household: "Elcanah, a Levite, one of a middle condition among his fellow citizens" (5.10.2). Elkanah is not as prominent as Manoah, but Josephus paints him as a Levite (which is not in the Bible) who frequents the priestly center in Shiloh. Hannah is an active participant in this version (as in the Bible), and she vows "to consecrate the first son she should bear to the service of God, and this in such a way that his manner of living should not be like that of ordinary men." This particular idea places the future child in a very special position. But before Hannah made this pledge, she "went to the tabernacle to beseech God to give her seed and to make her a mother." Eli, the high priest of the time, responded by saying that she indeed will get her wish. Josephus's retelling of this part of the story is strikingly similar to his recounting of the Samson pre-birth tale in that the woman retreats to a *hiding place* where she is alone with another man/angel who promises her that she will bear a special child who will have a special relationship with God. Moreover, in both stories the whole episode is firmly completed with a description of a semi-sacrificial rite involving a special meal and sometimes an actual sacrifice.

> So she came to her husband full of hope, and ate her meal with gladness; and when they had returned to their own country she found herself with child. . . . They therefore came to the tabernacle to offer sacrifice for the birth of the child, and brought their tithes with them; but the woman remembered the vow . . . and delivered him to Eli. . . . Accordingly his hair was suffered to grow long, and his drink was water. (Josephus, *Antiquities* 5.10.3)[44]

There is no indication that Hannah slept with her husband and then became pregnant; rather, as soon as they return, after eating the meal, she is with child. Samuel's position is symbolized, like Samson's, by water (rather than wine) and long hair. In the case of Samuel, wisdom is linked with his prophetic abilities.

In Pseudo-Philo's version of Samuel,[45] Hannah's voice is just as loud and clear as it is in the Bible: "Neither she who has many sons is rich nor she who has few is poor, but whoever abounds in the will of

God is rich" (*LAB* 50:5). Pseudo-Philo thus depicts Hannah as a righteous woman and her single-minded duty in the world is to obey God regardless of how many children she ultimately has. Hannah perceives herself to be "righteous" because she "walked before you [God] from the day of my youth" (50:4). On the surface, Hannah speaks as a spiritual person who has links with the deity, but she portrays herself positively because she desires so strongly to have a son: "Now what womb is born opened or dies closed unless you wish it?" (50:4). The author ultimately maintains that Hannah is beyond reproach and that her character and behavior are flawless. She boldly describes herself thus: "I am the wife of Elkanah; and because God has shut up my womb, I have prayed before him that I do not go forth from this world without fruit and that I do not die without having my own image" (50:7). Eli is even bolder than she when he claims: "your prayer has been heard" (50:7c). Moreover, Pseudo-Philo relates the birth of Samuel to a prophecy that had been foreordained. When Samuel is born Hannah names him, and Pseudo-Philo suggests that the name, Samuel, "is interpreted 'mighty one.'" In this quasi-perfect environment, the drama that ensues is quite remarkable because it centers on the woman who performs on behalf of the nation:

> You have not asked alone, but the people have prayed for this. This is not your request alone, but it was promised previously to the tribes. And through this boy your womb has been justified so that you may provide advantage for the peoples and set up the milk of your breasts as a fountain for the twelve tribes. (51:2–3)

Hannah's wish to bear "fruit" is now allegorized by Eli as a crucial moment in their history when God remembers and provides for them through his servant, Hannah. She becomes a prophetess, but only in the narrow sense of proclaiming to the world that a special son was born; she is a prophetess but with a limited agenda.[46] The original biblical Hannah had a clear voice as well, but the Hannah of Pseudo-Philo has more specialized power because she claims that she knows God (echoing "sexual knowledge"). When Samuel is born, she nurses him for two years: "And the child was very handsome, and the Lord was with him" (*LAB* 51:1). There are no sacrifices offered; rather, there is a very heavy emphasis on Hannah's words, like a "voice in the wilderness" (Isaiah 40), and her interpretation of the events that came to pass:

Come to my voice, all you nations, and pay attention to my speech, all
you kingdoms, because my mouth has been opened that I should speak.
. . . Drip, my breasts, and tell your testimonies, because you have been
commanded to give milk. For he who is milked from you will be raised
up, and the people will be enlightened by his words . . . and his horn will
be exalted very high. And so I will speak my words openly, because from
me will arise the ordinance of the Lord, and all men will find the
truth. . . . Speak, speak, Hannah, no longer be silent. Sing a hymn, daughter of Batuel, about the miracles that God has performed with you. Who
is Hannah that a prophet is born from her? Or who is the daughter of
Batuel that she should bear the light to the peoples? (51.3–6e)

Hannah is the wisdom/mother who is associated with milk and an
infant, as we saw above in chapter 1.[47] The Goddess references are
overtly displayed in this text in order to empower the woman in the
eyes of the people. She refers to herself as the daughter of Batuel,
which means "the daughter of God" or "the virgin of God" (*bĕtûlat
ʾēl*). The story of a barren or virgin woman giving birth to an extraordinary child is the story of immaculate conception. Though the
woman's voice is triumphant, she is still restricted to the circumstances surrounding her motherhood, except at the end, where she
prophesies as the one bearing "the light to the nations." Her son
shows the way, and "his horn will be exalted." Nonetheless, this quasi-
messianic speech is fairly astounding when put in the mouth of a
woman.[48] It could also be the product of a long tradition of reverence
toward what Pseudo-Philo describes as the representation of Wisdom.
In other words, the author is not enchanted with Hannah as a complete person who indeed accomplished spiritual feats but with Hannah the "virgin," "daughter of God," whose adherence to "virginity" is
the reason for praise. Pseudo-Philo's intellectual climate is almost the
same as that of the sectarians and their contemporaries, who
admired—indeed blessed—virgins *because of their sexual abstinence,*
hence their "perfection."[49] In the Wisdom of Solomon we find another
statement typical of the period:[50]

For blessed is the barren woman who is undefiled,
who has not entered into a sinful union;
she will have fruit when God examines souls. (3:13 RSV)

The barren/virgin is an undefiled woman because presumably she
had intercourse only for purposes of procreation and for the benefit
of the community. Philo (the Alexandrian philosopher) too alludes to

the possible association of the word "barren" (firm, solid, stern) with "virgin," which has similar associations in Latin (*virgo,* "strength to resist"):

> the barren woman, not meaning the childless, but the firm or solid [*steiran-sterran*], who still abounds in power, who with endurance and courage perseveres to the finish in the contest, where the prize is the acquisition of the Best, should bring forth the Monad which is of equal value with the Seven; for her nature is that of a happy and goodly motherhood. (*Quod Deus immutabilis sit* 13–15)[51]

He even goes so far as to suggest that this woman does have power and is looking for the "Best" and the "prize," reminiscent of winning a bet. Who is the "best"? The prize is the fruit of the womb (4Q173 frag. 2, line 1). Philo glamorizes the position of all virgins (male and female) and says that virginity is a prerequisite for being closer to God. For Philo, as for the sectarians, sexuality is polluting, and to attain the Godhead, in the mystical sense (an idea similar to communion with God), one must accomplish a measure of perfection that only virgins have.[52] We even find a virgin man in the Wisdom of Solomon's reference to a eunuch:

> Blessed also is the eunuch whose hands have done no lawless deed,
> and who has not devised wicked things against the Lord;
> for special favor shall be shown him for his faithfulness. (3:14 RSV)

Samson and Samuel are the two Nazirites who become leaders of their respective communities. The biblical record itself ponders their special characteristics and in the process describes their mother's position and contribution. We have seen that all of the narratives discussing these two heroes and their deeds and mothers (including the nonbiblical additions) attempt to come to grips with the Nazirite tradition itself. They portray the heroes of the tradition as holy, "chosen from the womb," and with very special tasks. Even though Samson falls short of perfection, he does redeem himself by becoming the savior of the people—ironically, through images and symbols that hark back to the world of the Goddess and fertility. There is no doubt that the Samson stories were popular not only because of the strength, charisma, and uniqueness of the hero but because he accomplished warrior deeds that resonated coherently and authentically with the people. The miraculous birth motif added a mystical flavor that further enhanced the popularity and magic of the narratives but also positioned the woman in the context of God, angels, and perfection.

Similarly, in the Samuel nativity stories the spotlight is on the mother, Hannah, the beloved wife of Elkanah. Hannah reminds the audience of Rachel, the compassionate mother who also had access to spiritual worship and also had charisma of her own. The biblical Hannah had a crystal clear voice; she sang and she prayed and she thanked; she also had self-worth and was attractive in her own right. Ultimately she paved the way for a more oppressive portrait at the millennium of "virgins" and "barren" women who become objects of male perfection. These newly discovered and newly narrated women are presented on the surface as basically the same as their biblical counterparts, but we have seen that this is not the case. By analyzing and studying the role of the biblical barren women, the sectarians and those affiliated with them reached their novel notions about intergender relations and about how to realize their greatest fantasy.

FATHER FIGURE OF THE NAZIRITES

Noah was more popular in intertestamental literature than in the biblical canon. *1 Enoch* describes the newborn Noah thus:

> And his body was white as snow and red as a rose;
> the hair of his head as white as wool and his demdema
> (Ethiopian for an afro, or, aura of hair) beautiful; and as for his eyes,
> when he opened them the whole house glowed like the sun . . .
> And when he arose from the hands of the midwife, he
> opened his mouth and spoke to the Lord with righteousness. (106:2–3)

In at least one other version of this same text (the Greek papyrus), when the pregnancy of Lamech's wife is introduced there is no reference to her sleeping with him.[53] In the passage from *1 Enoch,* Noah's birth is accompanied by the colors white and red. White is the color of perfection, righteousness, and innocence; it is also the color of the long linen robes that the Qumran sectarians were said to wear in imitation of shrouds and/or the garments of a groom before his marriage ceremony.[54] It is also the color of virginity and wedding dresses.[55] In another framework, white is the color associated with medicine and healing; priests usually wore white and were also the healers of the ancient world. Red, by comparison, is the color of blood and life and the red earth from which the first man was created. The newborn Noah is also portrayed as having eyes that caused "the house" to "glow like the sun." The baby's "righteousness," so important at Qumran, is immediately apparent, as is his closeness to God.

Lamech, Noah's father, *1 Enoch* continues, was afraid of his son and ran to discuss his "strangeness" with Methuselah (Noah's grandfather) saying,

> I have begotten *a strange son.* He is not like an
> (ordinary) human being, but he looks like the children of the angels
> of heaven to me; his form is different, and
> he is not like us. . . . It does not seem to me that he
> is of me, but of angels. (106:4–6)

Lamech speaks of "the children of the angels of heaven" as if there are a few of them that he knows of. Further, births associated with angels, by definition, must have been very different from human births. Although the woman's role is hardly a factor in the above scene, clearly she too must have been very special. Lamech's wife is not described as "barren" or as a "virgin," but the product of her womb is similar to that of the other barren women.[56]

Only after Methuselah consults with Enoch, who depicts the events as "*God will surely make new things*" (106:13), does he go on to suggest that the generation is corrupt to such a degree that indeed a special person (of the stature of Noah) is needed in order to cleanse the earth, or, "he will comfort the earth after all the destruction" (107:3). The phrase "new things" is articulated quite vaguely and recalls an apocalyptic, eschatological setting—like that of the millennium.[57]

Noah and his generation (end-of-the-world type) indeed witnessed new things and became partners to a new covenant. The concrete "sins" that people have committed and which presumably led God to the great destruction (the flood) are associated in Enoch's mind with sexual corruption: "they have united themselves with women and commit sin together with them" (106:14). *1 Enoch* in its sprawling apocalyptic vision reinterprets the Genesis "heroic" story to satisfy its own approach to human corruption and the possibilities for redemption.

We should note the affinity between this story (in *1 Enoch*) and Pseudo-Philo's rendition of the special birth of Samuel that was foretold and celebrated by the people with song and dance. *1 Enoch's* version of the birth of Noah is yet more fantastic and probably more to the liking of the sectarians, who produced their own version of it.

As in the Dead Sea Scrolls, companion literature such as *1 Enoch* reserved its ideal type of woman for the founding Nazirite mothers. Although they have some prophetic voice (apparently still necessary for legitimacy reasons), it is limited to their knowledge of the children that they are carrying in their wombs.

QUMRAN'S NOAH: LINEAGE IS THE CRUCIAL MATTER

The reason for Noah's importance in the Dead Sea Scrolls is that the covenant that was struck with him now preempts the covenant that was cut with Moses at Sinai. Therefore, there must be a special birth story for Noah as well, and there is!

In the *Genesis Apocryphon* (1QapGen), we find the following:

> Behold, I thought then within my heart that conception was (due) to the Watchers and the Holy Ones . . . and to the Giants . . . and my heart was troubled within me because of this child. (1QapGen 2:1–2)

Lamech is the speaker, and he associates the "conception" of the "child" with the Genesis episode of the "sons of God" and "watcher angels." We see that this version of the birth of Noah follows very closely the rendition of *1 Enoch*.

> Then I, Lamech, approached Bathenosh [my] wife in haste and said to her, ". . . by the Most High, the Great Lord, the King of all the worlds and Ruler of the Sons of Heaven, until you tell me all things truthfully, if . . . Tell me [this truthfully] and not falsely . . . by the King of all the worlds until you tell me truthfully and not falsely." (1QapGen 2:3–7)

The striking element in this statement of Lamech's concern is his wife's name, Bathenosh, no less than the daughter of mankind (ʾĕnôš)! Lamech's wife is a nonentity in the biblical story. Not only does she not have a name; she is never heard (as are all other wives of the sons of the genealogies of Adam).[58] Here she at least assumes a name, though it is a far cry from a real character. The other aspect emphasized in the Scroll is Lamech's fear about the child's paternity. He is asking her for the "truth," not "falsehood"; in fact, he is pleading with her to tell him the "truth" about the circumstances of the child's conception. The echoes of Manoah's earlier concerns about his wife's "relationship" with the man/angel, come immediately to mind. Lamech's anxiety, on the one hand, reflects a society that places a premium on firstborn sons. Lamech needs to know that indeed the child is his. But, by the same token, the whole patrilineal arrangement is based on the premise of the woman's virginity; she has to be a virgin because the man in the relationship can be certain about his paternity only if the woman is sexually "innocent." Since we assume that Noah is the firstborn of Lamech,[59] and since this rendition of the story is in line with the other miraculous births that we have examined, it stands to reason that Bathenosh was a virgin before giving birth to this "strange" child. Why was Lamech dubious? What is the truth he is asking for? And why would he focus on the "Watchers" and the "Holy Ones"? We have already seen that the Enochic literature dealt with the topic at length and concluded that, while indeed there is a connection between the birth of Noah and the "sons of God," it is linked positively here. Noah was presented in *1 Enoch* as the man who was appointed by God to save the righteous from annihilation. Qumran's *Genesis Apocryphon* seems to build on the same motif but treats the sons of God ambiguously. They are not considered by Lamech to be evil; rather, they are "holy," holy as angels. Is it then possible that Lamech, like others in this environment, speaks in coded language? Is he referring to a particular "holy" way of conception in which the virgin conceives with the help of the angels? Is this an immaculate conception? Bathenosh actually attests to that when she claims "with much heat" and righteous indignation as follows: "O my brother, O my lord, remember my pleasure . . . the lying together and my soul within its body. [And I tell you] all things truthfully."[60] Significantly, Bathenosh refers to Lamech as her "brother" and "lord," thus alluding to herself as his sister and handmaid (a sister of truth). These two concepts were closely tied to "barren" women in Genesis; their presence here hints at the sectarians' family roots. The description in the *Apocryphon* further emphasizes the importance of the "seed" and the "conception." It underemphasizes the act of sexual intercourse; in fact, it is hardly mentioned in the whole passage. When Lamech is still doubting, Bathenosh is outraged and speaks even more forcefully: "I swear to you . . . that this seed is yours and that [this] conception is from you. The fruit was planted by you . . . and by no stranger or Watcher or Son of Heaven." The one time that Bathenosh does refer to their "lying together," it is in the context of her "soul." The "soul" might refer here to the quality of the seed that is transferred to her in a mystery rite, one that is supposed to produce a "soul"-like experience. Indeed, the picture of a man "planting" his "fruit/seed" in the woman's body for purposes of conception as if she had nothing to do with it, is also found in other Qumran fragments such as "Rituel de Mariage"; there, we find that the sectarians regarded man's internal anatomy, his "bowels" even, as the sole source of procreation, and it is "his fruit" that is to be the product of the "marriage" of "the sons and daughters of truth."[61]

Our reading of the "secrets" in the story of the birth of Noah in the *Genesis Apocryphon,* as incomplete as it may be, which is very closely related to the *1 Enoch* nativity story, opens up a new door to a new sexually oriented ritual. In it there is a designated woman (preferably a virgin; from a priestly family) who does not have to be further identified (*bat ʾĕnôš* is the generic name for "daughter of humanity") but who has to be proved fertile. The ritual involves her in a procedure that aims at ultimately producing a *righteous* leader who will save the whole world from further corruption. The ritual demands that the "seed" which will impregnate the woman be of the right "root" and "branch," chosen by God from time immemorial, and more immediately from the woman's womb.[62] But that ritual also has a "new" twist, as befits the people of the "new covenant": it has to involve minimally the man whose role is indeed more crucial than that of the woman. If the time and place are right, both as far as the quality of the seed and the "garden" in which it is planted, then those who participate will surely reap the "holy" fruit. Noah's appearance is described as so extraordinary that his own father presumably did not and could not recognize him. For a moment, the text seems to stop in its tracks, and it pauses long enough to describe an unearthly creature who was the epitome of righteousness: one who will

> make atonement for all the children of his generation . . . His word shall be as the word of Heaven and his teaching shall be according to the will of God. His eternal sun shall burn brilliantly. The fire shall be kindled in all the corners of the earth. . . . Then the darkness will pass away . . . . They will say shameful things about him. He will overthrow his evil generation . . . When he arises there will be lying and violence, and the people will wander astray . . . . in his days and be confounded. (4Q541 2 iv 1–6)

HOLY, WISE, SAVING WARRIORS AND THE TEACHER OF RIGHTEOUSNESS

Virginity was significant in the ideology at the turn of the millennium and at Qumran because of the linking of sex with uncleanness. We have suggested that the office of a *nāzîr* as well as institutional virginity originated with the priesthood, where both resonated with specific ritualistic tasks. Both the *nāzîr* and the "virgin"—and the former could not exist without the latter—were officially dedicated to the deity and at times exclusively so.

Ironically, these strange stories, which focus on great men, are really about great women, even though they do not ultimately establish big families. Certainly, Samuel or Samson was not forbidden to marry and have a family, but, interesting, Samson (despite his various women) did not leave any offspring. It is as if his pent-up hormonal energies were concentrated on his head of "hair" that once "shorn" gave way to violence and revenge. Samson's legacy is Nazirite and salvationist, of the holy warrior type, and his character and actions live on and become transformed by the Dead Sea sectarians, who preach a similar message of salvation. We see that these Nazirites are not just monks who live in the wilderness like Bannous; they are active, militant participants in a war to eradicate evil: "A remnant will return . . . to the [mighty] Go[d . . . 'remnant of I]srael': it is [. . .] the leaders of his warrior band, and [. . . assembly] places of the priests . . ." (4Q161 frag. 1, line 1).[63]

Samuel's story seems to be purged of all women (except his mother), as he goes on to become the seer/prophet who anoints the ideal king David. Both Nazirites (Samson and Samuel) play a significant role in the literature just described, and their lives upheld ideals that the sectarians believed were necessary if an initiate were to adopt the ways of the new covenant—which is to be holy, wise, saving warriors.

In the most enigmatic (and controversial) thanksgiving psalm from Qumran, the birth motif is played in counterpoint: the special good son is born along with the extraordinary evil son (signifying a leading enemy for Qumran). The speaker identifies himself as the "I" who is beholden to God and who autobiographically identifies himself with the good son:

> And I was in distress as a woman in travail bringing forth her first child,
> for her birth pangs came suddenly and an agonizing (or, strong) pain

with her birth throes (or, orifice of the matrix; or, birth-stool) to cause
writhing in the womb of the pregnant woman, for children (i.e., *bānim,*
male children) are come to the throes of death; and she who conceived a
male child was distressed by her pains, for amid the throes of death she
shall be delivered of a man-child; and with infernal pains there shall
break forth from the womb of the pregnant woman a wondrous counselor in his might. And there shall come forth safely a male child (*geber,*
"man," in the sense of a hero) from the throes of birth by the woman
who was pregnant with him. (1QH 3:7–10)

Though there is no consensus as to the meaning of these lines,[64] the
language used in the hymn describes a special birth—of a man,
maybe a hero, certainly a firstborn child (hence probably related to a
virgin), whose "eruption" out of his mother's womb is an extraordinary event in its own right. The birth triggers a series of catastrophes
that culminate in its opposite, something in the dark:[65] "And they
shall shut the gates of the pit upon her who conceives injustice and
the bars of eternity upon all the spirits of nought" (1QH 3:18). The
point we wish to make is that the sectarians were absorbed by questions having to do with women, their sexual capabilities, and their
impact on the social framework. They were specifically perturbed
about the loss of virginity and what that meant for the fate of the
world. In this painful and violent poem, the male speaker attempts to
identify with a woman who gives birth for the first time to a quasi-
miraculous child who can almost be felt to emerge fiercely from the
womb. Like other miraculous births, this one is also referred to as a
"man-child" and he is "wondrous" (*pele*ʾ)—an echo of the wondrous
doings of the "angel" in the story of Samson. The imagery impact of
the poem is so vivid that the reader seems to be able finally to identify the "firstborn" of the pregnant woman. Is he the Teacher of Righteousness? Or is this just a parable dealing with the sectarian
community masked as the pregnant holy woman who "gave birth" to
a leader who took it out of the realm of evil and corruption and into
the wilderness and redemption?[66] Or is it both?

We find the Teacher of Righteousness identified with the royal
line of David in Qumran's Psalm 151 (11QPsᵃ 28:3–12).[67] The psalm
fits profoundly into the picture we are portraying of the Nazirite
heroes: "So he made me a shepherd of his flock and ruler over his
kids." David is from the right "seed," that is, "Son of Jesse"; he is
anointed by the prophet Samuel "to make me great . . . with holy

oil. . . . And he made me leader to his people and ruler over the sons of his covenant."[68] But the most telling sectarian Nazirite mark of all is the reference to David's "brothers"—by analogy, the sectarian community:

> Though they were tall of stature and handsome by their hair, the Lord God chose them not. But he sent and took me from the flock and anointed me with holy oil. . . . (11QPs[a] 28:6–13)

By emphasizing a special birth, the holy processes of creation and the punishment of destruction, the members of the brotherhood further isolated themselves from what they believed was the "world of darkness" and death. By getting involved with personal "signs" (the various horoscopes found at Qumran) and wishing to avoid "unclean" contacts to produce "new things," the Qumranites created new rituals that cleansed and purified the body sometimes in unexpected ways.

CHAPTER FOUR

Speaking in Tongues

Then I lifted up my eyes, and looked, and behold a certain man clothed in linen, whose loins were girded with fine gold of Uphaz: His body also was like the beryl, and his face as the appearance of lightning, and his eyes as lamps of fire, and his arms and his feet like in color to polished brass, and the voice of his words like the voice of a multitude. (Daniel 10:5–6)

BRIEF: ANGELOLOGY

Angels speak to some gender confusion in Western cultures. In Assyrian art, for example, winged beings appear as male warriors or male lions. Greeks, on the other hand, represent their female goddesses as angels, such as the famous Winged Goddess of Victory of Samothrace. In the Egyptian Tomb of Harpies in Xanthos archaeologists found "a number of winged creatures, half-women, half-birds . . . which calls to mind the Egyptian soul-bird Ba" (18).[1] Then there are the Egyptian winged sphinxes—their gender unknown. In early medieval European art, angels appear as young males; but by the time of the Renaissance, when classical Greek models resurface, we begin to find some female angels and baby angels—cupid or eros, for example—often with their little penises on display. Sometimes the angels are in pairs, usually "holding a medallion [or a mandorla] along with the Hand of God."[2] Angels are depicted with both feet always visible. This may be because angels perform a certain function; they are messengers and must be able to walk on earth as well as fly to and from heaven (see Rev. 14:6, for instance).

Since angels are depicted in the Bible and its companion literary works as heavenly,[3] it is interesting to note that they are always portrayed as youths, even boys. Sometimes they are not even recognized as heavenly beings (as in the biblical story of Manoah's wife and the angel). Their importance, then, lies in their service. Angels are so close to the realm of people that in Daniel, for example, they are periodically referred to as "man"; in fact, in that book they sometimes wear fine, priestly looking, linen clothes (Dan. 10:5; 12:7). The angels' heavenly connection is sometimes implied by their "strangeness," or otherworldly "handsomeness." Beauty here is more than skin deep.

The ambiguous world of the Apocrypha and Pseudepigrapha was full of angels, who were placed within a very elaborate hierarchy headed by archangels. Uriel (whose name designates light) was in charge of the underworld; Raphael, whose name is related to healing, was responsible for the spirits of humans; Michael was the angel who watches over Israel; Sariel's ("Prince of God" or "El is my ruler") duties are somewhat vague, whereas Gabriel (the root *gbr* is related to man, strength, sometimes in the sexual sense) ruled paradise.[4] There are also the angels of Presence, who play a role in punishing the fallen angels (*1 Enoch* 9:1; 10:1; 54:6). There are guardian angels (*ṣôpê šāmāyim*, "night watchers"); the Aramaic ʿîrîn ("watchers") is used in the *Genesis Apocryphon* to refer to the angels' possible copulation with the wife of Lamech. Her husband believes these angels impregnated her with Noah, the very special son, so important to the sectarians. We should not neglect to mention the presence of evil angels, who, interestingly, in the aggadah (Jewish legends of the later talmudic era) are expelled from heaven because they betrayed heavenly secrets (see *Genesis Rabbah* 50.13; 68.18). The Dead Sea fellowship was quite strict with those who divulged its secrets.[5]

In later developments, and especially in folklore, the Angel of Death confronts brides and bridegrooms on the night of their wedding and plots against them. The book of Tobit (fragments of which were found at Qumran) is an elaborate legend that introduces the angel Raphael (in human form) as one who thwarts the evil designs of Asmodeus, who is in the habit of killing the heroine's grooms on the night of their wedding. Tobit (on the advice of Raphael, the healer) mixes a concoction which Asmodeus drinks and which renders him ineffective; so Sarah marries Tobit and they live happily ever after. In the *Testament of Solomon* (a document that dates from as early as the first century C.E.[6]) the demons are associated with the stars; they reside in constellations and have the capacity to fly, even to heaven, where they uncover plans for people's lives. They frequent desolate spots and haunt tombs (*T. Sol.* 4; 6; 17) and generally are involved in mischief. The Angel of Death sometimes carries a knife and is described as an old man holding a sword dripping with poison (see *Aboda Zara* 20b).

Various angelic roles were played out at Qumran and not only because of an idealized view of the community. It seems to us that because of the very specific position that the tradition accorded angels, both the good and the bad, and because a whole host of legends developed around them, it was easier for the sectarians to adopt and transform them. Interestingly, the Angel of Death has been perceived to be the source of magical, medicinal knowledge. The book of *Jubilees* describes Noah as acquiring the art of medicine to cure "malignant spirits" (10:1–13).

Angels are essential characters in the wider mystical category. At Qumran, there are references to "seven paths" (4Q400 frag. 1, col. 2) representing "the rivers of joy" in heaven. There is an association with the imagery of the Garden of Eden and the later mystical association of the garden with the Pardes (orchard), which one is forbidden from entering.[7] Later Jewish mysticism, in particular the merkavah literature of the splendid angel-drawn throne/chariot of God, abounds with angelology.[8] Wings, also representative of the bird sign of the earliest Goddess and the hovering dove of the holy spirit, are literally necessary to accomplish this apocalyptic, mystical feat.[9]

THE *SÎRÔT*

The *Songs of the Sabbath Sacrifice* (Šîrot ʿÔlat Haššabbāt [4QŠirŠabb]) is a rare written record of a mystery rite surviving from the ancient world. Enough copies were found at Qumran to provide us with an almost complete document. The psalms are organized to lead the participants, initiates, and viewers gradually and hierarchically from the first to the thirteenth Sabbath. The songs (*šîrôt*) or psalms, when chanted in unison, must have inspired a feeling of triumph and fulfillment. The first seven or eight psalms present most of the symbols, but the whole scroll leaves an indelible impression of pageantry and ritual.

> In the 9th psalm the worshipper/initiate is brought into the "royal vestibules"; in the 10th he approaches the marvelous veil; in the 11th he views the figures on the brick pedestal of the throne; in the 12th the Merkabah is described, leading finally in the 13th to the climax of the burnt offering.[10]

From "vestibules" to "veil" to "brick pedestal," the images accumulate in a typically sectarian landscape that paid close attention to external matters as sometimes representing the internal.[11]

In this chapter we rely on the careful translation and commentary by Carol Newsom.[12] We agree with many of her sensitive insights, in particular the communal nature of the ritual and its intention to lead the participants toward ecstasy in order to achieve a heavenly communion. But in reading the songs and analyzing all the images they evoke, we come to a more radical conclusion about the function of the initiation mystery—one we think more befitting Qumranian beliefs.

Hypnotic Ecstasy

Up to this point, we have considered the historical and social background of Judaism at the turn of the millennium while pointing out the lingering traces of the Goddess in the region's culture. We have delved into the formation of a strong-minded faction, a warrior-priest brotherhood with its center at Qumran; and we have illustrated the obsessive mission of these sectarians to purify the nation in the face of grave threats by Romans to their culture and their very existence. In this chapter, we look closely at a text from Qumran that dramatizes how intense ideas were put into action and displayed to the community. We will begin to see what the sectarians' final logic was in their attempts to "solve" the problem of virginity.

In this chapter we will witness a high ritual, one with an intricate mystery related to angels. The setting is illuminated by the "highly descriptive content and the carefully crafted rhetoric [that] direct the worshipper . . . toward a particular kind of religious experience, a sense of being in the heavenly sanctuary and in the presence of the angelic priests and worshippers."[13] We pay close attention to the "particular kind of religious experience" that is conveyed by the *šîrôt*. In both tone and mood one can easily detect an urgency and an immediacy that account for the length of the description of the initiate, the priests, and the community participating in the gathering. The enormity of the experience is punctuated further by the time of the week (the Sabbath) and the regularity (at least thirteen) of the singing and possibly "sacrificing." These notions of a specific time and place as well as regular action illustrate the almost fanatical sense of order associated with the Qumran sectarians. Not only were they adherents of a nontraditional calendar, but they emphasized repeatedly the importance of doing the right thing at the right time: "He makes the fo[rm]er things [in their seasons (*môʿēd; môʿădîm*) and the latter things in their due time . . .]" (4Q402 4:13–14).[14] What they desired was nothing less than to commune with the angels, who travel back and forth from the stars and who are the saints who live in God's gated court.

To reach this heavenly communion required a "sophisticated manipulation of religious emotion in the songs."[15] There is sometimes a strong sense of presence associated with the description of the angels in the *Songs,* and at times one can detect a confusion between angels and real (though, holy) people. The relationship between the earthly realm and the heavenly realm is described in terms that are real enough to suggest that the humans discussing the angels totally identify with them. The forceful motivation in Qumran to establish a uniquely holy community might have led the sectarians to a deliberate attempt to envision the heavenly residents as earthly. They may have purposefully created the *Šîrôt* as if to witness physically the heavenly entourage and to demonstrate to the congregation that holiness had materialized among them. The vivid, detailed descriptions of the heavenly priests lavishly dressed and their celestial community singing and praising are very real and seem to be analogous to the meticulous sectarians themselves preparing for the right time, the appropriate words, and the applicable emotions. The texts manage thus to generate a certain perception of reality. Even more relevant is the *Šîrôt*'s literary flow, which enhances the response of the reader and creates a sense of theater. It is as if there is an audience, an assembly, which not only listens to the songs but also is watching the events that unfold on the Temple stage.

There are other texts also that articulate a relationship between the holy community gathered at Qumran and the angels in heaven and show the identification between "holy angels" and the "holy initiates" (e.g., 1QM 4:5–14; 9:15–16; 10:11; 1QS 10:8; 1QH 11:13). A popular notion of the sectarians was the idea of a human, holy community reflecting a heavenly, angelic community. In a sense, the discipline, rituals, and way of life undertaken by the Qumranites ideally made it possible for them if not to be transformed into angels then at least to be able to fully identify with the angels' status and mentality.

The idea of an earthly congregation mirroring a heavenly one is a classical, mystical concept that derives from the biblical view of chosenness.[16] The connection between "holiness" and the Sabbath is strong in biblical literature as well as in the Qumran writings. Therefore, it is no surprise that the Qumran community's reenactment of a heavenly sacrifice, a communion, is on the Sabbath, when the holy spirit is most accessible. This propitious timing allows access to the powers that be, in accordance with the quasi-solar calendar, at heaven's most permeable moment.[17]

But we wish to go one step farther. The dramatic ritual alluded to in the *Šîrôt* is not merely a priestly version mirroring a heavenly initiation of angels, or a circumcision of "joiners" or converts, as it has been interpreted.[18] On the contrary, the ritual mainly records the script of those who played the role of angels; furthermore, the words and the actions are presented from the perspective of angels. The angels are described as functioning within a clearly hierarchical order: the highest archangel, the Prince of light, is also the judge Michael or Melchizedek.[19] The seven archangelic counselors are a larger number of taskmasters, known as *ʾēlîm* ("Godlike beings").[20] Below them are the more ordinary angels living in the "camps," which indicates their human form. The initiates, their role being central to this drama, are designated as such by the crescendo of the seventh psalm.[21] Possibly there are the cherubim too who play the role of the babes in training.[22]

The Ritual

Before considering who the initiates are, we reconstruct the ritual that accompanied the Sabbath sacrifice. In attempting to clarify the symbolic code—the common person's evocative touchstone to profound thoughts—we harmonize the materials in the *Songs* and draw conclusions from the whole rather than from one psalm at a time (with the exception of psalm 7, which we examine in detail). This is necessary because of the secrecy of sectarians' rituals and their reluctance to divulge any of their activities to outsiders.[23] There is no reason to assume that even the clearest of rituals will be conclusively marked by a secretive group that, in fact, preferred to transmit such details orally.

The ritual begins: "O you godlike ones among all the holiest of the holy ones" (4Q400 1 i 2) and "the people (who possess) His glorious insight the godlike beings who draw near to knowledge" (4Q400 1 i 6). Thus are introduced the main actors of this spectacle: the initiates, those of "the sanctification" and their counterpart angels "of the presence" already imbued with the holy spirit. The emphasis on "holy" (*qōdeš, qādôš*) and "pure" (*ṭāhôr*) is constant, as is the focus on "king" and "god" (ʾēl), "prince" (nāśîʾ), and "priest" (kōhēn). The themes of holiness and purity run throughout the psalms; those who actively participate are viewed as the "holy ones," and those insiders who watch are vicariously benefiting.

The first six psalms form an introduction and a design. They repeat the main themes and words of the ritual, which will hypnotically induce the participants into an event that will bond them like no other. From "glory," "wonder," "royal," "God of knowledge," to "war in heaven," "wondrous new works," and "purpose" in the eschatological sense (4Q402 4) the *Šîrôt* move toward the climactic seventh-psalm event.

The vowed initiates undergo a "lengthy preparation,"[24] perhaps forty days (an appropriate number related to the testing and trials in the story of the exodus), a time for reconsideration, further dedication, ritual bathing, special diet, fasting, confessing, and maybe even exorcism—the casting out of any residual male and female demons.[25] The psalms are coordinated with the *Jubilees* calendrical cycles, and the ritual is performed in the spring of the year, when wisdom in terms of the law (the giving of the Torah to Moses) or in terms of the holy spirit (at Qumran) is most accessible. Once the initiates have been certified as physically and spiritually sound (a requirement of admission)[26]—and of course virginal—the climactic event of psalm 7 begins. The time is the "sixteenth of the month" (the second month is iyyar, which parallels our May/June).[27] The psalm's call to praise God "is expanded into seven distinct calls to praise." Phrases used include "praise," "sing," "give thanks," "elevate," and so on. Even the "animate structures and architectural features of the heavenly temple are called upon to praise." The end of the psalm describes the throne of God in the heavenly *děbîr* (holy of holies), the angels in the *debir*, and the angels' praise. "The passage concludes with a description of the praise uttered by the *merkābôt* (chariots), their cherubim (youthful-looking angels) and ʾôpannîm (wheels)."[28] "Let the holiest of the godlike ones sanctify the King of glory who sanctifies by holiness all His holy ones" (4Q403 1 i 31). The ritual is meant for "the holiest," to maintain their most holy status or possibly to bring about a most holy consequence. That statement at the beginning of the seventh psalm draws attention to a specific class of "angels" whose uniqueness is their special, extreme holiness. What distinguishes them from the others is their "choicest spiritual portion" (1 i 40). This difficult phrase apparently alludes to a "sacrifice," an "offering" that is sometimes made in the context of spices and holy oil (Exod. 30:23). Clearly, there is an offering made here that can indeed be compared with an "anointment" which is ultimately to represent "holiness" and completion.[29] The initiate is involved in a sacrificial act that renders him "holy" and "anoints" him in a most sacred (and secret) ceremony. The accumulation of images that tell about "purity" and "purity of purities" (1 i 42) is quite striking and further directs the audience to the mystery at hand.

> Sing with joy, you who rejoice . . . rejoicing among the wondrous godlike beings. And chant His glory with the tongue of all who chant with knowledge; and (chant) his wonderful songs of joy with the mouth of all who chant . . . [For He is] God of all who rejoice . . . forever and Judge in His power of all the spirits of understanding. . . . Sing praises to the mighty God with the choicest spiritual portion that there may be . . . a celebration with all the holy ones, that there may be wondrous songs together with e[ternal] joy. (4Q403 1 i 36–40)

All of these utterances combine to create a feeling of grandeur and splendor. But it is the "chanting" and the repetition that involve the whole congregation/assembly in a ritual that only they have witnessed and only they can therefore sing about. They alone "understand" it; they "celebrate together"; it is they who "know" and record "with their tongue."

On this crucial Sabbath eve (calendrically situated between Passover and Shavuot, Pentecost), the congregation waits by torchlight outside the sanctuary for the rising morning star—the cult sign (as distinct from the traditional sunset and moon orientation of Temple Judaism)—described as "perfect light" (*ʾôr tôm*),[30] the mingled colors of a most holy spiritual substance" (4Q403 1 ii 1). Then "from between them godlike beings (*ʾēlîm*) run like the appearance of coals of fire" (4Q403 1 ii 6). The vision of "coals of fire" in relation to holiness and the Presence of God and his angels has been utilized by both Isaiah (chapter 6) and Ezekiel (chapters 1; 10). In Isaiah coals were used to remove the "impurities" from the prophet's "lips," and afterwards he (Isaiah) was officially consecrated as God's messenger. The "angels" in the Qumran ceremony are also consecrated, but in a new situation.

Then there is an additional description of the presence of angels: "and divine spirits, shapes of flaming fire round about it" (line 9).

"Flaming fire" too is a traditional symbol of sacredness and sanctification, though it is also an image of separation. In this context, those who are holy are separated from the unholy; in fact, the holy seem to be afforded the opportunity to remove figuratively the "flaming sword" which bars entrance into the Garden of Eden, a place that was inhabited by the first two people, the man and the woman (Adam and Eve), and also the first untainted "virgins" (Gen. 3:24).

Further, there are references to "mingled colors" (*roqmâ*, or *riqmâ*). Such imagery is used in Ezekiel in two specific contexts: in chapters 16 and 17) the prophet accuses Israel of harlotry and idolatry and uses bright colors to illustrate the Israelites' commitment to the Goddess. The second context of a "variety of colors" is the oracle against Tyre, which was famous for its royal dye industry (see Ezekiel 28).[31] There, too, the idolatrous context should not be missed. The phrase "mingled colors" was used to deride the worshipers of the Goddess, whose priestesses were famous for their spectacular, colorful dress.[32]

This part of the psalm is mainly descriptive and wishes to impress on the viewer (reader) the spectacular nature of the light (rather than just dress), but it would certainly recall the biblical associations, well known to the sectarians. Here, the poet distances himself from the Ezekiel usage even though he clearly evokes the prophet's words and memory. The context here is positive, prophetic, and holy; those who partake of the "spirit" (*rûah*) of "the most holy" become holy themselves.

The other reference to "fire" is reminiscent of Moses in the wilderness confronting Yahweh in an "unconsumed fire" (*lahab ʾēš*) (Exod. 3:2). There Moses is verbally anointed as God's messenger to the pharaoh.[33] As an image of the divine, fire fits this particular setting and also provides a grandiloquent spectacle that people will not soon forget.[34]

Meanwhile, the initiates in their short (for a reason) sleeveless tunics,[35] possibly smeared with excrement (if following the tradition of Joshua in the book of Zechariah),[36] symbolizing their rededication from early vows to the higher state of purity here ordained, are blessed. That process of rededication is the prescribed order because "they are part of his glorious works; before even they existed, they were part of His plan" (4Q402 4:15). The sect's belief in predestination is evident, as well as their adherence to concrete directives that must be fulfilled by those who are called to be reborn, that is, to receive a new status and a new name.

> And there is a voice of blessing from the chiefs of His *dĕbîr* ... and the voice of blessing (is heard) is glorious in the hearing of the godlike beings and the councils of. ... And all the crafted furnishings of the *dĕbîr* hasten (to join) with wondrous psalms in the *dĕbîr* ... of wonder ... with the sound of holy multitudes. ... And the chariots of His *dĕbîr* give praise together, and their *cherubim* and thei[r] *ôphannîm* bless wondrously ... (4Q403 1 ii 12–15)

The moment of "blessing" is as spectacular and concrete as the rest of the procedure, and its climax is expressed communally, with everyone "blessing wondrously." The "wonder" and the "mystery," which are revealed to those who "know" and who are ready to "sacrifice," are a running motif throughout. But there is also "the mingled color of a most holy spiritual substance" (4Q403 1 ii 1), which may be the description of a sign painted on their hands and feet as initiates of a bridal ritual. (A similar practice is followed today among some traditional Middle-Eastern Jews, as well as Yemenites, Arabs, and Indians.) These initiates are preparing to become reborn to be qualified as the virginal brides of the Holy Spirit, "the spirits of holiest holiness." (4Q403 1 ii 7). In accordance with the notion of a dazzling, special celebration are various descriptions of a colorful dress which signifies festivities:

> In their wondrous stations are spirits (clothed with) many colors, like woven work, engraved with figures of splendor. In the midst of the glorious appearance of scarlet, the colors of most holy spiritual light, they stand firm in their holy station before the [k]ing, spirits in garments of [purest] color in the midst of the appearance of whiteness. (4Q405 23 ii 7–9)

This is not a traditional description of the priests' vestments; rather, it is a special "colorful" moment which blends two basic colors (red and white) with the power of the sun.[37] That "blending" of colors and dye, when applied to the head, helps to produce a golden red glow which proclaims their angelic glory in "shapes of flaming fire round about it" (4Q403 1 ii 9). At the same time, the initiate's head is kept covered, if not fully veiled from sight, "[while] he is unclean" (4Q402 frag. 4, line 4), until the appointed time for "making new things":

All these things He has done wondrously together with those things which are eternally hidden. . . . And from His knowledge [and His purposes have come into existence all the things which were eternally appointed.] He makes the fo[rm]er things [in their seasons and the latter things] [in their due time]. (4Q402 frag. 4, lines 11–14a)

At dawn, a light from the fire outside, understood as a flame from the everlasting sun, is taken by a runner angel into the sanctuary to signify the beginning of the act of sacrifice. There is a ritualized equivalent in the church today, where lighted candles function as a replacement for the lamps in the holy of holies in the Temple in Jerusalem. There is also a "fire ritual" related to Holy Saturday, when the church "prepares for the rising of the Christ on Easter Day. 'New fire' is struck from a flint as a prelude to the ceremonies, and coals lit from it outside the church. The fire is blessed and brought into the church, eventually to light one candle in which five grains of incense have been placed."[38] In the *Šîrôt,* the initiates and the full fellowship drink the wine, which is specified as having an "odor": "and the o[do]r of their drink offerings according to the num[ber of . . .] of purity with a spirit of holi[ness]" (11QŠirŠabb frags. 8–7, line 3). The odor is probably to be associated with drugs appropriate to the ceremony.[39] The participants then eat the loaves, the sacred meal of their communion. The initiate is supported by his appointed "best" friend, like the best man of a wedding ceremony. Perhaps the initiate is veiled by the best man, a duty of the husband in traditional Jewish weddings.

But the angels' speech is not recorded. Why do we not hear what they are saying?[40] One commentator has suggested that the big difference between the "tongues of men and of angels" rendered their idiom unintelligible.[41] Perhaps also, at such auspicious moments the sectarians themselves spoke in tongues (an ecstatic incomprehensible language), a chanting that would drown out what was going on. The sectarians' taste for the esoteric is evident elsewhere in their use of magical incantations written backwards and in circles.[42] In any case, the *Šîrôt* represent "an implicit call to imitate the angels."[43]

In the same context, one should consider the question of silence and its relationship to mystical ecstasy.[44] This rich "silent" tradition preoccupied the sectarians as part of their wish to imitate the divine in the most minute details.[45] In other words, maybe we do not hear the angels because of the vow of silence undertaken by the initiates (and the other sectarians), who may not speak about the ritual until after it is over. In addition, there is the basic "silence" of heavens that are far too remote, radically different, and therefore "silent" to us, humans. Above all, the silence of the participants draws attention to the ritual and pageantry taking place in the presence of other members who may wish to imitate those who are actively involved: "They are honored among all the camps of godlike beings (*ĕlōhîm*) and reverenced by mortal councils" (4Q400 frag. 2, line 2). There are also the godlike ones, other angels (those not yet initiated or those already in heaven), those with specialized duties, "those of the Presence and those of Sanctification,[46] and "holy ones" (probably a cast of priests and rechabite monks),[47] each with his particular vows and water rites of purification—all witness that which transpires: the secret. But even those who witness "know." It is therefore no accident that the comment that those involved in the ritual are "those that know" or "those that establish knowledge" (gnosis) is repeated almost unrelentingly in the *Šîrôt* (almost as often as the virginal number seven).[48] The most outstanding (yet typical) example is present in the first psalm:

> In the assembly of all the *ēlîm* of [knowledge and in the councils of all the] godlike [spirits] He inscribed His statutes for all spiritual creatures and [His glorious] judgments [for all who establish] knowledge, the people (who possess) His glorious insight, the godlike beings who draw near to knowledge. (4Q400 frag. 1, lines 5–6)[49]

There is irony in the use of the verb "inscribed" (*ḥrt*) because of its intimate link with the covenant that God "cut" with the Jews and presumably the sectarians. Circumcision was the sign of the original covenant (involving a cut); this ritual represents another covenantal "cut," which will be "inscribed" forever not only in the hearts of the initiates but also on their flesh. It is the greatest sacrifice: castration. Crucial diagonal cuts are made on the tied off areas (perhaps for prepubescent boys the testicles alone; or, for the most zealous of men, full castration of testicles and penis with a reed placed in the urethra to maintain an opening). The wounds are cauterized with fire ("shapes of flaming fire round about it" [4Q403 1 ii 9])[50] and anointed with healing oils. Then the physician/priest proclaims: "Thou art nigh to (God) and nigh to all His holy ones. Now be thou pure in thy flesh from every defilement of all men" (*Aramaic Testament of Levi* v. 18)[51] and then, "they announce in the stillness" (4Q401 frag. 16, line 2)[52] to the crowd outside. The "stillness" is appropriate because of the reality of the moment rather than the ineffability of the mystical experience.

"Stillness" represents tension and expectation, as well as an inability to articulate a profound experience. Marking the moment, the incense covering the smell of the holocaust of the fleshly sacrifice wafts outside to the crowd. This is a solemn moment when everyone realizes that there are "wonderful mysteries" but that the angels will now "make known hidden things" (4Q401 14 ii 2–6). They reveal secret knowledge "for those who cause knowledge to shine among all the *ʾēlîm* of light" (4Q403 1 ii 35). And as the "Hymn to the Creator" asserts: "When all his angels had witnessed (it) they sang aloud, for he showed them what they did not know" (11QPsᵃ 26:5–6).[53] In other words, what the initiate shows is the way God reveals to the community a process by which a man, born of woman and the flesh, can become a newly born "angel" by undergoing a procedure, painful as it may be, which renders him virginal, newly born forever and thus perfect.[54] The angels celebrate loudly: "with the tongue of all who chant with knowledge and (chant) His wonderful song of joy" (4Q403 1 i 36). However, it is unlikely that everyone who participated in the ritual actually survived it; and although there are no concrete references to blood and death in the *Songs,* the bloody echoes of the Angel of Death can be subtly heard. In another psalm from Qumran (11QPsᵃ 27:10) there is a clear reference to providing an outlet for those who have been stricken by demons or evil spirits. The Qumran psalmist tells his audience that "David" wrote thousands of psalms "and songs for making music over the stricken."[55]

The initiate's hair, with its sublime radiance, may be revealed only after the officiating priest pronounces: "You have purified a perverse spirit of great sin so that it may stand in assembly with the host of the holy ones, and enter into community with the congregation of heavenly beings" (1QH 3:21–22). Lifting the veil or mantle, the congregation can then see the initiate's hair "dyed with a most holy spiritual light" and his robe exchanged for a "splendid vestment," also "dyed" but with various colors and patterns: "multicolored like wo[ven work] purely blended, dyed garments" (11QŠirŠabb 8–7, line 5). These represent the rainbow sign of Noah. In biblical literature, "multicolored" fabrics are usually worn by women and kings.[56] The robe of the godlike ones is distinctive, quite appropriate for transvestites serving God and the new age by making the greatest fleshly sacrifice.

Also envisioned in the script are many colored stones, the opals and turquoise reflecting the sky, "the perfect light, the mingled colors of a most holy spiritual substance," and "crafted" artifacts overlaid with gold to catch the sunlight. All of this is evocative of the stained-glass windows and gilding of later churches and synagogues. These treasures of the *Šîrôt,* if factual (and the word crafting suggests they are), may account in part for the astonishing inventory in the *Copper Scroll.*

The godlike ones ("wondrous new works. . . . He has done wondrously together with those things which are eternally hidden" [11QŠirŠabb 1:1]) are carried on a litter outside (similar to religious processionals today as well as Arab weddings and circumcision rituals), and with timbrel and other musical instruments, their new status is announced: "Standing before you [celebrants] with the everlasting host." Paraded in jubilation and glitter, the celebrant "will cry joyously" (11QŠirŠabb 2:15)—"Hallelujah!" to the crowds.[57]

The final act may be a blessing by the priests of the congregation.[58] The appearance of the chariot (*merkābâ*), which may function here as a bridal chair, is anticlimactic. A later *Šîrôt* psalm for another occasion, forty days later, describes another processional carriage for the new *ʾēlîm*—or, at least, for those who survived the radical surgery of these physician-priests.

For the reader who thinks that our proposal is too unbelievable, consider that a similar tradition of total castration still takes place in modern-day India among the transvestite Hijras. This highly esteemed sect of eunuchs is dedicated to the service of the Goddess and perform musical rituals at weddings and births. Interpreting their status, too, as having been "reborn," they follow the same rules and procedures we have just finished describing: forty days of mental and physical preparation, a mantra to produce a trancelike state during surgery of penis and testicles (and they claim no pain), postceremonial henna, bridal clothing, processional, and a forty-day recovery period.[59] The old, unified, widespread Goddess system has left us a remnant.

Speaking of Tongues

The tongue imagery of the songs, repeated throughout, is the telling symbol of this rite of passage:

> And the offering of their tongues . . . And the tongue of the first (angelic prince) will grow strong sevenfold (joining) the tongue of the one who is

second to him. And the tongue of the one who is second with respect to him will grow strong. . . . And with the tongue of the seventh it will grow strong . . . holiness of the sanctuary. (4Q403 1 ii 26–29)

Even though the coherence of the phrases is not always maintained (it is a great secret after all!), the key words are "offering" and "grow strong." The first denotes a sacrifice, and the second suggests acceptance and accomplishment. The final "holiness" is the personal and communal outcome.

It is now our task to understand more fully what the sectarians did with their "angels" and how they attempted to "correct" the debased world, at least within their own ranks. As befits the frame of mind of the Qumran fellowship, the roles played by the sectarian priests reflect a rigid hierarchy. The highest archangel, the Prince of Light, is Michael, or Melchizedek, who is quoted as saying:

[My] des[ire] is not according to the flesh, [and] all that I value is in the glory of . . . [. . . the pl]ace of holiness. . . . And who can deal with the issue of my lips? . . . [F]or I am reckoned with the "gods," and my glory is with the sons of the King. (4Q491 frag. 2)

In keeping with Second Temple levitical practice, in which cultic song accompanied sacrifice and circumcision and conforming to yet more ancient rituals, we assert that all parts of the *Šîrôt* are scripted; all are roles, played out at the appropriate time, "each in their season" and "in their due time" (4Q402 frag. 4, line 13). To be most efficacious, the enactment is made precisely, exactly, and all by fleshly beings. We believe that this script is not about a circumcision, the traditional mark of distinction, as alluded to by the official editor, nor about priestly sacrifice for the initiation of heavenly angels. Certainly, "joiners" would not be circumcised within the inner sanctum; as Qumran's *Temple Scroll* suggests, they cannot even worship there, nor are they allowed to function as holy men or priests. As for Jewish infants, who are not mentioned in the text of the *Šîrôt*, they would not be the beneficiaries of such an elaborate secret ceremony which was (and still is) commonplace in Judaism.

Priests and angels are linked in that both are supposed to be "without blemish," namely, without the sin of sexual emissions, as well as without any physical deformities (or tattoo which normally accompanied all mystery sects of the Greek and Roman world; the longest surviving cult wounded one of the initiates' feet).[60]

The tongue imagery of the *Songs,* is the most telling symbol; it is also one mark of this order among sectarians; in fact, it is the key to the function of the ritual. The use of the "tongue" is culturally and psychically loaded because it is first and foremost associated with circumcision. We remember that it was said of Moses that he had "lips circumcised" (Exod. 6:12, 30), when he is offered the mission by Yahweh to free the Israelites from slavery in Egypt. He is reluctant to accept God's command because of his presumed speech impairment or shyness or poor rhetorical abilities—or all three. It is ironic that Moses, who is called "the greatest of all prophets," is first introduced to the Hebrews as someone whose speech capabilities are questionable. Further, Moses was the son of a Levite man and woman (Exod. 2:1) and thus the heir to their (Levites) elaborate Israelite tradition of "singing."[61] Finally, Moses accepts the task and is accompanied by Aaron, the priest, who was supposed to assist his "brother" in negotiating with the pharaoh. Aaron becomes Moses' "tongue," not only because of his perfect speech but also because of his priestly capabilities.[62]

The "tongues" in *Šîrôt* is not the only image that harks back to a ritual evocative of a certain perfection (which Moses seemed to have lacked). Ecstasy-producing chants along with swinging and sweet-smelling incense to cover the "odors" of the drugs accompany a rite of passage to the purest male bodily state, that of the eunuch. One can compare the early church, which was referred to as an "angelic choir" and comprised soprano-voiced eunuchs (presumably only their testicles were removed in childhood) and some famous founding leaders, also castrated (to whatever degree) by their own choice in adult life.[63] Their distinction as almost godlike beings is befittingly symbolized by the notion of "circumcised lips."

The sectarians were seriously searching for an atonement for "the first sin"; they thus elevated the sacrifice of the firstfruits to new levels because they believed that there they could find the answer to the human problem—male virginity. We suspect from another dedication mentioned in the Dead Sea Scrolls (and from biblical histories of other Nazirite sons adopted for priestly training, e.g., Samuel and even the prophet Jeremiah) that the small group selected for the angelic choir or other "holy" asceticisms were so appointed from early on, even "dedicated from the womb" (Jer. 1:5) as "firstfruits" and, if born male and physically fit, trained and conditioned to accept their status accordingly. But the most zealous, who made the extreme choice to become castrated as adult males (in whatever degree), to stand with the angels in the highest degree of purity, must have been fewer still. Qualified by commitment and schooling at Qumran, as well as by health, age, and ability to keep secrets, these eunuchs probably became the elite cadre among the "Angels of the Presence" in the camps. It may very well be that this concept was best articulated for Western consumption by Matthew in the Gospels:

> For there are eunuchs who have been so from birth, and there are eunuchs who have been made eunuchs by men, and there are eunuchs who have made themselves eunuchs for the sake of the kingdom of heaven. He who is able to receive this, let him receive it. (19:12)

It is noteworthy that in Third Isaiah, the most influential book of prophecies at Qumran, a text that scholars have long held was composed during the Second Temple period, eunuchs are also given an uncharacteristically positive value:

> and let not the eunuch say, "Behold, I am a dry tree." For thus says the Lord unto the eunuchs that keep my sabbaths, and choose the things that please me, and take hold of my covenant; . . . I will give them an everlasting name, that shall not be cut off. (Isa. 56:3b–5)

At this point, we can see what the sectarians were after. The *Šîrôt* speak of "a perverse spirit," which is presumably a spirit betrayed by his core of passion, namely, "abominable uncleanness or faithless guilt" (1QH 11:10). We have already seen that the Qumranites and their contemporaries (and later Gnostics—including some surviving today who still make themselves into eunuchs![64]) believed that the first Adam knew no carnal knowledge before the woman came into the world. According to the sectarians, her mortal sin subverted human perfection and therefore the second Adam, that is, the "son of man," by celibate example, repenting for the sin of mortals, would reverse that judgment. In the "firstfruits" sacrifice of the *Šîrôt*, the angels, the *děbîrîm*, the chariots, all "give praise together" (4Q403 1 ii 15); they "sing with one voice," monotonally, without distractions (like the liturgical hymns of the early church).[65] Indeed, the impression one gets from reading the whole corpus of the Scrolls is the tightly controlled terminology—the consistency of it and the crescendo to future "light," which is not too far off. We see in the *Šîrôt* that feminine nouns are changed to the masculine form but not vice versa;[66] that, too, is quite consistent with the message that eunuchs are highly honored men (*almost* godlike) and should be divorced from sexual associations with women, who are regarded as tainted.

Body defilement comes from any bodily emissions,[67] but spermal emissions (and thus their testicular source) are the foremost offenders because they are uncontrollable.[68] In a recently published fragment (4Q477) titled by the authors "A record of Sectarian Discipline,"[69] there are "reproving" words addressed to those whose vows may be limited to celibacy and who "love their bodily (or, fleshly) emissions" (i 8).

Unlike the angelic orders that eliminate the problem "in hand" (a euphemism in rabbinic literature for penis), the "priestly/angelic" parallel castes are pious in the sectarians' mind because they exert their will over matter. They are "saints," or "the righteous ones," those with the "purest souls," the ones having the "most light" according to their horoscopes; they exemplify perfection of mind. The description is related to degrees of purity that have been adopted by the sectarians; not everyone is of the same station, though all have to aspire to a significant degree of holiness.

Therefore, by comparison (and contrary to Christian practice), water baptism in the Dead Sea Scrolls is intended only for the purification of the body, to wash away any of their uncontrollable bodily emissions; the souls of the elect have already been saved from sin. All must be so (by water) baptized, even the high priest on whom rests the holy spirit.[70]

We also see that the angels have a variety of necessary, human tasks besides singing: specifically, serving the priests and the angelic elite daily (we think to prevent "contamination" by the women living at Qumran, but not in the all-male camps); making special announcements, such as who is chosen to bear special children. Moreover, it is the "angels'" mission to maintain the purity of the Temple and execute judgments. Watching for impurities among those in the camps and in Temple practices, guarding the elite like pedestal virgins, executing judgments, a role that may have been limited to the master, titled Melchizedek or Michael, are some of their other duties.[71] Godlike beings "do not tolerate any whose way is perverted. There is no unclean thing in their holy places [their "camps"] . . . [with] good will for all those who repent of sin" (4Q400 i 14–16). They make their daily prayers, and now, purified in the flesh, they serve the Saints, the

Just Ones.[72] According to the *War Scroll,* both groups are held to the rear in the final battle plan: the "hosts" of angels are there to prevent the saints' defilement because no priest may have contact with dead bodies:

> The Priests shall depart from among the slain and stand on either side next to the . . . and they shall not profane the oil of their priesthood [by the blood of the s]lai[n]. (4Q493 = Mc)

Predestined to be "part of His plan" (4Q402 frag. 4, line 15) are men: Jews and converts keeping the Law (as the sectarians understood it), separated from the Gentiles under the mark of circumcision; godlike beings separated from ordinary sinners by the sacrifice of their "hand." They see themselves as "holy" and deserving holiness because: "What is the offering of our mortal tongue (compared) with the knowledge of the *ʾēl[îm]*? . . . (4Q400 2:7). This is the council of Just Men, separated from all others in the community to teach the Law and to atone for the sins of their people through their pious will.

Isis and Horis, mother and miraculously conceived child. *Gift of Mrs. Horace L. Mayer. Courtesy, Museum of Fine Arts, Boston.*

Egyptian surgical instruments depicted in the Temple of Kom Ombo, ca. 200 B. C. E.

Circumcision, Egyptian
Temple of Kom Ombo,
ca. 200 B. C. E.

Isis on the birthing stool,
Temple of Kom Ombo.

The Virgin of the Dead Sea Scrolls, The Truth about Immaculate Conception, and the Pseudepigraphic Romance of Joseph and Aseneth

And Pharaoh took off his ring from his hand, and put it upon Joseph's hand, and arrayed him in vestures of fine linen, and put a gold chain about his neck; and he made him ride in the second chariot which he had. . . . And Pharaoh said to Joseph, "I am Pharaoh, and without thee shall no man lift up his hand or foot in all the land of Egypt." And Pharaoh called Joseph's name Zaphnath-paaneah; and he gave him to wife Asenath the daughter of Poti-phera priest of On. And Joseph went out over all the land of Egypt. (Gen. 41:42–45)

BRIEF: THE *HIEROS GAMOS*

The most valuable cache of wisdom of a peasant society relates to planting, harvesting, and preparing for the much-needed rains. The *hieros gamos,* the "holy wedding" of the great Earth Mother (via her priestess or handmaid) to her "brother," the land's shepherd/king, was remembered in the wedding ritual of humans. It is the Goddess via her priestesses who doles out immortality. In both the surreal and the real, there is a dedication of firstfruits or newborn ones. Recent scholarship places the traditions of Sarah, Rachel, and Rebekah in that same priestess role along with their "handmaids," who mate with their "brothers," the patriarchs.[1] We add to that list of righteous women not only the mothers of Samson, Samuel, and Joseph (Rachel), but now one more, Aseneth—an out-and-out fertility priestess, but one, as luck would have it, from the Egyptian court of the sun in Heliopolis (the biblical On).

Joseph and Aseneth (= *Jos.Asen.*) is a model romance featuring sex without sex and miraculous happenings. As pseudepigrapha, the parable takes great liberties with the few lines about Joseph and Aseneth in the Bible. We think the work commemorates an actual event and a core ritual worthy of ongoing public acknowledgment. The tale's most striking attribute is its "pure" sexuality, which marks a turning point in a tradition that had been searching for ways and means to overcome the "pollution," the associations of original sin with the sex act.

Based on a literary Egyptian import and on elements from the ancient erotica the Song of Songs in the Bible, *Joseph and Aseneth* apparently succeeded in taking hold on the popular imagination. For we find several other versions from the turn of the millennium (one by the Jewish historian Josephus and another by the hellenized Jewish writer Philo). We propose that the roots of this creative tale go back to Qumran and the sectarians who were searching for a way to wipe out "pollution" and "iniquity." We believe that the legend of *Joseph and Aseneth* was constructed as a popular gloss on exotic, secret practices at Qumran. While no scroll of *Joseph and Aseneth* has yet been identified among the Dead Sea Scrolls, the similarity of the language, imagery, concepts, and even the use of pseudepigrapha are extremely suggestive of the brotherhood's prolific hand.[2]

The other literature that dovetails precisely with *Joseph and Aseneth* is, most important of all, the Dead Sea Scroll's fragmentary Marriage Ritual—a quite unique description of an actual ceremony but, as we will see, not for common (marriage) purposes. In addition, there are other crucial Qumran fragments, the testaments of the righteous dreamer Joseph and the priestly Levi, which are highly stylized biographies thought to belong to a work known as the *Testaments of the Twelve Patriarchs*.[3] We use all of these materials to interpolate, tentatively, what may be missing from Qumran's corpus. This literary trio (*Joseph and Aseneth,* the Marriage Ritual, and the *Testaments*) makes the case better than any other that one cannot understand these materials in isolation. Moreover, this unity of theme and metaphor shows how profoundly these documents are linked; for the Dead Sea Scrolls are a puzzle that requires joining many pieces.

We also quote other books written before, contemporary with, and after *Joseph and Aseneth* to clarify our major thesis—for example, books of the Apocrypha, Pseudo-Philo, the *Odes of Solomon,* and the Gnostic *Gospel of Philip.* We even call on some particulars in Egyptian mythology from the era to help uncover the true meaning of *Joseph and Aseneth.*

On the surface *Joseph and Aseneth* is not too unlike the sensuality in the ancient liturgical Song of Songs and the miracles of the special birth stories treated above. But *Joseph and Aseneth* reveals what the Scrolls call "the Mystery of Existence." Here, played out in detail but in code is the secret ritual of immaculate conception, in which the sectarian orders of "Daughters of Truth" and "Sons of Truth" play their respective roles. What is so tantalizing is that this romance and the ritual it marks appear to have been constructed to appeal to a populace still revering the centuries-old *hieros gamos* of the Goddess religion performed at the winter solstice (by today's calendar, December 22).

In explaining the main points of *Joseph and Aseneth,* along with its key symbols, as well as the allusions to the deeper "mystery of existence" (meant for inside "knowers"= Gnostics), we keep in mind that this story about a special virgin and a distinctive birth is after the fact, after the successful birth of a "son" who proved to be a great leader. We believe that the heroic birth theme, which permeates this work, records none other than the birth of the Teacher of Righteousness, the *nāśîʾ* leader), or Zaddik, of the Dead Sea Scrolls' sectarians at Qumran. Naturally, it glorifies his heroic lineage and alleges an eventful sign, a star-struck birth.

> he is born in the night and he comes out Perfect . . . with a weight of . . . it left a mark on him . . . he will become wise and will be discreet . . . a vision will come to him while upon his knees in prayer . . . he will know the secrets of mankind . . . he is the Elect of God. His birth and the spirit of his breath . . . his [p]lans will endure forever. (4Q534–536)[4]

In this chapter, we examine the four main steps of the ritual in the legend of *Joseph and Aseneth:* annunciation, two initiates (including the miraculous conversion preparation of the "Bride of God" and lineage proofs), the enactment of pure sisterly love along with the grace of a pure meal; and the act of creation (or what the Qumranites called "the mystery of existence"). We clarify the meaning of the Egyptian setting of the story; the connection of "truth and righteousness" with virginity (i.e., chastity); the "angelic" roles, sun time (versus the lunar calendar of traditional Judaism);[5] and, as always, the ancient symbols that are newly adapted to this special practice at Qumran.

These concepts and symbols introduce us to the much more intricate world of *Joseph and Aseneth;* they place the work within a time when people were curious about the meaning of a better world inhabited by better men and women. The Jewish flavor of the tale is unquestionable, not only because it deals with characters that have Jewish connections but because it attempts, on the surface, to tackle the issue of conversion, thus explaining away the biblical fact of Aseneth's foreign Egyptian origins.[6] Curiously, though, the concrete way of conversion, its detailed rituals as well as intellectual preparations for it, is missing in the text. Aseneth's decision to "convert" is expressed in language that is reminiscent of a radical change of life-style and role, but it does not detail the official procedure of conversion. All is not what it seems. Very personal changes occur to the heroine, internally and externally, which presumably furnish her with some inner strength that is demanded of her for a very unusual event. There are few clearly "Jewish" matters that she embraces and focuses on. The Jewish community is totally missing from the tale, and there is no human authority to instruct her in the way of conversion. On the surface, Aseneth is merely intent on having Joseph, thus abandoning her status as virgin. But the virginal and priestly emphasis is never dispelled in the story; neither are the various glittering symbols associated with the heroine's life as a virgin. By telling the reader that Aseneth's main activity is conversion and by totally remaining silent about the detailed (and sometimes intricate) procedures involving conversion, the author adopts a symbolic code which leads the tale in a surprising direction, as we will see. Obviously, the story is about the "conversion" of a virgin, but not necessarily to Judaism or any other religion. The secret will ultimately have to be related to the enduring metaphors used in this text and others, which are, as we have just suggested, related to virginity, priesthood, and holiness.

Aseneth is the legitimate heroine of the tale: she is the one who "converts"; she is the one who falls in love with "the Son of God"; and she is the one who takes it upon herself to do the right things and say the correct words. Above all, the angel of God appears to her "at the right time": "behold, the morning star rose out of heaven in the east" (14:1). The angel alerts us and her to the heavenly sign (once belonging to the goddess Ishtar) and to her selection at this propitious astrological moment.[7] Aseneth is described as "a virgin of eighteen years, (she was) very tall and handsome and beautiful to look at beyond all virgins on the earth" (1:6). The heroine's status as virgin, her Egyptian connections (daughter of the priest of Heliopolis, Pentephres), and her rather "mature" age (eighteen), might forewarn us of the broader significance of her role. She is not a "normal" woman; rather, she is an important character in a great political and spiritual drama. When she is first mentioned in the text, she refuses to abandon her state of virginity: Aseneth "was despising and scorning every man" (2:1). She is thus portrayed as a woman who refuses to get married (even to the son of the pharaoh), presumably because she believes she is too good for any man ("she was boastful and arrogant," 2:1b).

Given this initial information about Aseneth, it is easy to be skeptical about the possible connection between her story and character and the Qumran brotherhood. But the ideas that lie behind *Joseph and Aseneth* reflect a major movement that was not limited to Qumran and its environment; intellectual links and conscious affiliation with other writings are widespread. In fact, the main conversation of the tale, particularly its main symbols and images can also be found in various other texts, including the Dead Sea Scrolls.[8] Although no copy of *Joseph and Aseneth* has yet been found in any of the Qumran caves, there is a possibility that the brotherhood not only knew about this work but had something to do with its composition. Further, the three themes of *righteousness, truth,* and *chastity,* which are prominent in the Qumran writings, appear also in this story, which deals with a "righteous" and chaste patriarch, Joseph, who is likely to be one of the "Sons of Truth."[9]

In the *Testament of Levi* (Aramaic version, 4Q213–214) Joseph is described as: "Joseph my brother, who taught Torah and interpretation and wisdom. (He received) honor and became a great man, both to kings . . ." (4 i 11).[10] We should note that Joseph was, potentially, an extremely appealing character model for the sectarians because of his links with two key concepts: he was a righteous man—a phrase that smacks of a title of membership (as his name signifies a particular role)—and an exile. The concept of exile, closely tied with Joseph's biblical story as well as that of the *Testaments* and *Joseph and Aseneth,* is even more intriguing because it is suggestive of the hero being at Qumran as one of those in exile from Jerusalem. It also points to the sectarians' Egyptian connection and their grasp of the meaning of exile, cleansing, and redemption. These basic notions at the millennium about punishing the Jews for their sins recur in the full fragment about Joseph that was found in Cave 4, where Joseph is afforded a voice that echoes that of the psalmist requesting God to help him in his hour of need: "and he said, 'My father, my God, do not abandon me into the hands of the nations'" (4Q372 frag. 1, line 16).[11] The same ideas are at the heart of the tale of Joseph and Aseneth.

Aseneth reflects all of the sectarians' images regarding feminine purity. Thus, in *Joseph and Aseneth,* when the heroine asks for "pure water from the spring" (18:8), she washes her face and then sees herself in the mirror (of the water):

> And it was like the sun and her eyes (were) like a rising morning star, and . . . her lips (were) like a rose of life (red) . . . and the hair of her head (was) like a vine in the paradise of God prospering in its fruits. . . . (18:9)

There are echoes of the woman/lover in Song of Songs, but the imagery is also typically sectarian: the sun, the morning star, the hair of the Nazirite, and the "vine" recalling the vineyard oracle of Isaiah, where the people of Israel are referred to as God's vineyard that went sour and that had to be destroyed. The sectarians' retreat is their answer to that vineyard prophecy.

Joseph and Aseneth in Josephus and Philo

Both Josephus and Philo have their own versions of this important story. Josephus's rendering of the roles and characters of Joseph and Aseneth is as follows:

> Joseph was now grown up to thirty years of age, and enjoyed great honors from the king . . . out of regard to his prodigious degree of wisdom; for that name denotes *the revealer of secrets*. He also married a wife of very great quality; . . . the daughter of Pentephres, one of the priests of Heliopolis; she was a virgin, and her name was Asenath. (*Antiquities* 6.2.1; emphasis added)

In his matter-of-fact tone, Josephus, whose interest in Joseph is greater than his interest in Aseneth, focuses on the hero's age (thirty), his wisdom, his ability to decipher "secrets" (rather than just dreams, as the original story in Genesis has it) as well as his marriage to a woman/virgin of "great quality." In both the Pseudepigrapha and in

Josephus, Aseneth has some relationship to priesthood; her father is the priest at Heliopolis in Egypt, and she is his "virgin/daughter." Neither of these stories emphasizes the role of Aseneth as priestess, even though in *Joseph and Aseneth* she is actually portrayed in this particular fashion, as we will see. "The revealer of secrets" points to the more turncoat side of Josephus (perhaps identifying with his namesake); he brags about his own spiritual knowledge of the main "philosophies" of his time, including a mystical one.

Just like his contemporary Josephus, Philo too was much more interested in Joseph than in Aseneth. Accordingly, Philo tells us that Joseph is a pseudonym, a man with "another name in the language of the country" (the Country of Qumran?) and is a man of splendor.[12] Aseneth is described as "the most distinguished of the ladies." Like the Egyptian title Son of the Sun, Joseph in *Joseph and Aseneth* is no minor character—he is sometimes referred to as "the son of God." Philo reflects this same, holy tradition but is also enamored of Joseph for being a chaste young man:

> he bestowed on him the royal seal and put upon him a sacred robe and a golden necklace, and setting him on his second chariot. . . . He also gave him *another name in the language of the country,* based on his art of dream interpretation, and betrothed him to the most distinguished of the ladies of Egypt, the daughter of the priest of the Sun. These events happened when he was about thirty years old. (*De Iosepho* 121; emphasis added)

Philo is also enamored of Joseph for being a chaste young man who resists through discipline and self-control the advances of "his master's wife."[13]

> Before the lawful union we [Jews] know no mating with other women, but come as virgin men to virgin maidens. The end we seek in wedlock is not pleasure but the begetting of lawful children. To this day I have remained pure. . . . (*De Iosepho* 43)

In all three versions of *Joseph and Aseneth,* something special, something holy and priestly is taking place. In all three accounts, there is also an emphasis on the holy place associated with the Sun and Heliopolis. But none of the authors at the turn of the millennium directly refers to Aseneth as a priestess, even though her family tradition and her name are priestly—"belonging to Neith." Much is made of her virginity (sometimes a priestly requirement), which is emphasized both in the romance and in Josephus's account. Virginity was the most desirable state for a woman (as well as for a man) because as soon as virginity was lost "original sin" came into play more starkly. To be born of a woman is to be born in sin and to breed iniquity.[14]

> When the breed of iniquity is shut up, wickedness will be exiled in the face of righteousness; like the exi[le] of [dark]ness before light; and when the smoke clears and is no [more], so shall wickedness perish forever and righteousness will be revealed like the su[n] governing the world. (*The Book of Mysteries* [1Q27] lines 5–7)

The message here is related to birth (*môldâ*) and barrenness (*hissāgēr*), and the imagery that is evoked harks back to a woman's closed womb. Presumably, the author discusses the ideal world, where "righteousness" is fully recognized and wickedness (or the wicked seed) will be no more—as if those women who become pregnant would give birth, via the "mystery of existence," to righteous people who will not be tainted by the wickedness of original sin.

First Step of the Ritual: Annunciation

Aseneth's uniqueness was not just her beauty but also her seclusion; she was fully sheltered from the outside (polluting?) world "because Pentephres had a tower adjoining his house, very big and high, and on top of this tower was an upper floor including ten chambers" (2:1). The ten chambers are described in some detail, emphasizing their gloriousness. Words such as "precious stones," "gold and silver," "costly stones," and so on convey the splendor of the tower. The words "ornaments of her virginity" (2:4) suggest first that virgins were sometimes in the habit of wearing special clothes; but in this case it also implies power and eminence that are not simply physical. On another level, when read within the context of a time and place that prized the state of virginity, the virgin herself is an ornament that must be kept in her "tower," or safe haven, where her virginity can more easily remain intact. One must keep her whole—indeed holy— as a symbol of perfection. In a more concrete framework, this particular phrase suggests physical health, and maybe even pharmaceutical means used to enhance Aseneth's beauty.[15] There are seven other virgins, less distinctive and less visible, who occupy seven of the ten chambers. These virgins are described as waiting on Aseneth; that is, they are her handmaids: "And they were very beautiful, like the stars of heaven, and no man ever conversed with them, not (even) a male child" (2:6b). The hidden virgin and those who assist in keeping her concealed are consistent with the view that there is a unique function for the virgin and one must keep her intact as representing the essence of perfection. Possibly, the seven additional virgins symbolize a whole "pool" of women/virgins who were trained for various temple functions. The use of the number "seven" is also quite telling, not only because of its biblical echoes but also because the sectarians were specifically enamored with this "motherless" number as relevant to their commitment to virginal propagation.[16] We note too that in Qumran itself there was an actual tower whose purpose is not yet agreed upon.

> And there were three windows to Aseneth's big chamber where her virginity was being fostered. . . . And there was a golden bed standing in the chamber . . . and the bed was laid with gold-woven purple stuff, interwoven with violet, purple, and white. (2:7–8)

The three windows are familiar motifs in the temple of the Goddess of Love, whose priestesses used to sit by the window waiting for the right moment to accomplish their tasks. Aseneth's chamber is of singular importance, because it is an intimate reminder of her environment, which is full of splendor, riches, and color. The bed, in particular, is literally dazzling. The three colors are emblematic of innocence/wholeness (white) and fullness and fruition (violet and purple). All of these colors are also typically priestly and royal. On a more realistic level, the picture portrayed in relation to the "aloof" Aseneth is one of security whereby the virgin/priestess is not only "hidden" from the rest of the world but carefully guarded and pampered by other virgins and "strong men."

The first section of the story ends with a precise description of the court surrounding the house:

> and a wall was around the court, very high, built from big square stones . . . and eighteen powerful armed young men guarded each of the . . . (gates). And handsome trees of all sorts and all bearing fruit were planted within the court along the wall. And their fruit was ripe, for it was the time of harvest. And there was in the court, on the right hand, a spring of abundant living water, and below the spring was a big cistern receiving the water of that spring. From there a river ran right through the court and watered all the trees of that court. (2:10–12)

The most outstanding feature of the court is its paradisal quality and even more specifically its water and trees. The concept "living water" is repeated later in the tale when Aseneth is instructed by the angel to prepare herself for the actual "conversion." She is instructed: "wash your face and your hands with living water" (14:12), which she does (v. 15). While the description of the court falls in line with the idea of the virgin's seclusion, it also serves another purpose. By reminding the reader of ideal, solitary environments and by focusing on water, trees, and idealized beauty, the author is pointing to other thoughts and perceptions related to them. Since this story deals with a woman's fate under unique circumstances, we are first of all reminded of the woman in the garden, who for all practical purposes was a virgin too, the first virgin. But the woman in the Genesis story was not as well protected apparently as was Aseneth in this tale. Ultimately, both women do acquire "special knowledge" by conversing with an unworldly—or an unusual—agent, who guides them in the direction of sex and fertility.[17]

But one of the critical differences between the two stories involves pivotal symbols: in the Genesis myth, sexuality (along with other "knowledge") is depicted in a tree; in *Joseph and Aseneth,* it is found in the curious phrase "living water." At first glance, "living water" might be contrasted with a more restricted, artificial type of water, like "*mikva* water,"[18] which is related to sexual matters as well. The *mikva* was used for ritual purification of women, before undertaking sexual activity, as well as after pregnancy and childbirth. But *Joseph and Aseneth* presents us with a scene that emphasizes a different source of water, which is narrated as being more "natural" as well as more powerful.

Aseneth's guardians, "eighteen powerful armed young men" are placed by the gates, presumably to assure the safety of the woman. The emphasis is on the power and youth of these men. Surely not every virgin was so carefully watched over! What is hinted at is the presence of watcher "Angels." They watch for the "ripening" of both the fruit of the trees and Aseneth, blending the woman and the environment as if they were interchangeable. Aseneth is being prepared for a "conversion" that, as we implied before, is of a sexual sort, not a formally religious one. The language of sexuality, splendor, and priesthood is consistently maintained in the tale; this suggests formal links with a goddess-oriented virginal fertility ritual, a type of *hieros gamos* ceremony that would ultimately take place in that temple. We will see that Aseneth's wedding is also an extraordinary event that, although associated with other holy weddings, turns out to be quite different. However, the tale maintains tension and credibility precisely because it alludes to rituals in which the audience is well versed. At least one of the eighteen "angels" has yet another role at the right moment in the ceremony, as revealed in a sacred scroll from Qumran, the Marriage Ritual, where "the man (Adam) and his wife [were commanded] to make seed."[19]

Aseneth's priestly role is emphasized by the way she communicates with and commands the angel as well as by the way she dresses and by her possible rehearsal for the ritual she is to undergo.[20] But her status as priestess is most evident in the scene where Aseneth prepares to welcome her parents and, as it turns out to have a party for Joseph himself.

> she put valuable ornaments and costly stones which hung around from all sides, and the names of the gods of the Egyptians[21] were engraved everywhere on the bracelets and the stones, and the faces of all the idols were carved on them. And she put a tiara on her head and fastened a diadem around her temples, and covered her head with a veil. (3:6)

The "tiara" and the "veil" are clear signals of a powerful priestess, although the symbolic engravings would have been quite different from the "pagan." Even Tamar in the biblical story of Judah and Tamar (Genesis 38), who was posing as a *qedēšâ/zônâ* (holy prostitute) on the side of the road, was wearing a veil that was symbolic of priestly action. Astoundingly, we learn that when the daughter is prepared for the "coming" of Joseph, she is referred to as "a bride of God" (4:1)! The parents, one of whom at least is associated with the priesthood, present her with "all the good things" they have brought from "the field. . . . And Aseneth rejoiced over . . . the fruit, and the grapes, and the dates, and the doves, and the pomegranates, and the figs, because they were all handsome and good to taste" (4:2). The paradisal echoes are hard to miss.[22] Neither should we overlook the Goddess's reverberations. The setting of perfection and innocence serves the purpose of further elevating and surrounding the heroine with images of purity and virginity. The emphasis on the various fruits, and possibly nuts,[23] is also sexual in nature and suggests sexual anticipation and preparedness.[24] Aseneth is at a ripe age, and the ceremonial change in her life requires offerings of special foods, which she accepts accordingly.

There is no question about the linguistic and cultural connection between the "handsome and good fruit" here and the "handsome and desirous fruit" of the tree of knowledge in Genesis. In both stories, the woman is being presented with special food, which ultimately impacts her relationship with the man (here, Joseph) as well as with God. Both stories describe a radical change that occurs to the woman after she eats the fruit. The only difference between the woman in the garden and Aseneth is one of process: the first woman in Genesis is transformed rather quickly, whereas Aseneth's transformation is more detailed and ritualized. Both transformations are accompanied by images from the world of the Goddess and her fertility.[25]

Our claim of a relationship among these materials is supported in the Marriage Ritual, which actually quotes a passage from another scroll (1QS) regarding visitations.

> These are the counsels of the spirit (*rûaḥ*) to the sons of truth in this world. And the visitation (*piqqûdâ*) of all who walk in this spirit shall be healing, great peace in a long life and fruition of seed together with every everlasting blessing and eternal joy in life without end, a crown of glory and a garment of majesty in eternal light. (1QS 4:6–8)

Again we find "the spirit" and "truth" and the eternal reward of crown and garment. But it also alludes to at least two sexual conditions that are related to propagation by way of miracles. The "visitation" immediately brings to mind the angels' appearance to Abraham and Sarah and the results, "And Yahweh visited (*pāqad*) Sarah" (21:1), referring to the promise that he made (via the angels) a year before. At Qumran, too, the "sons of truth" can be associated with special births as well because they are so distinctly different from the "wicked." They are blessed with eternal life and curiously with "fruition of seed," a phrase that is distinct from birth and procreation. The text seems to imply that in the right secluded environment (peace and healing) and with the help of the "spirit," the sectarians' "seed" will come to fruition. There seems to be a deliberate withholding of sexual intercourse in the passage even though Adam and his wife (presumably Eve) are mentioned. The brothers are clearly described as privileged and "blessed." Likewise, in the Marriage Ritual, there is a privileged ceremony which is held in "a period (*môʿēd*) of our happiness" associated with "our earth and all its yield . . . and all of the fruit of its tree

... with deep waters" (4Q502 frags. 8 and 9). The presence of images of fertility cannot be mistaken; nor is the mood to be misunderstood. At least on one level the ceremony described may be a traditional agricultural festival of the firstfruits, but here in the context of an "Assembly of the Righteous." Indeed, the whole "festival" is described communally; it is not celebrated in private, and it includes both men and women of all ages. The fragment also remarks that the man (or, Adam) and his wife are "to make seed," which links very well with the fecundity of the earth.

The Marriage Ritual fragments at our disposal use words such as "holy," "seed," "knowledge and understanding," which are repeated again and again throughout Qumran literature. The presence of "Adam and his wife," who serve as models for the couple(s) getting together in this "festival," speak to a very special "wedding," one that is appropriate for someone of the caliber of the first Adam from the supreme royal lineage who, like the first woman, was also a virgin.

Second Step of the Ritual: Two Initiates

When Aseneth hears that her father wishes to "hand her over" to Joseph to be his wife, she is furious because he is socially lower than she. Moreover, she describes him as a foreigner who "was caught in the act . . . sleeping with his mistress, and his master threw him into the prison of darkness" (4:10). Aseneth's speech is priestly in tone and content; she perceives Joseph as someone who is beneath her socially, politically, and spiritually. Joseph's virginity seems to be as much an issue as her own, and it is Pentephres who is just as sensitive to it when he describes Joseph to his daughter as "a virgin (Greek *parthenos*) like you" (4:7). The father's comment on Joseph's virginity is fairly apologetic, as if trying to pacify his daughter, who points out to him that this man (Joseph) is no match for her. The script and the role imply that Joseph evolves into a deserving mate—perhaps initiated through degrees of purity into the status of priest, one who ultimately deserves the title "Beloved One of Israel." He becomes thus deserving only when he comes in contact with Aseneth.

In the *Testament of Levi* (4Q213–214), Joseph is upheld as a most desirable man; he "taught Torah and interpretation and Wisdom . . . and became a great man" (line 11). In his own *Testament,* Joseph elaborates on his status in the household of Israel as "the one beloved of Israel" (1:2) echoing the "beloved of God."

But the most detailed descriptions in the *Testament of Joseph* deal with his moral stamina as depicted in the confrontations the biblical hero has with Potiphar's wife, who "tempts" and "lures" him almost with the "wiles" of the Qumran "Seductress" (4Q184). By comparison, Joseph is adamant about remaining a virgin: "I was unwilling to have intercourse with her" (3:1b). He fasted "for those seven years," "drank no wine" (3:4b), and gave his food to the poor and ill. The Nazirite link is revealed, and Joseph enters into the ascetic mode, as does Aseneth, to mourn the old habits and to make way for the new— namely, their initiation into the "mystery of existence." This initiation is about becoming "perfect," both righteously (with regard to behavior) and spiritually—and more so for the man. In other words, perfection is extended as far as possible; virginity is hers and his, which implies that imperfection and nonvirginity belong to both as well.

However, Joseph's perfection goes beyond his virginity and is finally matched with Aseneth's.

> and Joseph entered . . . and four horses, white as snow and with golden bridles, were harnessed [to the chariot he was riding], and the entire chariot was manufactured from pure gold. And Joseph was dressed in an exquisite white tunic, and the robe which he had thrown around him was purple, made of linen interwoven with gold, and a golden crown was on his head, and around the crown were twelve chosen stones, and on top of the twelve stones were twelve golden rays . . . and in his right hand he held outstretched an olive branch, and there was plenty of fruit on it, and in the fruits was a great wealth of oil. (5:4–6)

From horses to oil the idealized images associated with the hero have significant meaning not only to the story at hand but to the whole environment in which it was written. The literary aim is to impress the audience with its majestic sweep. The four horses are symbols of power, prestige, and authority from the four ends of the earth; they point to Joseph's closeness to the source of Egyptian power, the pharaoh who could afford war horses.[26] The purebred, fit-for-a-king, white-as-snow horses were even more highly prized. Joseph, the virgin, is riding on a white horse, with gold accessories, and he wears purple and white linen, the priestly vestments. Thus, when Joseph is allied with Aseneth and her family, he too becomes associated with priestly power.

We also learn of Joseph's entry into the house of Pentephres. The crown, "the twelve chosen stones," "twelve golden rays," and, above all, "a great wealth of oil" are the most outstanding of all the symbols. They ring with some truth of distinct rituals that have to do with the crowning of a very special priest/king or leader/*nāśîʾ*—like David over the twelve tribes of Israel/Judah. The oil that Joseph holds in his hand ("and in his right hand he held outstretched an olive branch, and there was plenty of fruit on it," 5:5c) is priestly in origin; it is the oil that is used to anoint the kings as well as the priests. It is the oil that marks the uniqueness of a particular holy community and/or dynasty; it sets aside a certain segment of the populace linking it with God.[27]

When Aseneth sees Joseph for the first time—that is, when it is clear to her and to the audience that she has to prepare for something new on the sun's day—she is completely overwhelmed and expresses her astonishment at his grandeur in messianic terms:

> And now, behold, the sun from heaven has come to us in its chariot and entered our house today, and shines in it like a light upon the earth. But I . . . did not know that Joseph is (a) son of God. (6:2–3)

In a rather extraordinary statement, Aseneth then goes on to ask, ritually, whether Joseph's lineage is good enough to give birth to "a son of God," namely, who his mother was: "and what womb of a woman will give birth to such light?" (v. 4a).[28] The peculiar emphasis here is on the "womb" rather than the woman, hinting at a radically different scenario for the birth of the "son of God." A special chore is implied, one involving a class of dedicated virgins, even a pool of them, all available, almost like surrogate wombs. Certainly, since Aseneth wonders about the mother of Joseph, she is also asking a question about herself and whether her time has come to function as a "womb" for the children of a "Joseph."[29] There is no question about the special status of a woman/womb like that. The tale's use of "light" in a sun-divine framework demands that the "womb" that guards the future child as well as the woman that finally gives birth to him, be treated with care and special attention. Aseneth thus reveals to us that in the temple of the Goddess there were some priestesses who were dedicated to a particular service which was perceived to be of utmost importance. Possibly, too, when the ritual of impregnation took place, it might have involved more than one virgin to make sure that at least one pregnancy would be successful in yielding a viable, healthy, male child. As a matter of fact, in the Qumran Marriage Ritual the subjects are not just one man and one woman; the text suggests that "in the holy community (*sôd*) there sat with him a blessed seed, old men and women and virgin women and boys and girls all of us together" (4Q502 frag. 19, lines 1–4). Some age hierarchy is designated in this assembly: old men and women[30] (*ʾāšîš* rather than *zāqēn*, which might mean only thirty years old or more and who were presumably celibate at least at that point); older brothers (*ʾaḥîm*), mature enough to keep secrets, teenage virgins (like Aseneth), and youths.[31]

It is therefore ceremonially appropriate that, after Aseneth recognizes the uniqueness of "the womb that gave birth to Joseph," she wishes to become Joseph's "maidservant and slave" rather than his wife. The connotations with the former positions are quite different from the latter, especially if we bear in mind that the famous biblical "maidservants" functioned as surrogate mothers who bore sons for the "barren" matriarchs.[32] Aseneth humbly expresses her unworthiness of Joseph, using a dialect that was distinctly priestly, related to fertility. While this in itself is not unique in a romance, it does become important later on, when the heroine is visited by a man/angel who is, curiously, Joseph's look-alike: "And Aseneth raised her head and saw, and behold, (there was) a man in every respect similar to Joseph, by the robe and the crown and the royal staff" (14:9). This moment is articulated as an epiphany, for Joseph is now recognized by the priestess/virgin as equal to the task at hand. But, even more important, Joseph is now acknowledged as someone who is ready for a uniquely holy experience. The fact that he looks like the angel (to Aseneth) means that he is dressed like one and therefore is justified in performing the very important act that is to follow.

Joseph's new power and position are the most discernible to the awe-struck and obedient Aseneth, who, we must remember, was completely unimpressed with him when he was first mentioned by her parents, as she herself said. What is now revealed in Aseneth's speech is akin to a tightly held secret; she talks about "the son of God" and "the sun" and "chariots," which bring to mind Qumran and apocalyptic literature, especially the description of the "Teacher of Righteousness" as a "son of God" (e.g., 1QpHab 1:10) affiliated with the sun and a horse-drawn chariot. We think it not a coincidence that the Teacher was invariably portrayed as a "star" that fell from heaven and was preparing himself and the newly elect community in the desert to be totally purified on behalf of the poor and the multitudes awaiting the final days.[33]

Joseph and Aseneth is replete with symbols of power and fertility for both the man and the woman; the woman seems to appropriate to herself much clout and independence—so much so that even her parents are somewhat helpless in the face of her determination to remain a powerful virgin. But since the tale changes course and finally deals with a confrontation and a relationship between Joseph and Aseneth, it does become a story about two special people fulfilling special roles. In fact, as the tale progresses and the main topic focuses on "conversion" the characters are locked into certain "righteous" positions (i.e., obedience) from which they are unable to free themselves. While in the beginning, the woman, for example, is absolutely free to maintain her status, she does change with the appearance of Joseph. As soon as that happens, she is interested in only one thing, thus losing her three-dimensional, humanistic persona. From then on, she is objectified as "a city of refuge," who can provide life forever. What we are suggesting is that even though the story begins by dealing with individuals and their fortunes and seems to be "romantic" in nature, there are various broad hints and powerful symbols that point in another direction—namely, in the direction of a rigid fertility ritual that sometimes requires right behavior of the characters. Granted, the characters in this story are presented as real—and we believe they are historical persons—and as crucially important to their families and their respective nations.

Third Step of the Ritual: Pure Sisterly Love
and the Grace of the Pure Meal

In the next stage of the tale, we find Aseneth brooding and internalizing her change of attitude toward Joseph. As soon as this happens, the emphasis of the story shifts from her condition of freedom and pleasure to that of restriction and obedience. Aseneth's role as priestess and conveyor of ritual, love, and immortality does not inherently change; rather, it is now channeled into one stream, which happens to include Joseph as almost the superhero of the tale. Aseneth's poetic articulation of Joseph as someone spiritual who can see everything and everywhere "because of the great light that is inside him" (6:6d) accentuates Joseph's role in the narrative. For a moment, some of the negative attitudes toward women take over; specifically, Joseph "remembers" his father's admonition: "My children, guard strongly against associating with a strange woman, for association (with) her is destruction and corruption" (7:5). This statement is certainly much more in line with the negative attitude of the Qumran brotherhood toward women, again showing the coherence of these stories. The same statement occurs also in the *Testament of Joseph.* The audience would have remembered that a significant part of Joseph's biblical story concerned a "strange" woman, presumably his surrogate mother, who attempted to seduce him; but he managed to narrowly escape, kept his virginity, and landed in jail, whence he proceeded to greatness. Joseph still remembers that episode and therefore must be absolutely certain that Aseneth is "a virgin hating every man, this (girl) will certainly not molest me" (7:8b). Curiously, though, he goes on to say that as a "daughter" to Pentephres—that is, the priest of Heliopolis—and a virgin, like himself, she is "a sister," hardly a stranger, and "I love her from today as my sister" (v. 8d). A spiritual link is established between these two characters on the basis of priesthood and virginity—two states of being that were perceived to be as close to holiness and perfection as humanly possible. In the Israelite priestly tradition, and in Qumran specifically, it is possible that all the dedicated virgins and all the brides were closely related to the brotherhood's stock and not to foreign outsiders.[34]

But what is much more important, the "sister" motif places both characters (and particularly Aseneth) within the framework of priesthood. Besides the brother-sister relationship of Sarah and Abraham and her maidservant (Hagar), Qumran was apparently quite taken with Miriam (or Miramme),[35] the great prophetess/priestess of the exodus who is the sister of both Moses (the redeemer) and Aaron (the priest). She travels with her brothers, though she is closely allied with Aaron. Since the latter is described as the priest, Miriam, by association, is a priestess and indeed she performs as such especially when the Israelites are in the desert and confront various hardships related to water shortages. Miriam (whose name signifies "bitter water") safeguards the community's water sources, the ubiquitous well of fertility and knowledge and, by implication, their legitimate offspring.[36] When she dies, the Israelites mourn her deeply, though the Bible, which is more interested in the heroic exploits of Moses, treats her ambiguously.[37] At Qumran, the very mention of a woman's name has to be examined very carefully, and since Miriam is alluded to as "Hur's wife" we see that her lineage is of the essence, not her exploits. In Song of Songs, the woman/lover is sometimes referred to as "sister." We have already seen how the sectarians in the *Genesis Apocryphon* present Sarah in the same Genesis light, namely, as a powerful quasi priestess who presides over a fertility ceremony in Egypt at a time of "great famine." Bathenosh in the *Genesis Apocryphon* refers to her husband, at one point, as "brother." In *Joseph and Aseneth* too the brother-sister motif (mentioned by Joseph) is just as significant because of Aseneth's status as a virgin-priestess.

The first physical encounter between Joseph and Aseneth is expressed negatively; namely, she attempts to open her lips to kiss him, perhaps the grand moment expected in the *hieros gamos,* but not here. Because, the text explains:

> It is not fitting for a man who worships God, who will bless with his mouth the living God and eat blessed bread of life and drink a blessed cup of immortality and anoint himself with blessed ointment of incorruptibility. (8:5)[38]

It is endemic to prophetic biblical literature, which inherited the tradition from the fertility practices of the Goddess religion, to include a ritual meal (as well as oil). The cycle of the year is also accounted for because all of the rituals dealing with fertility were dedicated to the agricultural cycle and the productivity of the land.[39] In the Dead Sea Scrolls, too, the pure meal is central: "When they set the table for a meal or prepare wine to drink, the priest is first to put forth his hand to invoke a blessing on the first portion of the bread or wine" (1QS 6:4–6). The "hand" used for blessing or for vows (like that of a Nazirite oath) is certainly evocative of a very old tradition enumerated in the Bible and specifically relevant to the story of Joseph, whose father (Jacob/Israel) blessed his grandsons by crossing hands and placing the right hand (meant for the firstborn) on the head of the second born (Gen. 48:14).

Josephus describes the pure meal of the Essenes in detail:

> while they go, after a pure manner, into the dining room, as into a certain holy temple, and quietly set themselves down; upon which the baker lays [for] them loaves in order: the cook also brings a single plate

of one sort of food, and sets it before every one of them; but a priest says grace before meat, and it is unlawful for any one to taste of the food before grace be said" (*Jewish War* 2.8.5)

At Qumran, partaking of food was so important that a first-year novice who did not complete his initiation into the group's activities was not allowed to join in the communal meal. He had initially to eat in isolation until he proved himself ready to enter the "holy congregation." We identify a ritualized communal meal, the "Pure Meal" of Qumran and the Essenes, in *Joseph and Aseneth*.

Returning to Joseph's refusal to kiss Aseneth, which is couched in both religious and sexual language, it centers on Joseph's position as a worshiper of the Hebrew God who does not look favorably upon a Hebrew man kissing "a strange woman who will bless with her mouth dead and dumb idols" (8:5b). The sexual aspect of the kiss is verbalized in Aseneth's arousal by Joseph, who "stretched out his right hand and put it on her chest between her two breasts—but not on them, suggesting mind over matter, spirit over sexuality. This is more than just sexual arousal: "and her breasts were already standing upright like handsome apples" (8:5). In a way, this description implies that both of them are preparing for a sexual encounter which is also coupled with religious overtones, especially when the man who arouses the woman places his "right hand" on her chest and later on her head: "And he lifted up his right hand and put it upon her head" (v. 9a)[40] to bless her as a priest would. But, in the sensual Song of Songs in the Bible, the "hand" is purely sexual.[41]

But the more important part of Joseph's "blessing" can be found in his statement about Aseneth's "spiritual renewal," which here appears to be a kind of Eucharist for the initiate's acceptance into the "Mystery of Existence."

> You, Lord, bless this virgin,
> and renew her by your spirit,
> and form her anew by your hidden hand,
> and make her alive again by your life,
> and let her eat your bread of life,
> and drink your cup of blessing,
> and number her among your people
> that you have chosen before all (things) came into being,
> and let her enter your rest

which you have prepared for your chosen ones,
and live in your eternal life for ever (and) ever. (8:9)

The passage evokes images of creation and transformation; words such as "renew," "form," "make," and "hidden hand" focus on the active participation of the deity in the process of transforming Aseneth. The heroine's transformation is articulated by using expressions such as "your life," "bread of life," and "cup of blessing." The "bread" and the "cup" are immediately associated with the former references to the communal ritual of bread and drink conducted by the priest. In that context, Joseph prays for Aseneth's acceptance into his own community of Jews.

But the symbols could be read differently. It seems that the chant or prayer deliberately associates images of creation and birth in order to draw our attention to a new way of dealing with those concepts.

"Renew her by your spirit" and the accompanying "form her anew by your hidden hand" as well as "make her alive again" are statements (prayers) not normally used in conversion ceremonies; they do imply, though, a "new" formation which is more "spirit"-oriented. The concept "your hidden hand" is associated with sexuality, and the picture portrayed here is of God using his sexual "hand" to "make her alive," or to impregnate the woman. Added to the "spiritual" references and the "eating" of the "bread of life" and drinking "the cup of blessing," the highly stylized and poetic passage discusses another construct of the immaculate conception.[42] Eating the "bread of life" and drinking the "cup of blessing" hark back to the rituals mentioned before; but since this whole context involves "new" things, the food and drink references are also beyond the merely ritualized meal eaten before a pivotal event is taking place. Because the "bread" and the "cup" are closely affiliated with God's "hidden hand," they too carry sexual connotations.

Not too long from this point in the ceremony Aseneth is to be engaged to Joseph, the son of God, and she is being told overtly about the oncoming sexual encounter when the "cup," the semen/"drink" and the still intact "mouth" of her body will be involved; this procedure will certainly "make her alive."

If we accept Joseph and Aseneth's special wedding as an embroidery on the actual script of these events revealed in Qumran's Marriage Ritual, we can understand why the images are so closely related: "seed," "holiness," "holy of holies," "blessed seed," "the God of Israel who helps in promoting life amongst an eternal people (4Q502 1:4, 6; 9:10; 19:2; 24:2–3)." If placed within a context of special weddings aided by the "holy spirit" of God who ultimately provides the "blessed seed" and/or "bread" in order to further assist those who aspire to perfection, we see that this community expects greatness and special treatment (by God); but a community that is also strongly aware— consciously or unconsciously—of the ancient roots of a ritual which promised immortality. Both Qumran's Marriage Ritual and *Joseph and Aseneth* play the chords of an ancient melody in which the Goddess in her gracious bounty offered her worshipers the fruits of immortality. It is thus also no accident that the "mouth" and a "drink" (and "kiss") are of absolute importance here. At this point, however, the God of both *Joseph and Aseneth* and the Qumran sectarians steps in to play the role of a bounteous, fertile male who produces "seed" that will impregnate the willing virgin. The innovative miracle of artificial insemination that takes place is the outcome of the ceremony where the participants and the "Assembly of the Righteous" realize with not a shred of doubt that the woman who just received God's "bread" is nonetheless a virgin.

Fourth Step of the Ritual: The Act of Creation,
Or the Mystery of Existence

"Know from Where You Come: From a Stinking Drop" (Abot 3:1).   Before continuing with the story of *Joseph and Aseneth* we need to clarify the religious view of gender relations regarding the act of creation at the millennium. While in *Joseph and Aseneth* the emphasis is on the appealing portrayal of the woman, in Qumran literature there is no placing of a woman on a pedestal. Yet we believe that because of the ideological premise of virginity and the very narrow realm that the sectarians did afford women, it is plausible that a woman of the stature of Aseneth who could have performed an extraordinary service for them would also have been treated, at least on the surface, with a measure of dignity. We still must emphasize, however, that Aseneth too and/or women like her, basically provided a service of a very oppressed sort and in that sense, they were denigrated and abused.[43]

Qumran's Marriage Ritual refers to six kinds of women: wife (ʾiššâ), with whom a man "makes seed"; companion (raʿyâ), who is maybe the same as a wife but with an emphasis on relations that are not necessarily sexual; daughter of truth (bat ʾĕmet), which may have been in the company of "sons of truth," a favorite phrase of the sectarians; possibly, this "order" of women also indicated mature age (truth and wisdom related to age); virgins and girls (*nĕʿārôt*)—the difference between those two "classes" of women is their respective ages, though *nĕʿārâ* was mostly perceived as mature enough to conceive, especially if she was well prepared.[44] Finally, in the Marriage Ritual there is an order of older women who are comparable to the "older men" and who may denote a class of mature or aging virgins who preferred that position as a part of their "holiness." There is also a separate community (*sôd*) of mature elders (frag. 24). We have hinted above that the "older" people may have been those who could be fully discreet and because of that were also revered. In addition, the fragments refer to *ʾašîšîm* in the context of "righteousness" and "holiness" as well as that of "a blessed seed" (frag. 19, line 2). While the official translator of this text prefers to render the word *ʾašîš* as "old," it is entirely possible to refer to it as the Bible usually does and to suggest that possibly the fragments of the Marriage Ritual deal with a ceremony that included the taking of drugs/estrogenic aphrodisiacs for the purpose of fertility—indeed, like the teenage Esther, who was given special foods and was rubbed with special oils in order to be ready for a marriage ceremony, as was the woman/lover in Song of Songs.

The sectarians' view of creation is expressed in their *Manual of Discipline*, which concludes with a sobering, humbling series of expressions about the greatness of God and the worthlessness of people. It is almost an anticlimactic utterance; after all, these people perceive of themselves as the real, zealous "sons of Zadok and men of their covenant" (1:2), who "kept his covenant in the midst of wickedness so as to atone for the land" (1:3). At the end, in a rather reflective and telling statement the author declares the greatness of God:

> And who can grasp (contain) your glory (honor), and what is indeed man amongst your wondrous deeds? And [he] born of a woman what does he sit before you? [he appears low and humble sitting before you] And he is limited by the dust and lives by the bread of worms. He who is saliva which has been emitted, clay which was nipped off and he who desires dust. What can clay and that shaped by hand be reckoned (responded to), and what counsel does it understand? (1QS 11:20–22)[45]

The "dust" and the "worms" are the writer's appropriate images signifying how much he detested the flesh as well as those "born of a woman" for their corruptibility. Humans come from "a stinking drop."

The Chosen Life. By comparison, in *Joseph and Aseneth,* Joseph, while agreeing in essence with the source of human mortality, chooses to focus on a more positive aspect of existence. He begins (in 8:9) by acknowledging that life came from "darkness," but the tone and imagery of the rest of the passage are full of "light" and "spirit" metaphors. Note Joseph's use of "bread," which is not that of "worms" but its exact opposite, namely, "life." The hero further proclaims eternity for those who have been "chosen" (like the sectarians in exile and their star, Noah, who was saved from extinction), and he hopes that Aseneth will be among them. While in *Joseph and Aseneth* the bread and the cup are glorified, the sectarians, in a comparable passage about clay and water, the stuff Adam was made of, prefer to emphasize the negative aspects of the process of birth. But, at the same time, it is important to examine some of the more personal statements attributed to the people (if not leaders of the group) of the Scrolls where they seem to hint at other things that are much more in line with the goings on in *Joseph and Aseneth.*

We left the story with Joseph departing from Aseneth after his blessing; she is totally shattered and retreats to her tower in preparation for "conversion." The next section of the tale is a detailed description of Aseneth's shedding of her old self; she wept and fasted and brooded "and kept being filled with great fear and trembled (with) heavy trembling" (10:1c). The heroine, who has rarely seen a strange adult, is in an agitated state even though she is in control and knows how to behave. Interestingly, in addition to her crying and brooding, which are general activities, she is also engaged in ritual: "Aseneth hurried and took down from the window the skin (which hung there for a) curtain [Greek *katapetasma* = veil hanging in the Temple] and filled it with ashes from the fireplace and carried it up into the upper floor, and put it on the floor" (10:2). Aseneth is in a state of mourning and she performs the ritual associated with it. The curtain she uses for a ritualized reason points to her quasi-priestly position and suggests further that something about her status will soon be changed. The "veil" that she carries (and later on wears and removes) to her chamber is like the veil of Isis, the Egyptian Goddess; that veil is a blatant reference to hidden things—particularly the hymen. Removing the veil was a symbol of another level of knowledge and true consciousness; only the initiates had access to the veil and only they could remove it at the right time in order to accept and understand the mysteries of the Goddess. Ashes speak of death. When she throws away her clothing and jewels, her power as virgin/priestess, Aseneth signals the completion of the external part of the ritual of transformation. Falling and crying upon the ashes as well as girding her waist with sackcloth seem to be the main activities in which she is immersed for seven days. The result of so much weeping and crying was "mud." Again we see the Egyptian connection. It is clear here that Aseneth is imitating a ritual performed by Isis, who mourned the death of Osiris (the Egyptian god of the resurrection) and who at the same time was getting ready to search for him in order to bring him back to life. Isis's crying ultimately caused the Nile to rise signaling a hopeful beginning to her search, which culminated in the resurrection of Osiris. Aseneth, who seems to be mourning her old self, is thus also preparing for her own resurrection—but as another Aseneth ready to perform other rituals associated with a holy kind of birth and resurrection. It should be recalled, though, that in one of the most puzzling myths of Isis she is said to be able to give birth to Horus without actually having intercourse with a male deity. Aseneth, tired and "out of her power" (11:1), now has to undertake the long and arduous journey to the nether world in order to "die" and only then reemerge as a revitalized virgin ready to perform in a new capacity. The death experience is as vital to the representative of the Goddess as life is and only after that harrowing confrontation can she really renew herself and hopefully her community.[46] In the whole of the Hebraic tradition, the notion of removing the old, sometimes by very violent means, in order to make way for the new, is strongly present–for example, in Noah and in the forty years wanderings of the exodus. The sectarians themselves envision repairing the scenario when the "Sons of Darkness" are defeated in the war that will last forty years with the "Sons of Light."

The climax of Aseneth's address to God is in her characterization of Joseph as the son of God: "For who among men will give birth to such beauty and such great wisdom and virtue and power, as (owned by) the all-beautiful Joseph?" (13:14). Finally, she claims that she is ready to be completely subservient to him "and be a slave to him and serve him for ever (and) ever" (v. 15h). In other words, Aseneth submits by a vow of obedience, which is the essence of righteous behavior. She recognizes Joseph as her master and as a man with special powers for whom she is ready to abandon her power and station in life. Aseneth portrays herself more and more as a willing subordinate, ready to participate in a great drama which will be initiated by her master, Joseph.

The hero's blessing of the heroine with its sexual overtones, her meticulous physical and spiritual preparation for the change that is about to occur to her as well as the Goddess echoes throughout the tale, combine to present the reader with a startling procedure for its time.

Living Water.   The story of Joseph and Aseneth now moves to a spectacular ecological change: "the morning star rose out of heaven in the east" (14:1). This star is the sign of the birth of the Teacher of Righteousness in the Dead Sea Scrolls (CD 7:18). The star sign is taken from the Pentateuch: "A star is emerging from Jacob, a scepter is rising from Israel" (Num. 24:17). In the *War Scroll,* when the Sons of light encounter the Sons of Darkness, their hope is that the God who assisted the biblical heroes (like David against Goliath) to defeat their enemies will also help them in their militant pursuit. The star is used again in order to convey their success in that war (1QM 11:6).[47]

But the next event is supernatural: "the heaven was torn apart and great and unutterable light appeared" (v. 2). Accompanying that light, "a man came to her from heaven" (v. 3b) and addressed her in a rather direct fashion: "Aseneth, Aseneth" (v. 4). To be called by name by God is of utmost importance. The overt recognition of the woman is significant at this juncture of the story; it empowers her on the one hand and subdues her on the other. The "man" who appears to the heroine is described as the angel Michael "commander of the whole host of the Most High" (v. 8b).[48] While the "angel" appears to Aseneth in her own environment (in the tower where no one can enter), thus signaling her independence and identity, the message that he ultimately delivers is one of nonfreedom, maybe even oppression.

The most notable aspect of the man/angel is his likeness to Joseph: "in every respect similar to Joseph" (v. 9b). The description that follows is culturally, symbolically, and ritually relevant, "by the robe and the crown and the royal staff, except that his face was like lightning, and his eyes like sunshine, and the hairs of his head like a flame of fire of a burning torch, and hands and feet like iron shining forth from a fire, and sparks shot forth from his hands and feet" (14:9).[49] The robe, crown, and royal staff belong in the realm of power—though a "robe" can also be ritualistic, as we have seen in other examples. The sunshine brings Egypt back to mind, but the fire, especially from the feet of the messenger is messianic.[50] And since the whole story of *Joseph and Aseneth* is first associated with Heliopolis, this city of light fits the ecology of the events.

The angel proceeds to instruct Aseneth about her mourning attire: "put off your black tunic of mourning" (14:12b) and the ashes "and wash your face and your hands with living water" (v. 12c).[51] The man/angel tells Aseneth to perform a purification ritual which is typical among Jews and some sectarian Egyptians in this period. Many of the sects of the time practiced purification by water; the Qumranites were literally obsessed with purity and we have already shown how they used purification images to their advantage. The practice of purification derived from a rather negative view of women and sexuality, but the phrase "living water" seems to imply more profound, maybe secretive, matters. While the phrase is used in a matter-of-fact, almost innocent fashion, it seems to distract the audience from something that is more meaningful and maybe problematic.

To further understand the phrase "living water," we have to examine, in some detail, significant passages in which it occurs. The Bible invariably refers to God's words and injunctions as "living waters." Jeremiah, in his description of "the man" who trusts God, proclaims that he (that man) "will be like a tree planted on water" (17:7–8). The language of Jeremiah is rather curious emphasizing "manly" in the sense of virile (*geber*, "man"; also associated with virility in the sexual sense) and focusing attention on the man's security during a "drought year" when "he will not have to worry about not producing any fruit" (v. 8). The prophet describes a righteous, committed man whose trust in God is like a tree on water as opposed to idolatry (implicitly, the Asherah), which is practiced "on young trees and high hills" (the high places). Jeremiah advises that God is "a source of living water," the real God of fertility—and not the Asherah. Similar metaphors can be found in other prophetic texts (e.g., Isa. 40:24; Ezek. 31:6) as well as in Job (14:8) and Daniel (4:9).[52]

It is further no accident that the author of *Joseph and Aseneth* as well as the sectarians in their *Thanksgiving Hymns,* use the phrase "living water" to make their points. Jeremiah, though viewed by the tradition as a prophet, is himself from a priestly family and, like other key heroes, was "dedicated from the womb" to perform a godly duty

(Jer. 1:5). He never got married, did not have a family of his own, and did not participate in any communal ritual that might have involved the drinking of wine (16:1, 5). For all practical purposes, Jeremiah fits the Nazirite category and, because of his prophetic and priestly status as well as his links with Egypt, he might even be the founder of the sect. Significantly too, Jeremiah, who witnessed the destruction of Jerusalem in 586 B.C.E., went into exile in Egypt.

In the Dead Sea Scrolls "living water" is referenced frequently. For example, in their characterization of the enemy party, those who "returned and became traitors and turned away from the well of living water" (CD 3:23). Also in the *Thanksgiving Hymns* there is a whole array of water and tree imagery used to justify the sect's way of life: "and he opened his trunk to living waters" (1QH 8:7c) and, "so that a stranger will not enter into a well of life" (8:12c), as well as, "a source of living water that does not disappoint" (8:16b). All of these poetic phrases can be firmly anchored in the biblical tradition as we have just seen. But, as the sectarians were in the habit of using the text for their own purposes, here too there is an attempt on the part of the sectarian author to describe something different, more relevant to his life and to the life of the sect:

> I [thank you O Lord for] Thou placed me in a source of running water on land; and a spring of water in an arid land and a watered garden [which Thou planted] a plantation of cypress pine and cedar together for Thy glory (honor). (1QH 8:4–5)

Running water, a spring, and a garden are contrasted with "arid land" and that which is barren, and he thanks God not only for his chosenness and distinction in the midst of evil and pollution but also of providing him with a "source" that can enable him to exist in a hostile world yet function as "a spring of water." The sectarian, who "knows" what others do not, can serenely be anchored in the garden that God provided for him. The "plantation" is teeming with life (the various trees, like the cedar, traditionally referencing the Jerusalem Temple) because of God's providence. These trees are "trees of life beside a mysterious fountain hidden among the trees by the water and they put out (*lĕhapriaḥ*) a shoot (*nēṣer*) of the everlasting plant" (1QH 8:6). The "mysterious fountain" is, on the one hand, a typical sectarian analogy which emphasizes the secretive, mysterious, and mystical nature of some of their activities. It distinguishes between the special "fountain" that is hidden in the midst of other kinds of trees and water that presumably are not as pure. "Trees of life" echo the Garden of Eden and immortality, whereas "trees by the water" are more shallow and death-oriented. The emphasis is on the "fountain," which, in the midst of all that uncertainty and treachery, finally "brings to fruition" a *nēṣer* ("shoot," also related to *nāzîr*). The allusions to the classical Isaian messianic text are quite obvious: "And there shall come forth a shoot from the stump of Jesse and a branch shall grow out of his roots" (Isa. 11:1). Since the sectarian imagery is so close to the original Isaian oracle, and since that oracle became traditionally associated with the "roots" of the Messiah, the Qumran hymn should be placed within a messianic/christological context. More than that, in this hymn the author tells his audience, in terms couched in the language of water and fertility, that the "father" of the Messiah is a part of the *sôd* (community and secret). Moreover, since he is dealing with a special *nēṣer*, the "planting" is special as well. In the "Exhortation to Seek Wisdom," the Qumran author speaks about similar motifs and points to the "hiddenness" of "wisdom" as well as those special people (like Moses, who was hidden in the "ark") meant for the work of salvation: "They shall seek him but shall not find him . . . become wise through the might of God. Remember His miracles which He did in Egypt" (4Q185). The actual "planting" of the chosen is also "water"-laden: "But before they did so, they took root and sent out their roots to the watercourse that its stem might be open to the living waters and be one with the everlasting spring" (1QH 8:7–8a). The process of "taking root" is crucial in any planting, particularly where the Messiah is concerned. The "living water" must reach the "stem," which, in turn, must be "open" to the water. Metaphorically, the author describes a fertilization procedure that is particularly acute because of the use of the verb "to open," reminiscent of God's "opening" of barren/virgin women's wombs (in *Joseph and Aseneth,* the "kiss" opens the mouth).

The hymn proceeds with what seems on the surface a typical description of the group's xenophobia. Although they did seek and accept new members and "joiners," they were furious with those who took advantage of their teachings and abused them among outsiders, who at times abandoned the *sôd* (group); that is, they became heretics.

> And all [the beasts] of the forest fed on its leafy (netser; translated as nesher=leaves that drop off) boughs; its stem was trodden by all who

> passed on the way and its branches by all the birds. And all the [trees] by the water rose above it for they grew in their plantation; but they sent out no root to the watercourse. (1QH 8:8b–10a)

These lines in the hymn compare the shallow trees that grow by the water with the eternal tree; the former seem to grow faster and "rise above" the tree of life. But this is merely an illusion, and since they ultimately "sent out no root"—that is, they have no links with the sources of truth and eternity—they will perish. In the metaphor of "new births" and "new conceptions" which seems to be alluded to in this hymn, the poet suggests that indeed the old way of conception and birth is shallow because it leads to corruption and death whereas the sectarian "way" will produce fruit that will last forever.

> And the bud of the shoot (*nēṣer*) of holiness for the plant of truth was hidden and was not esteemed; and being unperceived, its mystery was sealed. Thou, O God, hedged in its fruit with the mystery of mighty heroes and spirits of holiness and the whirling flame of fire. (1QH 8:10–12b)

The "hidden," secretive "truth" is known to only a few who are obliged to "seal" it because it is "not esteemed" (presumably by outsiders who follow traditional legitimacy means).[53] The phrase is placed within an environment that is reminiscent of the "closed" Garden of Eden after the banishment of the human couple. We may remember that in Genesis God placed a "flaming sword" at the entrance to the garden so that the people would not be able to return and eat of the fruit of the tree of life (Gen. 3:24). Here too the poet mentions powerful men (maybe watchers/angels) and "holy spirits" who guard against the stranger, or any of the sect's enemies, and who are being helped by the flame of "a turning fire" (8:12).[54] The allusion to Genesis contributes to the feeling of closure, exclusivity as well as separation from the rest of the world. The "fire," in addition, is a symbol that denotes the group's notion of holiness but also of a necessary cleansing destruction before that perfection can be arrived at. The landscape described in the hymn is one which, at least in the poet's mind, is linked with Eden and specifically the Tree of Life, presumably the tree of immortality.

> No [stranger shall approach] the well-spring of life or drink the water of holiness with the everlasting trees, or bear fruit with [the Plant] of heaven, who seeing has not discerned, and considering has not believed

in the fountain of life, who has turned [his hand against] the everlasting [bud]. (1QH 8:12c–14)

The statement about a stranger "not approaching the well-spring of life" is consistent with the sect's perception of itself as holy and mystical and therefore closed to the outside world that might contaminate it. Once again, the "living water" or the "well-spring of life" is related to fertility.

In one of the most intriguing expressions in another fertility text, the biblical Song of Songs, we find that the woman is represented as "a garden closed":

> my sister, my promised bride;
> a garden enclosed,
> a sealed fountain
> . . . .
> Fountain of the garden
> well of living water,
> streams flowing down from Lebanon.
> Breathe over my garden,
> to spread its sweet smell around.
> Let my love come into his garden,
> let him taste its most exquisite fruits. (Song 4:12–16)

In one of the most explicitly sexual exchanges, the author of the Song of Songs considers the relationship between the two lovers and assigns to the woman the role of a virgin who has not been violated and whose virginity is enclosed in a garden. The "key" to that garden is, of course, in the "hand" of the male who pursues the woman. Appropriately, his sexual overtures are discerned by the woman to be the "well of living water," which "streams flowing down from Lebanon." The sexual act itself is described thus: "breathe over my garden . . . let my love come into his garden" and, of course, "taste its . . . fruits." The garden is intricately used here to show the woman's surroundings, which are tightly controlled by her (and maybe by her society); the garden is finally available to the man when the woman permits him to come in. The "living well" is thus transformed into a symbol signifying the man's sperm, which is being "breathed" over, or into, the woman's "garden." We see that "living water" is given the emphasis because of the extra value in a patriarchal society on the man's regenerative abilities.[55]

At Qumran, we hear the following fertility song:

> But Thou, O my God, hast put into my mouth as it were spouting rain
> for [those who thirst] and a fount of living waters which shall not fail.
> When they are opened they shall not run dry. . . . [The trees shall sink
> like] lead in the mighty waters, fire [shall burn among them] and they
> shall be dried up; but the fruitful Plant [by the] everlasting [spring shall
> be] an Eden of glory [bearing] fruits [of life]. (1QH 8:20)

The hymnist declares that he is "the spouter of rain" (probably in
opposition to Qumran's infamous "Spouter of Lies"), which connects
very well with a known early rabbinic assertion that "semen which
does not spout like an arrow cannot be brought to fruition" (*b. Ḥag.*
15a). While the "fount of living waters" performs its task ("he shall not
fail"), those who are now considered fruitful "trees"—that is, those
who engage in normal sexual intercourse giving birth to normally
corrupt people—"shall sink and burn and be dried up." In this statement the speaker completely rejects the fallen world in favor of a radically different one governed by "water," in which fertility is not
available to the iniquitous. The "fruits of life," which were forlorn and
abandoned for so long, can now be finally tasted. And there is more of
the same in other hymns; for example:

> By my hand Thou hast opened for them a well-spring and ditches [that
> all their channels] may be laid out according to a certain measuring
> cord, and the planting of their trees according to the plum line of the
> sun that [their boughs may become a beautiful] branch of glory. When I
> lift my hand to dig its ditches its roots shall run deep into hardest rock
> and its stem . . . in the earth; in the season of heat it shall keep its
> strength. (8:21–24a)[56]

In another hymn, a leader (we suggest the Teacher of Righteousness
himself) speaks of his lineage:

> For Thou hast known me from (the time of) my father, [and hast chosen
> me] from the womb. [From the belly of] my mother Thou has dealt
> kindly with me (protected me), and from the breasts of her who con-
> ceived me have Thy mercies been with me. [Thy grace was with me] in
> the lap of her who reared (nursed) me, and from my youth Thou hast
> illumined me with the wisdom of Thy judgement. (1QH 9:30–31)

Isaac and Samson and Samuel (as well as the prophet Jeremiah too)
were known to God "from the womb." We have seen that their births
were special, indeed miraculous. In the case of Samson and Samuel,

the Nazirite legacy was part and parcel of their upbringing. The speaker in the hymn places himself within that tradition of being *dedicated from the womb* as well. The mother remains in the shadows of the youth's experience and is cited as "womb," "belly," "breasts," "lap," "nurse" (*ʾōmenet*). The woman involved in the birth process is anonymous, and the emphasis is on the end product.

The "well of life" in *Joseph and Aseneth* can now be understood as a sexual symbol which describes the virgin, who has to stay in her virginity and not be violated by a "stranger." Some virgins were intended to stay intact forever; others were meant for pure pro-creation with selected members of the community. The sectarians who used water imagery to describe purification and rebirth also dif-ferentiated between water and "holy water" and, of course, "living water"—which is, quite simply, sperm. And, like Jeremiah's holy source of "living waters," the semen of the elect is superior and there-fore must be preserved for special purposes and occasions. The Qum-ran *Thanksgiving Hymns* begin by giving voice to an individual who portrays himself as close to God, like a high priest or prophet convey-ing God's message to the community. Perhaps this is the same person described here as "the spouter of rain to all those who are thirsty" (8:16), who in *Joseph and Aseneth* is marked by a star from birth and who enables the heroine to "flourish like flowers of life from the ground of the Most High" (16:16).

The Honeycomb, or Bread of Life. Stripping her mourning clothes and getting dressed "in her distinguished (and as yet) untouched linen robe, . . . [Aseneth] girded herself with the twin girdle of her vir-ginity, one girdle around her waist, and another girdle upon her breast" (14:14). The two girdles signify the transition to a new status. The waist girdle is the more traditional while the breast girdle, a brassiere, is a custom denoting modesty during intercourse for respectable women in the Roman world.[57] Aseneth then washes her hands and face "with living water" after which she takes an "un-touched and distinguished linen veil" and covers her head (v. 15). One thinks again of Isis and her star-covered veil of the universe: "I am all that has been and is and shall be, and no mortal has ever revealed my robe."[58] The "man" in Joseph and Aseneth instructs her to remove the veil, in line with the promise embodied in the myth of the veil of Isis: "you will be renewed and formed anew and made alive again . . . and drink a blessed cup of immortality" (15:5). Aseneth sheds her mortal image by removing the veil and uncovering the secrets of nature and procreation. She is "new" in every sense of the word and is about to become a fitting model for Qumran, a "City of Refuge": "because in you many nations will take refuge with the Lord God, the Most High, and under your wings many peoples trusting in the Lord God will be sheltered, and behind your walls will be guarded those who attach themselves to the Most High God in the name of Repentance" (15:7).[59] The main talk of retreat for reasons of "renewal" and deep change is identical in both *Joseph and Aseneth* and in the Dead Sea Scrolls.[60]

When Aseneth removes the veil, the man prepares her for a wedding; accordingly, he instructs her to wear her "wedding ornaments" and "dress in your wedding robe, the ancient and first robe which is laid up in your chamber since eternity" (v. 10). These are echoes of predestination and of the "first" wedding "since eternity," namely, the *hieros gamos* (holy wedding). The groom to be is Joseph. One can almost see how satisfying this point in the tale would be to its folk audience.

When Aseneth asks for the name of the man/angel who looks like Joseph, he responds that it is too "unspeakable" and "exceedingly great and wonderful and laudable."[61] She wishes to establish parity between them; she "reveals" herself to him by removing the veil and becoming who he wants her to be. All the while, the man is somewhat obscure, and Aseneth wishes to publicly identify him. In addition, since she is preparing to invite him to a meal, Aseneth wishes to create a more comfortable, intimate setting. Above all, she wishes to maintain a measure of power over him.

The meal scene that follows is loaded with sexual connotations and references. From the very beginning it is a scene of intimacy (though also highly ritualized and traditional).

> And Aseneth stretched out her right hand and put it on his knees and said to him, "I beg you, Lord, sit down a little on this bed, because this bed is pure and undefiled, and a man or woman never sat on it. And I will set a table before you, and bring you bread and you will eat, and bring you from my storeroom old and good wine . . . and you will drink from it. . . ." (15:14)

The familiar placing of the hand on the man's knee and the proposition to sit on a "pure bed" are obviously suggestive. Both Aseneth and the man are assumed to be virgins; hence, it is important for them to be associated with "undefiled" objects, especially of the sexual kind. Setting the table in preparation for a sexual act or a miraculous pregnancy, or even a magical seance—all are events recorded in the Bible and all are relevant to *Joseph and Aseneth*.[62]

Aseneth offers to bring "good wine" that "exhales" (or smells) so well and goes "up till heaven." In many ways, the wine fits into the ritual meal as well as water, but its relationship to the vineyard and a new stock puts it in a different category. New wine is important in the context of a holy wedding because the old, impotent king is discarded and the new one is put in place. In other words, the ruler who cannot fertilize the land must be sacrificed before the new, virile king is crowned. It is the role of the priestess, as a representative of the Goddess, to officiate during the proceedings.[63]

The man who is in Aseneth's company agrees to the meal but with a slight though important variation: "Bring me also a honeycomb" (16:1b). While Aseneth initially protests that she has no honey in her "storeroom," she does find it there. "And the comb was big and white as snow and full of honey. And that honey was like dew from heaven and its exhalation like breath of life" (16:8). Honey is a classical symbol of the Goddess, and it is always associated with sexuality. Bees and butterflies combine to signify the Goddess of regeneration. The Dead Sea Scrolls too recall the symbolism of bee and honey[64] as appropriate to "the Queen of Heaven" and a "mother of Israel."[65]

While all of the bee associations are quite appropriate for the narrative of *Joseph and Aseneth,* thus suggesting rather overtly that the woman is preparing for sex—not conversion in the conventional sense of the term—the emphasis ultimately in this passage is on the honeycomb. The latter is closely tied to the honey, but it has imagistic qualities that are different from honey. First, the honeycomb is the place where the honey is either manufactured or contained. It is a tool that serves a specific purpose, and Aseneth is convinced that she does not have it in her storeroom because presumably, in the past, she never needed it. Nevertheless, she knows where to obtain it and is ready to send a "boy to the suburb" to get it for her. The "angel" insists that the comb is where it is supposed to be, and he is obviously right. When Aseneth tries to rationalize and explain the source of the honeycomb, she says: "Lord, I did not have a honeycomb in my storeroom at any time, but you spoke and it came into being (or, it happened). Surely this came out of your mouth, because its exhalation is like breath of your mouth" (16:11).

The narrative now overwhelms the reader by the sheer number of images used in describing the initiation of Aseneth:

> And the man smiled at Aseneth's understanding, and called her to himself, and stretched out his right hand, and grasped her head and shook her head with his right hand. . . . Sparks shot from his hand as from bubbling (melted?) iron. And Aseneth looked . . . at the man's hand. And the man . . . said, "Happy are you, Aseneth, because the ineffable mysteries of the Most High have been revealed to you. . . . For this comb is (full of the) spirit of life." (16:12–14)

The ritual being performed by the "angel" and Aseneth is quite amazing.[66] The angel, who is constantly present, commands the woman and "does" various things to her that are not always in line with seemingly angelic missions. Generally speaking, this angel is unlike any other angel in other "angelic" texts; he seems to be intimately involved with Aseneth: touching her, talking, explaining, and commanding.

The honeycomb is described as a container of honey that, in the hands of a holy servant, provides Aseneth with the "bread of life." In a more sexually active environment where the two people involved indeed engage in the sexual act, the combination of honeycomb and "bread" and "honey" and "water" would have vividly portrayed a moment of penetration and/or sexual ecstasy. But this angel/man cannot sleep with this special woman. The only thing he can do is simulate the sexual act by performing a service that will enhance his status as well as the status of the virgin. Thus, the container/honeycomb is a vessel that carries the "bread/water" (i.e., semen) of a holy man who does not wish to contaminate himself with sexual intercourse but who also does not wish to "spill his seed to the ground." It is spilled instead into the comb from whence it is "breathed into" the body of the virgin. The nineteenth *Ode* of Solomon articulates the procedure in a poetic idiom:

> And he who was milked is the Father
> and he who milked him is the Holy Spirit.
> His breasts were full
> and his milk should not drip out wastefully.
> The Holy Spirit opened the Father's raiment

and mingled the milk from the Father's two breasts

. . . . .

Those who drink it are near his right hand.
The spirit opened the Virgin's womb
and she received the milk.

. . . . .

She bore him as if she were a man,
openly, with dignity, with kindness.

The ode may have originated in a time and place similar to the setting of *Joseph and Aseneth.* The main idea is indeed virginal conception, and it details the process by which the "Holy Spirit" in anthropomorphic garb literally extracts "milk" (semen?) from the "Father's breasts," or testicles. Even more explicitly, that "milk" is taken after the "Father's raiment" is opened. In other words, the ode describes a stripping process that is necessary if the "milk" is to be reached. As in *Joseph and Aseneth,* the "right hand" plays a significant role here, and the climactic moment is the opening of the "virgin's womb." This specific ode, which puzzled scholars in the past, is clearer in a context that, we suggest, describes a ritual of artificial insemination where no significant penetration takes place. Rather, there is a ritualized "extraction" of semen from the willing and prepared male candidate, who gives what he has to offer to a serving messenger/angel who proceeds with the intricate transaction. The ritual seems to be performed within a communal setting with other people participating, all of whom, we speculate, were in a state of ecstasy induced by earlier consumption of drugs and new wine.[67]

The sectarians' Marriage Ritual may contain within it the complete ritual performed at Qumran; it is undoubtedly about some kind of "wedding" involving various people (young and old, wise and holy; men and women), and not only males. The various fragments that are legible speak about the stars in the skies (frag. 27, line 4) as well as a "plantation" (*maṭṭāᶜ*). The document refers to "seed" (in the sense of semen) three times; the most explicit reference designates it as "blessed seed" (frag. 19, line 2), similar to the "living water" and "blessed bread" in the *Thanksgiving Hymns* and *Joseph and Aseneth.* There is communal rejoicing in the Marriage Ritual, which is partly ascribed to the possible consequence of the ritual enacted, that is, "prolong your life amongst the eternal people" (frag. 24, line 3). There is also a reference to the "father of the girl" (frag. 108, line 3) who, whether father, or "God father" (one appointed for the occasion), is traditionally in charge of this daughter (of truth) up to the time of her marriage, and there are a few references to "fruit of the womb."

It is therefore reasonable to say, as does Justin Martyr (110–166 C.E.) of Mary and Christ, that "she conceived not by intercourse but by power" (*Apol.* 1.33); or that Christ was "born of God in a peculiar manner, different from ordinary generation" (*Apol.* 1:22); or that he was born "a man from men" (Greek *anthrōpon . . . ex anthrōpōn*), since the men's role in this affair is much more significant than in the normal process of sexual union.[68]

But we still attribute the origination of the concept of ritualized artificial insemination to Egypt. Going back to what scholars referred to as "a strange and unusual" passage, we hear Isis say to Osiris:

> I am thy sister Isis. There is no other god or goddess who has done what I have done. I have played the part of a man though I am a woman, in order to make thy name live on earth, since thy divine seed was in my body.[69]

Isis is almost explicitly saying that it was the combination of her unusual "activity" (with a papyrus reed or cylindrical drum), which is under normal circumstances assigned to the man, and the "seed in my body" that led to her impregnation and delivery of Horus. "She stirred up from his state of inactivity him whose heart was still, she drew from him his seed (or, essence), she made an heir, she suckled the babe in loneliness" (*Hymn to Osiris* lines 16–17). Isis operates as a regenerative Goddess who uses Osiris's sperm to give birth to Horus.

By comparison, the Pyramid texts narrate the myth about an earlier (than Ra) sun-god, Tem, who supposedly masturbated in order to "give birth" to Shu and Tefnut. Thus:

> I brought together my members, they issued from me myself. After I produced excitation with my fist, my desire was realized by my hand. The seed fell from my mouth. I spat out Shu, expectorated Tefnut. Whereas I was One, now I am Three.[70]

It is left to the so-called Gnostics, who are in many ways the spiritual—and, we think, the real—heirs of the Dead Sea sectarians, to articulate a doctrine about perfection and how it can (and is to) be accomplished: "For it is by a kiss that the perfect conceive and give birth. For this reason we also kiss one another. We receive conception from the grace which is in each other."[71] The kiss alludes to the non-traditional method of conception; it also includes "water" elements within the "mouth," which make it possible for the carrier/performer to transmit the necessary "properties" to the womb of the virgin. The result and the method of that "kiss" are "perfect." In an overt reference to nontraditional marriage and intercourse, the Gnostic *Gospel of Philip* suggests the following:

> If there is a hidden quality to the marriage of defilement, how much more is the undefiled marriage a true mystery! It is not fleshly but pure. It belongs not to desire but to the will. (2.3.82)

Sectarian ideology, then, is that desire and the flesh are natural/animal; the will is an artifice of inspired men. In the trio of vows associated with the "kiss," we find an important formula: *knowledge* (gnosis), or wisdom, is equal to righteousness, right conduct, or obedience to the Father; *truth* is equal to the holy spirit, fulfilling while counteracting the flesh; and (reversing the Goddess's message) *virginity*, or chastity, equals rebirth or life forever.

Epilogue: Betrothal and Crowning

The Sacrament of Marriage in the Byzantine Rite. The significance of *Joseph and Aseneth* is attested to in the Orthodox, Byzantine marriage ritual still performed today; it is a sign both of the enduring legacy of this story and of the legacy that originated at Qumran. The impact of the images used in the ceremony reflect its importance and transmit to the participants the aura of holiness which is so pivotal to the original undertaking. The ritual is divided into two parts: the Service of Betrothal and the Service of Crowning. It maintains the balance between the various important symbols already introduced in *Joseph and Aseneth*, and it uses the typical "holy" terminology that was essential to the original story.

In the first part (the Service of Betrothal), the parties to be involved in the ceremony are "the servant of God" and the "handmaiden of God," who are about to join forces so as to "preserve them in a blameless way of life" (131). The language retains the sex-without-sex motif in that the proceedings, surprisingly, couple "an honorable marriage and a bed undefiled." The ring that is used as the symbol of binding the couple is placed on their "right hands," which played an important part in *Joseph and Aseneth*.[72] When the ritual is placed within its biblical context, it mentions Abraham, who sent his servant to look for a wife for Isaac. The "sign" used by Eliezer in that biblical story, which is emphasized in the present-day ceremony, is "the drawing of water," completed by Rebekah at the well of fertility. We remember that both Isaac and Rebekah are associated with miraculous births. Isaac is the son born to Sarah in her old age and Rebekah is one of the "barren" matriarchs who gives birth after appealing to God. The Byzantine ceremony refers to these two ancient characters as being engaged in "a holy union which is from Thee" (133).

The Orthodox marriage ritual emphasizes the importance of the ring (an image of immortality with no beginning and no end) because of its initial associations with Joseph, Daniel, and Tamar.[73] The relationship between Joseph and Daniel is highly suggestive as well as credible because of links with dreams and motifs of foreign power (Joseph with the pharaoh in Egypt and Daniel with Nebuchadnezzar in Babylon). The inclusion of Tamar in this prominent circle brings up the image of the priestess that is so evident in *Joseph and Aseneth*.[74] All three of these characters are important in the ideology of the community of the Dead Sea Scrolls.[75]

The second part of the ritual, titled "the Service of Crowning," is the actual marriage ceremony, which reaches a peak when both the priest and the choir pronounce: "Your wife will be like a fruitful vine . . . your children will be like olive shoots" (135). The "vine" and the "olive shoot" have been dominating images in the sectarians' canon, having both individual and communal overtones. When the priest goes on to recite the central prayer of the ritual, he reminds the couple of "our forefather Adam, of "opening the womb of Sarah," and of Isaac and Rebekah. The priest continues reciting and reminding the celebrants of the other famous couples in the Bible all of whom are associated with miracle births: Jacob and Rachel (both of whom, strangely enough, are credited with producing the twelve patriarchs) and Joseph and Aseneth (138). Zechariah and Elizabeth, the parents of John the Baptist, close off that prominent circle; they may be associated also with Hannah and her son Samuel.

When the priest "recites aloud" the second major prayer of the ceremony, he once again calls upon the genealogy of "God" parents: Abraham and Sarah, Isaac and Rebekah, Joseph and Aseneth, Moses and Zipporah, Joachim and Anna, Zechariah and Elizabeth (the parents of John the Baptist) and "Noah in the ark" (139). The overwhelming number of priestly personalities—to say nothing of Joseph and Aseneth themselves—on that list is surely not an accident; nor is the mention of Noah coincidental. Like Tamar (the Canaanite priestess who gave birth to the great ancestor of David), Zipporah, the Midianite priestess, is associated with a cleansing, covenantal act (circumcision) that saves the lives of her son and/or her husband. The priest presiding over the ceremony calls for the preservation of the couple along the lines of the preservation of Noah, thus suggesting that a sacred wedding has an impact on individuals as well as on the natural world.

The ritual also recalls the name of Helen (Helena), a memorable person at the millennium because of her charity during the great famine in Judea (140). Here the reference is to a later namesake, Constantine's Christian queen in the fourth century. Last but not least are "the groomsman" and "the bridesmaid," echoing the "strong men" and the "seven virgins" who watched over the precious woman/virgin and who are now ready to see them off on their new journey.

At the heart of the ceremony is the spectacular "crowning" of the bride and the groom: "Thou hast put upon their heads crowns of precious stones" (141). The kingly/priestly motif is another metaphor that appears in *Joseph and Aseneth* of splendor and precious stones as gifts presented to the couple in this ritual. When the "reader" in this contemporary ceremony attempts to comment on the significance of the celebration, he sums it up thus: "This is a great mystery" (142). The priest announces: "Preserve their bed blameless . . . that they may live together in purity" (144). And: "Receive their crowns into Thy Kingdom, preserving them spotless, blameless, and without reproach" (147). "Blameless" and "pure" are almost direct allusions to the Dead Sea Scrolls. There is also reference to the importance of the patriarchal couples: "These are the couples that brought forth the human archetypes: the masculine, John the Baptist, and the feminine, the Virgin, the 'unmarried spouse,' 'from whom the Savior is born without the intermediary of marriage,' the royal bridegroom of the banquet of the wise virgins. Marriage is thereby placed under the signs of the miraculous Birth, and of the Servant and the Friend of the one Bridegroom" (152).

Finally, there is a procession that is "a symbolic summary of the nuptial dance of former times. It is led by the priest who joins the hands of the bridegroom and bride" (158). Although the procession is in line with the tradition of the joyful celebration of marriage in the Goddess religion, this particular part of the ritual dramatically reenacts God's placing of the hand of Eve submissively in Adam's hand. The procession, led by the priest, advances three times in a circle, symbolizing eternity. "By reproducing the symbol of eternity, they change mere extension into sacred space" (158).[76]

CHAPTER SIX

Horse Power

And the Lord called those men, the seven chief white ones, and commanded that they should bring before him, beginning with the first star who led the way, all the stars whose genitals were like the genitals of horses. (*1 Enoch* 90:21)

BRIEF: SEX AND VIOLENCE

The use of horses for war in the ancient world can be compared to the invention of the wheel or the modern machine. Horses gave a great advantage to warriors straddling this strange, powerful machine of sheer energy and speed. Horses could move in swiftly on a population; they could also retreat before significant retaliation could be mobilized.

The first images of horsemen, perhaps remembered as half-man half-horse satyrs (before horse-and-wheel technologies were combined in horse-driven chariots), can be associated with the Indo-European invasions of Asia Minor in 2500 B.C.E.[1] It is believed that these fierce horsemen came from the Caucasus Mountains in Russia, where horses may have been domesticated about six thousand years ago. Horses became weapons of war for the powerful empires of Assyria, Babylon, and Egypt much later. In Egypt, the Hyksos, who possibly originated in Asia Minor, succeeded in their takeover of the pharaonic state in the seventeenth century B.C.E.[2] They are remembered largely because of their horse power. It should also be noted in this connection that of all the animals associated with the long-lived pantheon of Egyptian gods and goddesses, none are horses. The reason is indeed the late date of their introduction to the region. Even so, there is at least one demotic (popular) text from the turn of the millennium that mentions Horus (the solar son of Isis and Osiris) on a white horse, and a mounted Horus appears in later art as well.[3]

The Greeks and the Romans developed horse-drawn chariots for their wars. The story of the Trojan horse may be a popularized rendition of some sneak attack of early Greeks who utilized the innovative horse and chariot.

As far as we know, Israel/Judea, historically a poor, underdeveloped nation sandwiched between major empires, had access to large stables of horses only once.[4] Both the Bible and archaeological data show that the rich, trade-based kingdom of Solomon, son of David, owned and bred many horses. Horses thus became associated with the golden royal era of 1000 B.C.E. It is no coincidence that the horse, viewed as an almost supernatural creature with its thundering hooves and fire-snorting sounds, and even more awesome in the guise of the chariot of imperial Rome, became associated with the messianic apocalypse and the war to end all wars. The horse evolved into the sophisticated war machine of the ancient world.

Horses in the ancient world equaled power and wealth because they were rare and were thus reserved for warlords and kings. Several pharaohs were entombed with their favorite steeds along with other valuable possessions and persons. Horse-breeding techniques, like rights to competitive technology today, were kept a secret. Eventually, these valuable fertility secrets leaked out, and Arab tribesmen who developed the famous Arabian stallions knew all about artificial insemination. When this particular knowledge (artificial insemination) was developed is still unknown, but at least by the seventh century C.E., when Arabic writings proliferate, it was reported that the technique was accomplished with the help of cotton balls.[5] Another anecdote from the fourteenth century tells of Arabs stealing the semen of prize stallions and impregnating fine mares of rivals with semen from sick, inferior stallions.[6]

The horse was introduced to the Israelites probably via the Egyptians, but they may have seen horses from neighbors in the northeast too. In fact, there is an extraordinary recent archaeological find in Syria, "a 4,300-year-old clay figurine that stands as the oldest known sculpture of a domesticated horse."[7] It is not clear what the social function of horses was at that point in time. The sculptured figurine represents a stallion "with enlarged genitals . . . [which] may have been used in ceremonies to ensure the fertility of horses, much as full-bodied female figurines found at the same site appear to have been intended to promote healthy human births."[8] It has been suggested that the site's residents "probably concentrated on breeding horses with donkeys to produce mules, which kings and other royal officials considered most desirable for pulling chariots."[9] That mixed breed enabled men to engage in long-distance raids on settled regions with food stores, goods, and women; thus, the association of horses with masculine power and prowess is almost spontaneous. Although horses may have had a more functional use in Asia for their barbaric raids, in Mesopotamia their pulling of kings' chariots may have been more idiosyncratic than warlike.[10] It is hard to say how the chariots were used, but the innovation of horses with wheels certainly enabled a king to parade his power in front of the general populace. The focus of most interpretations about the role of early domesticated horses is on fertility, the breeding industry, and its usefulness to humans. Since the technologies of animal (and plant) breeding were well known to very ancient societies, experimenting with animal/horse "graftings" for more direct human purposes was a logical result.

HORSE MYTHS FOLLOW FUNCTION

Migration, trade, and war, the results of normal social intercourse, persisted as ideas in the Goddess religion as a widespread symbolic system for thousands of years. Localized adaptations incorporated the basic elements into their own fables, giving the false impression that each developed uniquely on its own. Recent scholarship claims that Indo-Aryan pillaging, raping horsemen brought along their male gods overlying the agrarian fertility goddess. The horse is the subject in many myths and folklore related to physical force, beauty, and—perhaps because they appear suddenly out of the blue sky from afar—to the sky.[11] Poseidon, the Greek sea-god, was powerless without his horses. Pegasus is the winged horse associated with the skies, poetry, and the muse.

Horses function also as fertility images in the Roman world. A fast horse is akin to lightning, which is associated with thunderstorms, which, in turn, are harbingers of rain and fertility. In Roman mythology the horse was sacrificed to Mars, thus impersonating the self-sacrificing god. In Mesopotamia, the love-goddess Ishtar reportedly had a stallion among her various lovers. In the Roman myth of Phaedra and Hippolytus, a male virgin consecrated to the love-goddess Artemis is falsely accused of raping his stepmother Phaedra and is banished from his land. As a further evil, a god is enticed to send a sea monster who terrified Hippolytus's horses (symbolizing his saved-up sexual energies), which crush him to death. From then on, maidens remembering Hippolytus's virtue in turning down an easy mark hang up a lock of their hair in the temple before marrying. This myth combines elements reminiscent not only of the vestal virgins who sacrificed their hair to trees but also of the virginal young Joseph, who was falsely accused of raping Potiphar's wife (and then banished, presumably for not doing so), and, of course, of Samson, whose testosterone power is signified not by horses but by his fetish for uncut hair. As we have previously shown, the much later Qumran literature that dwells on Samson recycles these same popular symbols.[12]

Even the great official church historian Eusebius, narrates a horse story in his report about Marcus Aurelius's triumph in one of his crucial battles; there God sent rain from heaven at the behest and prayers of many soldiers.

> And as this was a singular spectacle to the enemy, a still more singular circumstance is reported to have happened immediately; that the lightning drove the enemy into flight and destruction, but that a shower came down and refreshed the army of those that then called upon God." (*Church History*).[13]

Finally, in the same report, Eusebius tells his audience that this whole miracle led to the establishment of the fulminea "or thundering legion." In other words, the legion of cavalrymen saved the day for the Romans. The message of redemption through rain and the thunder of horses is not far from Qumran's own Noachic/messianic tradition.

It is likely that the ancient Egyptians, rather than anyone else, who fostered a civilization and a culture that encouraged more precise scientific reasonings and experiments and precise record keeping, and even had a zoo by about 2000 B.C.E., were the first to take their knowledge of breeding one step further. That ultimately led to a fairly sophisticated understanding of intricate anatomical and biological phenomena that assisted the Egyptians in enhancing human medicine. The case for a connection between animal breeding (specifically the horse) and human fertility was made much more persuasively by the observing ancient Egyptians, who were trying to protect their most prized animal/weapon.

Echoes of fertility, war, and glory allotted to the horse in the ancient world generally, and Egypt particularly, can already be heard in the Bible; they are much more of an issue for the Dead Sea sectarians.

HORSES, EXCESSIVENESS, AND THE HOLY BOOKS

All knowledge in the ancient world had a supernatural quality to it and was therefore restricted to very special elites, as if only appointed ones had been sent new revelations or technology to accomplish some historic mission. They thus believed that the spirit of the god or goddess came to rest on those with this special calling. Appropriately, when the prophet calls on the Israelites to convert their swords into plowshares as well as *not to follow the way of the Egyptians by multiplying horses* (Isa. 2:4–7; see also Deut. 17:16),[14] he actually alludes to horse breeding of some sort. Five centuries later, we believe, the brotherhood at Qumran was using this most secret gnosis, as signified by the totem animal of the Messiah, the horse, to get back to the Garden of Eden.

The part played by the horse in biblical literature is quite unique. On the one hand, horses are analogues for excessive power, like that of the gods. On the other hand, horses seem to stand for excessive sexuality, like that expressed by uncontrollable women. (We see that sex and violence were confused in people's minds even back then.)

One of the greatest battles that was fought and won by Joshua during the early settlement period (eleventh century B.C.E.) was against Jabin the King of Hazor and his allies; they are described as being: "as many as the sand on the shores of the sea . . . with many horses and chariots (vehicles)" (Josh. 11:4). Yahweh commands Joshua not to fear any of them and to "castrate (from the root ʿqr, associated with barrenness) their horses and set their chariots on fire" (v. 7b). Joshua is reported to have done as Yahweh commanded him (v. 9).[15]

In 1 Kings 10–11 Solomon is said to have had thousands of chariots and horses most of which were acquired in Egypt; he is also faulted by God for these acquisitions. In fact, horses are inextricably linked with Egypt and its culture, not only historically but also metaphorically. It is no accident that the biblical author warns the Israelites about having a king who will "multiply horses" and might "return the people to Egypt so as to multiply horses; and Yahweh told you [Israel] that you will not continue to return to that way (or, on that road) again" (Deut. 17:16). The Dead Sea sectarians often quote from Deuteronomy but use that particular passage for their own purposes; they emphasize the role of the foreign, non-"brother" king (whom we identify as Herod and his dynasty) who must be shunned by the people. But they also repeat the injunction against acquiring horses for purposes of war and riches. We are told by the biblical author that Solomon, who built the Temple to Yahweh in Jerusalem, also maintained the borders of the United Kingdom which was found by David. He established relations with the Egyptian government, which presumably supplied him with the horses necessary for military strength and prestige. Although there is still some controversy about whether there were stables or storehouses in Megiddo (where Solomon's horses were presumably maintained), it is nonetheless instructive that the text (in Kings and Deuteronomy) is quite leery about kings and horses. More than that, as we have just suggested, there seems to be an effort on the part of the editors to link horses and women and to thus imply that the overt physical power of the horse can be connected to another kind of power, which, though less obvious, is nonetheless quite perilous. Solomon's penchant for both horses and women is disliked by Yahweh, who is finally intent on destroying the king along with his kingdom. The biblical author is rather schizophrenic in his assessment of Solomon's position. Although the king is prone to women and horses, he is also endowed with God's wisdom: "And the whole world sought Solomon to listen to his wisdom which God put in his heart; and each one of them brought him presents: utensils of silver and gold and clothing and ammunition and perfumes, horses and donkeys year by year" (1 Kgs. 10:24–25). The Bible here acknowledges that horses were as expensive and valuable as "silver and gold" as well as "perfumes."

By comparison, the prophets treat the subject of horses in a rather hostile fashion, because horses represent in the prophets' minds the negative dependence of people on material things and earthly kingdoms and non-Yahwistic power. In that legacy, horses are symbols of earthly power that will have to be destroyed if Yahweh is to prevail. It is not coincidental that from the prophets' point of view the divided kingdom that is formed after the death of Solomon is evil; they believe that the divided kingdom came about because of Solomon's promiscuity particularly with "foreign" women, and his political excesses, symbolized by his ownership of an inordinate amount of horses. Both these elements (women and horses) proved to the prophets (and their adherents) Solomon's disrespect for Yahweh. Solomon is therefore perceived as a king gone astray (unlike the

unpretentious warrior King David, whose charm and charisma won
the people). Solomon disobeyed Yahweh, who demanded strict adherence to his laws and commands and who was particularly incensed
with those who attempted to find positive links with Egypt, the real
and mythical archenemy of the Israelites. Therefore, it is horses (signifying military power) that, for the prophets, denote reliance on
human frailties and, by implication, nonreliance on Yahweh, which
had to be given up. Isaiah's eschatological prophecy about "horses
and chariots" (chapter 2) as symbols of human pride that must be
eradicated before redemption occurs is in line with the Deuteronomic
injunction against "multiplying horses." But horses (like "swords into
plowshares") stood for more than this peaceful metaphor; one must
also consider the uses of horses in war and breeding techniques used
by the ancients to "multiply" them.[16]

It is left to the sixth-century B.C.E. prophet Ezekiel to articulate
fully the symbolic meaning of the horse for the biblical tradition.[17] In
chapter 23, which describes the sins, faults, and misdeeds of the two
kingdoms of Israel (the centers of which were in Sumeria/Israel and
Jerusalem/Judah), the prophet employs his most vitriolic adjectives to
describe the political arrangements that prevailed in both the South
and the North before the final destruction. The governing image used
by the prophet is of a whore, and the people's political connections
with Assyria and Egypt are seen as a prostitution of national sovereignty.

The picture painted by Ezekiel is one of intense promiscuity initiated by the woman: the Samarians in the kingdom of Israel court the
Assyrians while their Judean brethren appeal to the Egyptians. In
both cases the imagery includes horses and horsemen who are powerful both politically and militarily and, above all, sexually. The
prophet thus describes the political alliances of the divided kingdom
in personal terms which delineate sexual and political corruption.
Both sisters' names are associated with the root *ʾōhel* ("tent"), which
denotes intimacy and femininity. The Assyrian leadership, no longer
much of a threat in the time of Ezekiel, is the subject of the first sister,
Ohola (once the northern kingdom that became Samaria); her image
is one of aristocratic vanities, insincerity, and of corrupt intimacies
"wearing blue, . . . pleasant young men, horsemen riding on horses"
(23:6). But the prophet reserves the greatest invectives for the second
sister, the "heart" of the Jewish homeland, Oholiva (the southern

kingdom of Judah and Jerusalem); she is affiliated with the crudest sex: "she desired to become their [the Egyptians'] harlot, those whose flesh is that of a donkey and their flow is that of horses" (v. 20). The "flow" is the image of semen. In an extraordinary expression, the prophet links human sexual intercourse with horses' potency, and, although there is no attempt to describe bestiality here, the whole landscape is quite suggestive and implies a certain Egyptian know-how that seems already to be part of the national consciousness. At all times, the prophet's imagery is negative and accusatory. The final judgment that Ezekiel pronounces on the two "sisters" and on their excesses is devastating; they will have no access to repentance and no chance to "return." The whole chapter, which echoes major prophetic objections to women and their sexuality, curiously links women to treachery and to horses and to horsemen. The prophet seems to be addressing a specific issue that was clearly understood by his audience and was related not only to corrupt tribes as women but to their attraction to "horsemen," who were powerful people because of their training as well as their ability to control their animal and to afford it.

A good portion of the later reforms of King Josiah, a devout Yahwist, were dedicated to the destruction of pagan practices associated with the cult of the sun and horses. Archaeologists have located the desecrated remains of a frieze of a horse and the sun that is thought to have been on the entrance to the temple. The most prominent Goddess related to that destruction is the Asherah, who, according to 2 Kgs. 23:6–7, had a particular spot of worship within the Temple in Jerusalem. More specifically, the priest, Hilkiah, and his cohorts were instructed by the king/reformer to "prevent the horses which the kings of Judah gave to the sun from entering the house of Yahweh . . . and the chariots of the sun he burnt in the fire" (23:11). There is no clear indication of the nature of "horse offerings," but we know of the sun-god, who roamed around the heavens in his swift, horse-drawn chariots. In that same spirit, the Dead Sea sectarians, who claimed that they had a new covenant, appear to have linked the digressions and evils of their contemporaries in Jerusalem with, among others, sexual misdeeds, whether of a generally incestuous nature or more specifically with the house of Herod.[18]

The later postexilic prophets see horses everywhere, but in a new, purified form; they are the ones who ultimately formulate the popular concept of the "four horsemen of the apocalypse." In Zechariah's first vision "there was a man mounted on a red horse! . . . and behind him were red, sorrel, and white horses" (1:8). When the prophet inquires of the angel, who shows him the horses about their meaning, the response is intriguing: "These are the ones which Yahweh sent to roam about the earth" (1:10).[19]

In Zechariah's seventh vision, he sees four chariots drawn by horses: "With the first chariot, there were red horses; with the second chariot, there were black horses; with the third chariot, there were white horses; and with the fourth chariot, there were dappled horses; [all] mighty ones" (6:2–3). While in essence this vision is similar to the first one, the emphasis here is on power, swiftness, and omnipotence. The prophet claims that Yahweh employs the most significant symbol of strength in order to emphasize the universality of his message as well as the quickness of its delivery; the four horses that are sent to the four corners of the flat world (the four winds) are intended to disseminate the word of God. At this point in the development of prophecy, the horse is fully assimilated into Yahwistic discourse, the image is cleaned up. But what goes around comes around—and the horse now has attributes similar to those mentioned in polytheistic, goddess-oriented myths, namely, decisive supernatural strength and awesome swiftness of winners.[20]

The horse would have been a familiar evocative image to a wide audience in those times. To speak of "horse" and "chariot" focuses attention on the absolute power of kings and tyrants (who have access to horse and chariot) to accomplish almost any political goal and to be viewed as powerful by those who have to capitulate. The reality behind the myth of the horse's commanding abilities was the power of the king.

In the holy books of the Dead Sea Scrolls there are also references to pure horses in the context of war and political accomplishment. In the *War Scroll* the sectarians decree that only those who are thirty-five to forty—that is, "elders" who are wise and experienced—can be designated as horsemen—and as might be expected of the brotherhood, the preferred horses are stallions: "The horses advancing into battle . . . shall all be stallions (*sûsîm zĕkārîm*); they shall be swift, sensitive of mouth, and sound of wind, and of the required age, trained for war, and accustomed to noise and to every (kind of) sight" (1QM 6:10).[21] Since much of the *War Scroll* describes military tactics that are in the Roman mode, horses and horsemen play a significant role in the crucial apocalyptic battles. In fact, it is only fitting that the Sons of Light, who ultimately face the "Kittiyyim," also use similar horse techniques, albeit to their advantage. Only a small fraction of the graves in the Qumran cemetery have been unearthed so far, but the remains of a man identified as a horseman have already been reported.[22] What this small piece of evidence suggests is that horse talk was not a matter of doctrine alone. There is no doubt that, in addition to their militant ideology, the Qumranites were familiar with (if not well versed in) military maneuvers. This may point to links between them and the Egyptian corridor, which at an earlier time included the mercenary cavalry at Elephantine. We have suggested all along a paramilitary power structure beyond the settlement in the desert.

The Scrolls as a whole clearly indicate, among other things, that the people in the desert who dedicated themselves to a life of "nondefilement" (at least for some period of time) were also organized as a quasi commune, where all material possessions were shared by the whole group and where members of this order had to surrender their worldly goods to the community. Under these circumstances, the wealth of the group may have been quite considerable, especially if one accounts for their unwillingness to support the Jerusalem Temple as many diaspora groups did.[23] In a recently published article about the Qumran settlement, the official archaeologists now maintain that the whole settlement was more of a "villa" than a "monastery."[24] Specifically, "Elegant column bases at Qumran suggest a style of architecture that . . . [is] hard to believe for a simple quasi-monastic community. Other objects . . . glass unguentaria, elegant urns and fine pottery also indicate a somewhat luxurious lifestyle."[25] More specifically, because of the hierarchical nature of the Qumran sect, a few of the major priests may have come from wealthy families. The Qumran community also had a large popular following (if it turns out that "the many" spawned the later numbers of mystics, Gnostics, and major religious groups) who probably supported the movement with tithes.[26] In short, they could afford horses for their expected holy war. We also take into account the possible ramifications of the *Copper Scroll*, which lists great amounts of silver and gold and other treasures (maybe crown jewels and icons). Although this could be just a boast of the community's great wealth, we think it represents a reality. It is feasible that the *Copper Scroll* is a hidden inventory of actual

Temple treasures (and establishment priests with their Temple goods may have "repented" in the end, and joined the sectarians in the desert hideouts[27]). It is just as possible that it represents a Qumran catalog of the sect's own treasures.

THE MESSIANIC HORSEMAN

We turn to the book of Enoch, fragments of which were found among the Qumran writings. The complete Ethiopic version of the text may be later than the Qumran rendering with its preordained stars, or saints (reasons to preserve them accurately). There is thus no reason to assume that much (of this later version) was changed.[28] Here too we find horses, but, importantly, horses that suggest sexuality of an extraordinary nature. In the second dream "a single star fell from heaven. . . . Then I saw these big and dark cows . . . I kept observing, and behold, I saw all of them extending their sexual organs like horses and commencing to mount upon the heifers . . . and they all became pregnant and bore elephants, camels, and donkeys" (86:1–4). In other words, the author describes what he perceives to be a phenomenon contrary to nature but one that reminds him of humans. His general argument is that there was a breach of divine law associated with Eve's original sexual sin. Before that time, humans procreated spiritually as in *1 Enoch:*

> Surely you, you [used to be] holy, spiritual, the living ones, [possessing] eternal life; but (now) you have defiled yourselves with women, and with the blood of the flesh-begotten children . . . like them producing blood and flesh, (which) die and perish. . . . Indeed, you, formerly you were spiritual, (having) eternal life. . . . That is why (formerly) I did not make wives for you, for the dwelling of the spiritual beings of heaven is heaven. (15:4–7)

Original sin must be wiped out: "And the Lord called those men, the seven chief white ones, and commanded that they should bring before him, beginning with the first star who led the way, all the stars whose genitals were like the genitals of horses" (90:21). We take this statement as a blatant admission of horse breeding and human artificial insemination. Like everything else associated with the brotherhood at Qumran and those influenced by its literature and ideology, the sin offering had to be made precisely at the right time as preordained; that is the role of the "white chief" (Messiah): "The horse shall walk through the blood of sinners up to his chest; and the chariot shall sink down up to its top" (100:3).

In the symbolic, sex-obsessed landscape of the Hebrew imagination, the horse slowly evolved to be not just a tool representing the evils of foreign political association but, as the later prophets as well as intertestamental and rabbinic literature tell us, the animal that stood for a certain perfect beauty that will reemerge during an apocalyptic age. The symbolism of the horse placed it increasingly within a framework of perfection, which was sometimes unique to those who have special priestly duties.

The Hebrews had every opportunity to learn horse breeding techniques early on. Herds were raised at the edge of the Egyptian Delta, especially at Pithom on the Wadi et-Tumilat, which is the eastern branch of the Nile. Pithom, the House of Atum (the sun-god), is mentioned in Exodus as the store city for which the Hebrews made bricks.[29] We have already mentioned the role of the Jewish Elephantine community in relation to horse breeding. Certainly by the turn of the millennium, when temples known as "the House of Life" dealing in the "Mystery of Existence" were on a route to the sectarians' settlement, even into the Sinai (Hathor's temple and cave, for example), the more exotic techniques of fertility may have become known to the sectarians.

Ideologically, the religious fundamentalists seemed to have initially rejected such notions of increasing their stocks "artificially," because of their association with foreign ways and "strange" women. But there was always an underlying tension regarding the acquisition of horses (as all the prohibitions against them attest), and symbols have a way of becoming their opposite, so that excessiveness on earth could become rationalized as perfection in heaven, the home of the "stars." Furthermore, there was an ambiguous attitude toward horses precisely because the early Hebrews (and later Jews) might have known the potential embodied in horses who could be molded and formed to perfection with the right stud and mare. In a way, Qoheleth's statement about a time and place for everything under heaven is more than relevant here (Qoh. 3:1–8).

We also call attention here to the demand for priestly purity coupled with a pride in lineage parallel to the demand for the right breed of horse. The priestly profession, in which specialists communed with supernatural beings via sacrifices and magic, oversaw all medical knowledge and healing practices. Healing and medicine required a pure family line of descent; the priest had to be extremely careful about whom he associated with and whom he married. The Bible is adamant that the high priest marry a virgin from his own family (Lev. 21:14); he thus must be from a fairly select lineage. Certainly, the priest can never marry a widow or a divorced woman (she would be damaged goods).[30] Pure priestly "breeding" comes as close as literally possible to pure horse breeding. To succeed, both have to have the right "stud" lineage; any "mixed seed" (i.e., the wrong woman) is bound to produce either ordinary horses/priests or outright failures and corruptions (like mules).

Finally, the method of breeding is also of immense importance to those who think in terms of pollution and failure—the less "pollution," the better. Evidence of the importance of purity can be seen in the *Temple Scroll,* where many of the rules of priestly (and non-priestly) purity are listed. To describe the pure city and temple, the author frequently uses words derived from the root *ṭhr* (pure). From "pure cities" to "pure temple" to "everything pure" to "pure meat" and "pure body (flesh)" as well as "pure sacrifice," the author seems to be obsessed with that condition[31] (in the same way that the angelic *Šîrôt,* the sacred songs of the eunuchs, are obsessed with the purity of the motherless number seven). For the sectarians that meant that less intercourse was better; and, even more, no intercourse by "polluting" means was best. How could they have accomplished this? The most obvious answer was artificial insemination, and horse power—horse breeding—as their imagery tells us, provided the way. If we accept that conjecture, we then understand why, among other things, the apocalypse and the Messiah were closely linked with the imagery of horses. In the midrash (*Lamentations Rabbah*), the rabbis claim: "If you see a Persian horse tethered in Eretz Israel (land of Israel) look for the feet of the Messiah" (I.13:41).[32]

It is our main contention that the sectarian brotherhood's legacy, which stemmed from Qumran, is strong and abiding. The priest, to this very day, in his various manifestations, is almost synonymous with holiness. The Gnostic heirs expressed that sectarian legacy in concise terms:

> The priest is completely holy, down to his very body. For if he has taken the bread, will he consecrate it? Or the cup or anything else that he gets,

does he consecrate them? Then how will he not consecrate the body also? (*Gospel of Philip* 77:2–6; Robinson, 146)

Similarly, "For if a thought [of] lust enters into [a] virgin man, he has [. . .] being contaminated." Therefore, "a pure seed is kept in storehouses that are secure."[33] The "pure seed" echoes quite lucidly the image of a pure-bred horse which sometimes must be kept in an enclosed "storehouse" (perhaps the creche of a stable) in order to assure its desired performance.

WELL BRED: THE STATE OF ANCIENT MEDICAL KNOWLEDGE

The Egypt of the pharaohs, at its height, was well aware of the power of horse breeding and was particularly jealous of giving away prized stallions, which were highly regarded and protected. Because of their sophisticated scientific and medical knowledge, the Egyptians were resolute in maintaining a well-polished cavalry as well as fine stables which furnished horses to other countries as the diplomatic need arose. But the specific breeding technology used by the Egyptians for animals generally was, in fact, a secret. The Talmud mentions how devious such practices were: "Theodos the physician . . . who reported that in Alexandria every cow and sow to be exported from Egypt had its womb removed, in order to prevent breeding of these highly rated animals outside the mother country."[34] With regard to cattle breeding, the Egyptians "were no longer content to lead their animals to their pasture, and in other respects to leave them to themselves; on the contrary, they watched over every phase of their lives. Special bulls were kept for breeding purposes, and the herdsmen understood how to assist the cows when calving."[35] Other documents show that the castration of both males and females (animal and human) was also practiced in the ancient world.[36] Since animal technology was advanced and the cultural emphasis was on fertile women (i.e., the sign of beauty)—and on male control over both, it is highly likely that the Egyptians had an inkling of human artificial insemination.

It will be our task, at this point, to show the modern reader, who may be skeptical (and perhaps a bit presumptuous about our own technological superiority), the high level of Egyptian scientific knowledge and, of course, discoveries related to their use of horses for political and medical purposes.

Artificial insemination is fairly simple, particularly with a healthy, fertile woman. One non-medically assisted technique today involves using very rudimentary instruments: the sperm is kept warm in a jar (e.g., with a pillow over it) ideally for no more than two hours; it is then introduced into the woman with the help of an eye dropper, a syringe, or a turkey baster. Perhaps in ancient times the hot desert sun kept the sperm warm in an urn designed appropriately for the magic; for injection then a papyrus reed, for suctioning and blowing (as with a straw, or a clyster used for douching and medication, or a speculum scoop) would have sufficed. The woman's body must be inclined with her feet against a wall for about twenty minutes to ensure attachment.[37]

Because the main task of the ancient priests was animal sacrifice (and such animals had to be perfectly clean [Leviticus 11; Deuteronomy 14), they were first of all veterinarians. Their knowledge of animal anatomy from the slaughter house (and the kitchen) must have preceded that of human anatomy. In addition, the ancients derived their knowledge of human anatomy from observing external body parts and from the battlefield.[38] Let us not forget the anatomy lessons learned from the famed Egyptian embalmings. Even some hieroglyphs point to the Egyptians' recognition that there is an essential similarity between animal and human organs.[39] The Greek physician Galen (first century C.E.) was schooled in at Alexandria; he observed that "dissecting animals which are near to man . . . we may find out at once what is common to all and what is peculiar to ourselves, and so may become more resourceful in the diagnosis and treatment of disease."[40] The earliest talmudic rabbis although apparently uncomfortable with the idea of applying information about animals to humans were aware of it too.[41]

The Egyptians practiced medical specialties. Herodotus (a fifth-century B.C.E. historian) pointed to their achievements: "Some are physicians for the eyes, others for the head, teeth, abdomen, and for unknown diseases" (2.84). Some even maintain that the Egyptian pharaohs themselves performed autopsies.[42] The Egyptian doctors' skills included setting broken bones, dentistry, tumor removal, tracheotomy, sedatives, anesthesia, circumcision, possibly brain surgery, and more.[43] In the specialty of gynecology, the Egyptians referred to the uterus as *mwt rmt*, which is translated as "the mother of men," and in some documents the same terminology (*mwt rmt*) may refer to the placenta: "the Egyptians perhaps . . . thought that at each birth the uterus followed the child in the shape of the placenta, to re-form again for the next childbirth."[44] This calls to mind the early rabbinic legend about the barren matriarchs Sarah, Rebekah, and Rachel, who, the rabbis tell us, had no uterus and God had to mold one for them.[45] There is an early talmudic description of what to do about a woman's (unusual) bleeding: "How does she examine herself? She takes a tube (i.e., speculum) within which there is a painting stick (*makchol*) which has cotton on the tip . . . inserts this tube into the vagina" (*Niddah* 66a). The Tosefta (*Niddah* 8:2) suggests that the woman not examine herself; that is, someone else should perform that examination. The use of the "speculum" is intriguing here because some scholars believe that it was not known in antiquity.[46]

But the earliest rabbis of the diaspora (and their Christian counterparts (like Luke) often practiced medicine more in the sense that we know it (rather than the priestly, magical way). Apparently they kept no textbooks, perhaps relying on the Egyptian ones. Famous doctors still remembered are Samuel b. Abba Ha-kohen, or, Mar Samuel Yarhin'ah (165–257) who was of priestly descent (Ha-kohen). Theudas is mentioned as a famous doctor from Alexandria. "Aulus Cornelius Celsus . . . in the first century C.E., refers to salves compounded by skilled Jewish physicians. Galen reports on the Jewish physician Rufus Samaritanus in Rome in the first-second centuries C.E."[47] The Talmud mentions people whom we might characterize today as research scientists (*ʾaskan bidbārîm*), who dealt with the study of human and animal anatomy. Abba Saul, for example, describes the development of an embryo in its sixth week (*Niddah* 25b). Even surgery was performed by surgeons in "houses of marble" (*bātê šāyîš*) (*Hullin* 77b). Anesthetics were widely used (*sammê dešinta*) and there is a description of at least one caesarean operation.

The practical concerns about population size as well as the promotion of fertility in the ancient world made gynecology a very important field, and the surviving literature attests as much. It is well accepted that the Romans and many other ancient civilizations used birth control devices. As early as the sixth century B.C.E., "the Cyrenians were cultivating and exporting huge quantities of silphium, a kind of giant fennel plant. These plants were shipped all over the ancient world"; they were "crushed and turned into . . . 'Cyrenaic juice' which women took to prevent conception.[48] It turns out that some recent scientific studies indicate that "some of the plants used by the ancients to control fertility do have the capacity to affect female hormones."[49]

But the actual state of knowledge about reproduction, or "genesis," as Galen maintains was elementary: "The seed [is] cast into the womb or into the earth (for there is no difference)."[50] In other words, he sees no distinction between fertilizing the woman and doing the same to the "earth." "Casting" can be accomplished by sundry means; one does not necessarily have to have intercourse with a woman to do that. Galen also assigns the role of "nutrients" to tissues from the mother's menstrual blood; these are accessories for the fetus. The nutrients, says Galen, are ultimately altered by the organs and become bone and flesh (27). Galen even criticizes and debates other surgeons and physicians (as well as philosophers) particularly about so-called bladder anatomy, which he discusses at some length. His initial statement to support his claims is "practically every butcher is aware of this, from the fact that he daily observes" (51). But he goes on to argue by illustrating on animals that sperm cannot discharge when there is urine in the penis—all of which is in the context of a scathing argument about "spermatic ducts in the neck of the bladder" (51–57).

Both in myth and the medical records around the millennium the male was assigned the predominant role in procreation. When Galen asks "What is the semen?" the answer he gives is rather classic: "Clearly, the active principle of the animal, the material principle being the menstrual blood."[51] The early Christian scholar Tertullian wrote that when sperm is released from the man it is already a bona fide child.[52] Indeed, it was generally believed that the mother's menstrual blood was only for purposes of nourishing the father's offspring. In both Egyptian and Hebrew the verb "to know" (like the forbidden knowledge of Eden) is associated with copulation and pregnancy. Typically, as soon as the man "knows" the woman, she becomes pregnant. "In other legends, man's seed may develop even by abnormal access, as in the story of Seth and Osiris, and in the tale of 'The two brothers' in which a princess was with child after swallowing a splinter from the tree into which her husband had been changed."[53]

As for conception without intercourse, the early portions of the Talmud have at least three discussions about the unutterable, which, we think, show precisely what was on their minds.[54] In the first, the concern is the prohibition against a woman sleeping on the sheets of a man who is not her husband, because "she [may] become impregnated from his sperm and her child ends up unwittingly marrying his or her . . . paternal half-sibling."[55] The second reference, which is not framed as a legend, is most interesting; it is about a high priest marrying a virgin who became pregnant. "Do we [in such a case] take into account Samuel's statement, for Samuel said: 'I can have repeated sexual intercourses (*beᶜilot*) without [causing] bleeding;' . . . He replied: 'the case of Samuel is rare, but we do consider [the possibility] that she may have conceived in a bath into which a male has discharged semen'" (*Ḥag.* 14b–15a). It thus seems that, on the face of it, a woman who conceives in a bath is not regarded as having been rendered a nonvirgin; therefore, she may still marry a priest. Third, there is a legend related to the birth of Ben Sira, an important teacher whose story was circulated at Qumran. Ben Sira was supposedly conceived from the semen of his father Jeremiah (whom we identify as one of the first Nazirites), which was discharged in a bath; it impregnated Jeremiah's daughter, who bathed after him.[56] "Daughter" may be an allusion to the status of "sister" or to a "Daughter of Truth" in Qumran literature. All of these suggest a basic understanding of artificial insemination, of sperm living outside the body—of, in fact, "living water," even if their way of speaking about this issue seems bizarre today. The Dead Sea Scrolls mystery text titled by the translators "The Fountain of Living Water"[57] mentions "hybrid like a mule" (4Q416, 418 frag. 2, line 6), indicative of their priestly anxiety about almost anything "mixed."

The Hebrews considered the man's semen so valuable that it was a sin to "spill the seed to the ground,"[58] and it was certainly a grave problem to have a "seminal emission." The Dead Sea sectarians were particularly distressed about seminal emissions, and their "Torah" (the *Temple Scroll*) devotes a considerable amount of time to a discussion about these phenomena and how a man must cleanse thoroughly, if indeed he is thus "polluted," and do penance.[59] There is even good reason to assume that the desert brotherhood linked semen to sacrificial holiness and that some men could have holier (than other men's) semen, which could then be used for "holier" purposes. The same is reiterated in the Gnostic texts and in Boborite practices.[60]

Many historical references show that Egyptian medicine, while not always accurate, was the most developed among the ancients, scientifically and experimentally.[61] Further, medical books were widely available and circulating. There once was a whole medical library in the Egyptian port of Alexandria, to which doctors around the Mediterranean made their sabbatical.[62] In the Kahoun papyri we find descriptions of various gynecological diseases and treatments.[63] The Egyptians seemed to have come to the conclusion that the pelvic organs were not attached to anything else in the abdomen and that in order to treat them the physician had to put them in place again by performing a series of fumigations. "These fumigations were made of turpentine, dried excreta, or an ibis of wax . . . in the shape of the god Thoth. Pessaries and lavages made of vegetable extracts and beer were also used."[64] Obviously, some sort of douching device would have been necessary for fumigations, and there are two such objects in the Cairo museum. These objects were discovered at Dair el Medinehm: one is "a hollow horn, 30 cm. long, hermetically stoppered at the base by a wooden disc, and broadening at its point into a perforated spoon, 4 cm. in diameter. The other is smaller . . . it ends in a Hathor head capped by a spoon-shaped moon."[65] Some suggested that these instruments must have been used "as clysters to inject lavages and enemata." Others believe that they may have been utilized as perfume bottles (incidentally, perfume bottles were found at Qumran). Interestingly, "clysterophiles of the Middle Ages injected [enema] by means of a syringe."[66]

Physicians in the ancient world gave their patients very detailed instructions about medications and procedures. The Ebers papyrus describes how to give an inhalation which may have been an anesthesia or drugs that brought about altered states of consciousness:

> thou shalt fetch seven stones and heat them by fire; thou shalt take one thereof and place [some] of these remedies on it and cover it with a new vessel whose bottom is perforated and place a stalk of reed in this hole; thou shalt put thy mouth to this stalk, so that thou inhalest the smoke of it. Likewise with all stones. (Ebers 325; quoted in Ghalioungui, 145)

In another segment of Ebers (col. 70) inhalation was also used in conjunction with the plants Te'am and 'Amamu "to reduce them to fine powder, to put them on the fire, and to inhale the rising steam through a reed."[67] In yet another set of instructions, the physician suggests that one should "knock a piece out of the bottom of the pot and stick a reed into the hole. Put thy mouth to this reed so as to inhale the rising steam" (Ebers 54:8).

It is clear that from very early on people made use of specialized instruments in conjunction with "blowing" or "breathing"; these were utilized in specific circumstances to alleviate pain, to cleanse the body of polluting materials, or to reach a spiritual state appropriate to receiving a ritual of life.

EGYPTIAN ARTS AND THE "HOUSE OF LIFE"

Egyptian medical books show a range of interest from the mundane to the esoteric and a propensity toward professional secrets—from simple, almost Shamanic practices from recipes using dew (presumably the semen of the gods that make miraculous mushrooms appear overnight along with the morning star)[68] to sophisticated surgical technology; from treating simple maladies to performing complicated operations on all parts of the body. The scribes of these books were attached to temples involved in the mysteries of the House of Life.[69] Their pharmacologists, also known as magi (magicians) or wise men, were adept at concocting biochemical agents not just as medication but also as beauty enhancers for both men and women. The region is rich with estrogen vegetable sources, including, incidentally, decaying plant material in the mud at the bottom of the Dead Sea. They experimented with the urine of pregnant mares, excreta which we use even today in menopausal medications (like Premarin, short marketing name for "pregnant mares' urine"—yet another use for those unique horses!).[70] Contemporary specialists have noted that the female flower of the willow tree contains biologically active estrogen. So do a variety of other plants, twenty of which are fairly common foods, including: chick peas, soybeans, licorice, pomegranates, apples, and date palms; these can also initiate estrus in animals.[71] Estrogen hormonal treatments bring about sexual changes in women (early breast growth) and in men (boys) too.[72] There is no doubt that the Egyptians (and possibly the Dead Sea sectarians who made their headquarters in the Dead Sea region) made use of estrogen for fertility purposes because women were perceived to be "ready" for procreation as soon as they started their menstrual cycle. By age twelve to fourteen, a girl would have been considered ready to "ripen"; these very young women sometimes must have needed hormonal encouragement in order to be fully successful.[73]

There is some convincing evidence that Egyptians used hormonal drugs to improve skin condition as well as to retard the effects of old age.[74] Youth was essential not just because of its aesthetic appeal, as it is today, but because of its association with fertility and the ability to perpetuate the "race." In some rituals and some cults there was a demand for "perpetually" young men—for example, feminized eunuchs, who were valued for their soprano voices and as appropriate counselors, companions, and guards to queens/priestesses and their maids.[75]

Some of the medical information gathered by physicians was considered secret data and was highly guarded for the eyes of doctors only. The Ebers papyrus (88) refers to a secret book created by a physician. Clement of Alexandria (second century C.E.) refers to a secret collection devoted to medicine (forty-two volumes) that was kept in a temple. Secrecy of learning in the ancient world is usually associated with holy things and holy men who are believed to perform holy mysteries. The temples that acquired medical reputations were in Denderah, Deir-el-Behari, and Memphis. At Denderah, for example, water baths were used as a cure. These healing institutions (which may have associated with the first-century C.E. Therapeutae, with their curing waters; they, in turn, are associated with the Essenes) were fairly reputable, and a medical academy was still in existence in Alexandria in the third century C.E. (see Galen).

An Egyptian "magical" text dated to the time of the sectarians survives (Leyden papyrus); it is the script for a mystery initiation along with its medical components. The formula begins with a Qumranlike call to remove "darkness" and to "bring the light into me." The initiate in his girdled linen seems to be taking the part of Horus, "the good son of Isis," and is named a "pure boy" (or son?). Something is done to him with oil, with bricks, with magical utterances, including the number seven and the naming of birds. There is the laying on of hands around his ears, and it is specified that he is given a drug "prescription." Then the priest "binds" him. Isis is named as the "mistress of magic" and presumably to whom one appeals in casting the "spell" ("which you utter to it when you cook it"):

> O my beautiful child, the youth of oil-eating (?), thou who didst cast semen and who dost cast semen among all the gods . . . who cometh

forth as a black scarab on a stem of papyrus-reed; I know thy name, I
know thy . . . the work of two stars. . . . (Leyden papyrus XXI:27–29; Griffith and Thompson, 141)

A scarab is the sign of the self-begotten Khepera, who is an Egyptian
god associated with the rising sun, birth, and rebirth, with the flying
spirit and the earthly walk. We now understand the reference to a
papyrus reed and what is signified by "casting semen." The astrological sign referred to, namely, "the work of two stars," is the same as
that of the Teacher of Righteousness in the Dead Sea Scrolls—Gemini,
the twins. One can compare the Dead Sea Scrolls fragments of magical texts (4Q560, 467) including the "mystery of existence" (4Q416,
418). "The male poisoning-demon and the female poisoning-demon
(is forbidden) [to] enter the body. . . . (I adjure you) by the Name of He
who forgives sins and transgression, O fever and chills and heart-
burn" (4Q560 1:3–4). This quote, incidentally, follows a curious phrase
about "a new mother." In 4Q416 the statement about "meditating on
the Mystery of Existence" is coupled with the "knowledge of the
Secret of Truth" (frag. 8, lines 4–6; *Dead Sea Scrolls Uncovered,* 252).

In the Egyptian (Leyden) text the initiate is instructed essentially
to be like Horus (this is the Horus of the "verdure season, mounted
on a white horse") and to repeat: "Send me to the thirsty, that his
thirst may be quenched. . . ." We also read in the magic of this fertility
rite about a "love-man plant," which may be the mandragon of biblical lore related to special births[76] (often pictured in the shape of a
man) and that the initiate's mate-to-be is aroused, "she is mad for
him." The "foam of stallion's mouth" is used to "anoint a phallus"
before "amare coitum suum," and the way to test whether a woman is
enceinte is for her to "pass her water on this herb . . . in the evening;
when the morning comes and if you find the plant scorched (?), she
will not conceive; if you find it flourishing, she will conceive."
Although convoluted—for it is a magical secret—we identify estrogen
usage indicated here in the reference to her urine, and perhaps by the
"foam," the horse-breeding procedure.

Up to this point, we have referred to the early conflation of
horses, war, and sexuality, the result of a thriving industry of breeding horses. We have shown how a negative image about war horses
and sexuality in the Hebrew Bible became purified as the messianic
hosts of Qumran, eventually becoming, in their Egyptian form,
loaded with hints of artificial insemination. We have clarified the

logic of Qumran's obsession with lineage from their own words and have shown that they had the opportunity, the Egyptian connections and the motivation for learning how to have sex without sex in a House of Life, either in the Sinai or in Egypt itself via the ancient route of the "Horus Road" (Ways of Horus). We have detailed the medical knowledge of the milieu, particularly of sexual anatomy, the use of hormonal plants, herbs, and drugs, and located the type of instruments that would have succeeded in this fertility rite. What remains is a deeper understanding of the ancients' relationship with the sacred and how women's roles therein became at the turn of the millennium so limited and almost obsolete.

EONS

Reconstructing the past is always a precarious task, but more so when it comes to "secrets." While no two-thousand-year-old written record of artificial insemination has emerged (or any magical text decoded that might give precise directions), we believe that the horse—its many repeated references, its stupendous war status, and its actual fertility uses in antiquity—is the "smoking gun" of our case. The circumstantial evidence for artificial insemination, or a pure intercourse, is compelling. Qumran's mentality reveals the motive: the absolute necessity to defend a way of life under physical and ideological attack; a culture long embedded in the land of Judea about to be overwhelmed with its very roots dug up and exposed to the sun. The extreme ideological reaction is understandable: by sacrificing sexuality, which they decided was misguided fruitfulness, and by demonizing the struggle of man with original sin, the saints in their white linen shrouds hoped beyond all hopes to change God's mind, and they made a last-ditch effort in the wilderness to save the people.

Qumran had potential access to the means: ancient medical knowledge of anatomy was as intensely involved with the animal arts, and what humans might learn from them, as much as animal experimentation in laboratories today. Biotechnology and herbal chemistry were as well funded by military industrial complexes like Egypt as our own and for similar reasons: power and glory. As we have discussed, Qumran sectarians and their forebears appear to have had long-term connections with the Egyptian corridor, to say nothing of the influential Egyptian mystery cults in Judea itself, which were open to non-Egyptians.

Qumran had developed appropriate institutions to manage the artificial insemination process within ritualized, rationalized routines. A close-knit elite of Nazirite warrior zealots and physician/priests—maybe called Essenes[77]—guarding their professional knowledge (gnosis, or *da'at*) could mobilize popular support through the still-resonant motifs of the Goddess religion. Through a secondary institution, the veiling of women, they could hide away female powers of sensuousness and simultaneously prevent the birdlike spirit of the Goddess in her heavenly Wisdom from choosing female heads. In this way the brotherhood could simultaneously procreate their own kind and monopolize the status of life-givers. Once the possibility and probability of artificial insemination are recognized, the mystery of immaculate conception becomes quite mundane. The puzzle of Qumran's claims to celibacy, yet its official Marriage Ritual and its maintenance of a storehouse of women (and children), as grave-sites attest, are easily resolved.

Qumran's metaphors and its later renditions are the written evidence. They speak in tongues but flash the truth to all who are knowers. Joseph and Aseneth, Samson, Enoch, Daughters of Truth and all the other texts we have explored speak in tongues to a truly virginal presence at Qumran. The paradigm of worldly excessiveness—multiplying horses for war as whoredom—easily shifts at the end of history to salvation (*yĕšûa'*) and redemption from original sin, by the excessive sacrifice of flesh and even of life itself in the holiest of wars, to say nothing of the sacrifice of women's humanity.

There is one more reason why this then-exotic procedure was essential and pressing for Qumran. As the millennium approached—it was almost one thousand years from the glorious, well-intended, and free kingdom of David—a just man, a righteous Teacher, a second Adam formed from the nutrients of mother earth matter and the soul-breath of God was required by circumstances, and urgently due. The sectarians took the initiative into their own hands, hoping they would hear the thundering sound of powerful horses in the not too distant future.

CHAPTER SEVEN

The Sign

Pray let me swallow of the red stuff—that red stuff there—for I am famished. (Genesis 25:30)

BRIEF: EVERYTHING IS CONNECTED!

Western civilization is obsessed with dichotomizing and prioritizing everything: from mind/body, good/evil, unworldly/worldly, light/ darkness to male/female. The sectarians at Qumran succeeded, at least, in convincing "the many" that they knew the "truth" about the spirit, which was holy and stood opposite to the body, which, in turn, had to be disciplined.

The new movement, which by the millennium was headquartered at Qumran, thought of everything—everything of significance in the realm of their cultural time. Using a variety of literary forms conducive to their stock of "insider" metaphors, they created a complete and orderly statement about the world as they viewed it. The sectarian-priests who controlled knowledge, a new and vital part of which was borrowed from the "wisdom" of Egypt, had a scheme for the four elements of the universe (earth, water, air, and fire); the significance of colors and the absence thereof (darkness and pure light); magical numbers, an arithmetic mirrored in the stars; the esoteric function of timing for festival dates, sacramental acts, and daily prayers; and the artifice of purifying lineage. But that is not all.

Alongside the wealth of symbols of imperfection—such as the harlot representing corruption, infidelity to the covenant, and original sin—the holy angelic, number seven is as close to perfection as possible and specifically stands for the immaculate Sabbath. The role and the symbol of the Sabbath for the sectarians can be compared with the ideas of Philo, who essentially explained what the idea of "newly born" or "self-begotten ones"[1] strives for, namely, to be rid of unclean femaleness altogether: "It is in the nature of seven alone . . . neither to beget nor to be begotten . . . other philosophers liken this number to the motherless virgin. . . ."

Further:

> For he [Moses] found that she [the Sabbath] was in the first place motherless, exempt from female parentage, begotten by the Father (God) alone, without begetting, brought to birth, yet not carried in the womb . . . she was also ever virgin, neither born of a mother nor a mother herself, neither bred from corruption nor doomed to suffer corruption. (*Vita Mosis* 2.210; LCL 6:553).

The other major images, such as golden honey and bees, the snake, living water, the multiplication of horses, and white linen, stem from the initial ones above. They stand for the sectarians' strong commitment to a "new birth," "new conception," and pure truth—all within the realm of their technical, indeed scientific, capacities.[2] An array of color symbolism rounds up the Qumranites' perception of themselves as priestly Nazirites who carry the apocalyptic torch and wear the shining crown of spiritual authority.

These intricate metaphors assist us in identifying the Qumran community and their descendants as coherently focusing on a lifestyle that was different from that of Jerusalem. In traumatic times prophets of fundamentalist ilk and other zealous gamblers arise to make long-shot promises for unobtainable rewards. Convinced that the apocalypse was at hand, the saints in the desert planned to join forces with the angelic Sons of Light in a forty-year war effort that would ultimately produce a better, paradisal environment.[3]

But earthly events, being less than perfect, did not work out quite that way. In the Dead Sea Scrolls' version of the Davidic Psalms (which includes some new ones not found in the Bible),[4] we find a unique "memorial" Psalm (11QPs xvii) that is rather cryptic and subdued. There is no indication as to what (who) the "memorial" is for, though possibly, it may be related to the death of the Psalmist (David, or whoever was identified as the king/priest at Qumran—maybe the Teacher of Righteousness) whose words came to a close: "The prayers of David, the son of Jesse, are ended." But for his followers his ". . . testimonies are streams of honey" (12:129). They continue to live, which is why a ritual of communion was instituted in "Zikkaron," that is, in "remembrance of me."[5] A few of his last words, copied from the psalm in 2 Samuel 23, present David as a prophet and a wise man. The relationship between this psalm and the life and times of the Teacher is indeed instructive; the psalm describes the king as having "oracular" power, as being "sweet" and "just" and "like the sun." Furthermore, the interrelationship between the king and his subjects seems to reflect that of the Teacher and the sectarians:

> When one rules justly over men, ruling in the fear of God, he dawns on them like the morning light, like the sun shining forth upon a cloudless morning, like rain that makes grass to sprout from the earth. (2 Sam. 23:3–5)

The rain, dew, and sprouting images were used in the *Thanksgiving Scroll* in a very similar vein. Further, in a psalm of consolations (4Q176, *tanhumim*)[6] denoting intense pathos, a survivor of the Roman holocaust cries out: "he shall see the bodies of thy priests. . . . And none [left] to bury them." This means that God will judge the wicked for the sacrilege (none left to bury them), the ultimate indignity for religious Jews. The speaker fully humbled by God's not being on their side, adds (from Isa. 40:1–3) that Jerusalem's "[bondage is completed], that her punishment is accepted, that she has received from the hand of Yahweh double for all her sins."

But we have one more surprising insight from these histories of the messianic sectarian movement at the millennium. The innovations of the Dead Sea Scrolls also included a number of visible signs to mark membership in the community. We have already mentioned a few that have been decoded and are fairly well accepted, in particular, the sign of the morning star, the so-called "star prophecy" associated with the special birth of the Teacher of Righteousness along with the special vow or Nazirite oath of the sectarians. We have also focused on another, the sign of radical cleanliness, the removal of the red snaked "tongue" by a fiery rod, an act of unique holiness that makes a man into a godlike being and that goes far beyond circumcision, the older sign of Jewish separateness; it was viewed by the sectarians as the supreme sacrifice of a leader (like "Michael").

As alluded to in another new Davidic psalm about the confrontation with Goliath we can almost see the angelic ceremony of new fire: "I went out to meet the Philistine and he cursed me by his idols. But drawing his sword from him I beheaded him and removed his shame from the sons of Israel."[7] The "shame" of this utterance is focused on what is foreign and evil, and the "beheading" (a Samson allusion) is appropriate to a Nazirite who seeks total purity. We glimpse it again in a psalm that creatively combines two of David's traditional compositions dealing with his enemies, external and internal. 11QPs 27 opens with a statement associated with David's psalm, about those who support him and those who do not: "The shaft of a spear and the wood of an outside room, and they are utterly consumed with fire in the sitting" (2 Sam. 23:7). This line echoes the original expression about those who oppose the king "who will not sprout. . . . They are like uprooted thorns. . . . For they cannot be held in the hand, and a man cannot touch them, except with an iron or wooden tool; in the fire they will be burned up on the spot."[8] The final part of the Qumran rendition of the psalm is a cry to God to be saved:

> Deliver me . . . from evil men; preserve me from violent men, who plan evil things in their heart. . . . They make their tongue sharp as a serpent's, and their lips are the poison of a spider. (27:12-14)

In our closing commentary, which summarizes some of our insights, we follow the thread of the color red to show how it can be understood as the unifying sign of the Sons of Zadok, the Righteous Ones, at Qumran.

The first male sinner, Adam, is a man of red earth or red clay (like Hathor the dark, earthy red woman of earlier lore). "Yahweh shaped an earthling from clay of this earth, blew into his nostrils the wind of life and the earthling became a living being" (Gen. 2:7).[9] *'Ădāmâ* ("earth") means red clay; it is red because the clay has been infused with blood, the blood of the womb that nurtures the father's son in his fleshly life versus the spirit's (or the wind's = *rûaḥ*) godly life. Before this, blood was the stuff of the Goddess, as is remembered in red slip glaze, the ubiquitous form of pottery of the region for eons, and signified in the magenta pomegranate seeds within her womblike, favorite fruit. Only when a young female begins to bleed is she ready to be fruitful and multiply. At that point in her life she is also subject to various purity laws that were observed even more strictly by the sectarians. For example, we find that there were actual "record keepers" (*sōpēr*, "scribe" and/or "someone who counts"), uniquely here, of both genders who made sure that these strict standards were observed:

> At all costs she is [no]t to mingle during her seven days, so that she does not defile the camp of the Ho[ly O]nes of Israel. . . . And the person that is keeping a record of the period of impurity, whether a man or a

woman, is not to t[ouch the menstruant] . . . during the period of uncleanness, but only when she is cleansed [from her uncleann]ess. (4Q274 frag. 1, lines 6–8)[10]

While men are normally initiated into their social frameworks with festivities when they reach puberty (the male's *bar mitzvah*) the age of knowledge, a woman's initiation, at least within the sectarians' environment (not too different from Jewish law on the same subject), is the exact opposite. She is required to retreat or hide or be absent from social gatherings and public events, because presumably she is "unclean." By comparison, we can only wonder what sort of ceremony may have marked that wonderful event in a woman's life in the Goddess's ancient world.[11]

Blood also accompanies the birth of a child, in fact, profusely (another event that makes a woman's very presence in Qumran's holy places taboo).[12] The bloody afterbirth was sometimes buried in the earth, sometimes hung on a sacred tree (in the same way that women hung their tresses when they dedicated themselves to becoming vestal virgins).[13] Qumran remembers the significance of blood absorbed by the earth for fertility, life, and regeneration in the color red and retrieves for itself the wisdom of the Goddess to rest on the heads of the members. The sectarians' curious last rites seem to have included either the drinking of, or an infusion after death, of some red chemical, which subsequently turned the bones red (the bones that would some day "stand up" again).[14] The sectarians threw into the grave with its carefully preserved air space above the corpse some broken red bricks,[15] *Adam's red clay*, not just "from dust to dust" but, more precisely, from clay to clay. We add to this the older and much more established practice from the ancient world of the Goddess where brick platforms accompanied the birthing stool in a physical representation of the idea that death leads to rebirth (as does the white linen garment worn both for marriage and the grave).[16] No wonder a reddish-brown powder was found in the cave sites of the Dead Sea Scrolls. We suspect that the red stuff used at Qumran was predominantly henna (also possibly, as John Allegro insisted, the dye of the red-cloaked mushroom Amanita Muscaria[17] and perhaps for priests on the right occasions the precious royal red purple dyes of Tyre along with otherwise forbidden red sacramental wine). Henna is the name given to the dried and powdered leaves of *lawsonia enermis,* a plant that grows in Egypt, India, and parts of the Middle East. For thousands of years it has been used as a colorant to stain human hair, nails, or skin a blood-red color. The ancients combined henna with other natural colorants such as indigo, iron oxide, or lead salts in order to produce brown and black colors. The Hebrew Bible describes its respectable lineage, for Solomon used henna and indigo to stain his beard.[18]

Whatever its botanical source, the red substance was the sign for both earth and fire. The Teacher of Righteousness was marked by this sign of red at his birth. According to his astrological record, he had "red hair" (unlikely to be his natural Semitic color) and the "lentils" and "birthmark" on his hands and thighs were probably red too.[19] The Teacher of Righteousness—we think a high priest[20]—was anointed, or "smeared," with some holy oil (Messiah, of course, means "the smeared one"). This oil would have been "new," like everything else promoted by this innovative community, and it may have included in its preparation some red dye. The "oil of mercy" in *Joseph and Aseneth* (9:3; 13:1–2) is described in *2 Enoch:* "He anointed me with the delightful oil" and its appearance is "greater than the greatest light . . . like sweet dew . . . fragrant like myrrh; and its shining is like the sun" (A = 22:8–9).

As the Dead Sea Scrolls tell us, even purification by water (baptism) was not enough for severe sins. Instead, there was to be a sprinkling of the ashes of the red heifer, a sacrificed cow, added to the holy water, a priestly promotion in Numbers 19 (going back to a much more ancient Kohen/soothsayer rite and once related to a regional cow goddess, like Hathor).[21] We must remember that even though the "heifer" is a cow (*pārâ*), the ceremony always involved a "whole"—that is, "pure" and "untouched" both in terms of work and sex—perfect, virginal cow.

The echoes of the concept and ceremony involving the red heifer reverberate in the *Apocryphon of Ezekiel.*[22] The human-animal connection, which supports what we claim about artificial insemination, is made precisely here: "We read also in the writings of Ezekiel concerning that cow which has given birth and has not given birth." And in yet another version (which seems to be more reliable): "And the heifer gave birth and they said, she has not given birth."[23] In the *Ascension of Isaiah* there is a clear allusion to these bizarre statements about the heifer in the context of the pregnancy of Mary: "Some said, 'the virgin Mary has given birth . . .' and many said 'she has not given birth" (11:14).[24]

The red hair and beards of the serious-minded sectarians seem a bit idiosyncratic, even quixotic and amusing to us;[25] but to a dark-haired community without access to the closely held secrets of the chemists, hair that glowed in the sunlight in an unearthly way would be a reason for awe.[26] These halos, so well remembered in medieval pictorial art, would be marks of distinction,[27] as would the hallowed red hands and feet (reiterated in the flames shooting around the thundering feet of the horses that indicate the coming of the Messiah) that mark sacramental occasions such as "marriages," including the dedication of female virgins or male virgins, or those who would be eunuchs, "brides of God," with their "unutterable anointings." The *merkābâ* is their chariot of fire. These anointings explain why an angel is described as "a man who shone like copper" (Ezek. 40:3; *1 Enoch* 2:35) and why Samuel is seen as "the light of his people." In the *Odes of Solomon,* which in many instances sound like the Qumran *Thanksgiving Hymns* we read that the Lord "is my Sun / And His rays have lifted me up / And His light has dismissed all darkness from my face" (15:2). Further, when Aseneth sees Joseph for the first time, she is astonished, for his grandeur is like a "light upon the earth . . . the sun from heaven has come to us."

Another "mark of distinction" though not merely Nazirite, stems from that tradition; it "recognizes" the "holy man" from his very conception, who, as a result, has a mark on his face:

> And before they had existed, I recognized them; and imprinted a seal on their faces.
> . . . .
> And they are my own. And upon my right hand I have set my elect ones.[28]

The seal imprinted on the face of the newborn may be associated with the morning star (like a cross?) and describes an initiation that includes not just babies.[29]

The sun glow is the all-important thing, associated with the Nazirites' crown and flames around their head. The sectarians and the populace understood the continuing presence of the Goddess; like the Egyptian Eve, Hathor "the dark red woman," who is also interchangeable with Isis (and whose headdress/hairdo is copied in many final resting places in first-century Jewish tombs) and from the time when Hebrews became self-identified and intermingled with Egyptians at the boundaries (if not as Exodus's captives), they remembered not only reverence for the One God and the sign of circumcision, but Pharaoh Akhenaton (1353–1336 B.C.E.), who claimed to be the Son of the Sun and who excluded all other gods and beliefs. Thus, the holy men made ready to receive the Spirit of Wisdom, a gift from God's female essence from above, onto their gloriously gleaming heads.[30]

Sun worship, sun time, holy days, and daily prayers timed for the sun's course in the sky are evident at Qumran. When does Qumran celebrate the Sabbath? Not in the traditional Jewish way at the end of the week (Friday) after sundown. They begin just before the sun dips below the horizon and glows deeply red: "No man shall work on the sixth day from the moment when the sun's orb is distant by its own fullness from the gate (wherein it sinks)" (CD 10:14b–15a).[31] In line with Qumran's emphasis on the sun and its glow, the Sabbath is ushered in, appropriately, by the most magnificent sun gleam when one can actually focus on a "wheel" (*galgal*) of red fire.

We see other locations of red. It is even the color of their treasure map, the reddish copper scroll (distinctive from all the rest, which are made from animal hides); it is in the physician's healing sign of Moses' rod that struck new fire and the bronze snake of his Midian wife (identified as Miramme and his sister in Gnostic texts).

The blood-red cross, drawn on the white-garbed virgin with the rosy-apple cheeks so indicative of the fertile moment in *Joseph and Aseneth,* is her protection from Lilith's dark underworld with its sexy demons (ex-goddesses) and, in truth, readies the virgin for the role of bridal princess: an immaculate conception and the birth of a new Adam. Fertility of a special nature, manipulated to exclude human "evil" inclinations along with intergender love—and a babe fashioned by new knowledge to defeat the snake in the garden—had its day.

Eventually, the virgin birth as a holy icon may go the way of St. Nicholas. But the celebrative capacity of the winter solstice—the necessity for optimism in the depth of hemispheric winters for a new, more innocent beginning—is fittingly envisioned by the newborn infant of the human couple. The gift of the babe is the next generation, who, if well nurtured in the spirit of the Goddess, will improve our chances. The Day of the Infant, timed to the virginal ecological moment, will surely punctuate our calendars and remain resonant for centuries to come.

Qumran's Ritual
of Immaculate Conception

The man (Adam) and his wife (Eve) were commanded to make seed, a blessed seed. And God will bless the fruit of the womb with long life.

All of Israel in the congregation (*sôd*) of the holy thanks together. And virgin boys and girls and the holy of holies with all of us together will bless the God of Israel saying: "Blessed is the God of Israel who fixed a time of happiness to glorify His name."

The elder (*ʾašîšîm*) and *ʾašîšôt* and young boys (*nĕʿārîm*) and girls; and the daughters of truth; cattle and sheep; our flocks and even the fowl flying in our heavens and our earth and all its bounty and all the fruit trees and the waters of the deep. All of us blessing the name of the God of Israel who gave us a fixed time (*môʿēd*) for our rejoicing.

The Marriage Ritual is preceded by a water purification and the cutting off of the girls' hair, while the boys vow never to cut their hair. There is also a last joint feast outside, cursing the forces of the moon (the dark Lilith powers that connect with Belial and menstruation). Both girls and boys, now with new names, are sealed with vows of chastity—virginity, their purity, in exchange for salvation.

The appearance of the morning star, Venus, which marks the transition from the evening to the day (or moon power of the Goddess submitting to the sun power of the most high God; it is also a symbol of renewal and regeneration) is the signal for the first part of the ceremony. The "angel," Gabriel, makes the announcement at daybreak. He has carefully studied the astrological timing as well as the records of the most suitable virgins. The chosen virgin must now proceed with the prescribed "conversion" steps. She ultimately takes the vow of obedience and gives up control over her body to the will of the *sôd*.

Both virgin and holy men emerge from their separate quarters splendidly dressed. The virgin and her protective "sisters" (maid-servants) have been preparing for this ritual for the appropriate period of time. The woman/virgin's cycle is fully taken into account. She must be at her peak, and she must be completely "receptive."

The wiser (older) Daughters of Truth surround the virgin on this, her day of glory. They have all been praying together for the last few days, and on the very last day of preparation, she has been fasting, focusing all of her energies on "the moment of truth." Now, at last, she is allowed to wear the white wedding robes; she is also fully veiled, head to toe. The ritual meal she shares with the others is made up of bread, wine, and honey. The virgin who is at the center of the ritual keeps her eyes downcast throughout so as not to contaminate the holy men. She knows, though, that God will miraculously bless her womb. She now begins to understand more fully what it means to be "Miriam," though she knows nothing of the secret ritual itself. Every-thing must be fully completed before sundown because her time is ripe. Groggy from the wine and special herbs that have been given to her, the virgin is readied for the singular moment of the Immaculate Conception. She is led by a host of "angels" to the holy candle-lit grotto, "the marriage chamber" on the cliff, where she is stripped of her ornate clothing. The subtle veiling of the girdle around her waist and the brassiere over her breasts remain. She is placed prone, body tilted with legs upward and bent in a receptive position.

The holy "Son of Truth," the righteous man, "Joseph," is totally prepared. He too, on a parallel path, is escorted by his entourage to the top of the cliff where he confronts another "angel" (Rephael), who will bless him and be ready to collect his holy seed; not a drop will be lost, nothing will be cast to the ground. After all, the "angel" has been training for just this moment, and he is committed to execute it with deep concentration and the right amount of humiliation. His "angelic" role is about to be crucially expressed. He is learned in the movement of the constellations and he knows the secrets of "new creation." He is also well versed in the magical arts of medicine. "Joseph" and the "angel" slowly approach each other. In the twilight, after the blessings have been uttered and the semen carefully placed in the warmed up elongated container, they seem to blend into one. The "angel" is now on his way, clutching the precious "holy water," ready for the second and most holy encounter with the virgin.

"Raphael" enters the "chamber" reserved for this holy occasion, and he now faces the pure, innocent, as-close-to-perfection-as-possible, chosen woman. She is young (about twelve or thirteen) and radiant though not fully conscious. The "angel"/eunuch is the only man who actually touches the virgin because he cannot be "contaminated" by her womanly essence.

He first places an amulet on her stomach to ward off the "male and female-poisoning demons"/serpents and unclean spirits that might attempt to enter her body during the upcoming penetration. He then proceeds to write a propitious spell, which is enclosed in the container. He anoints the virgin with his special red oil and waves incense to further these protective effects.

He gently sucks in the holy breath and then inserts the warm elongated device within her, three times, with great care so as not to cause bleeding. All of the semen fills the virginal uterus, while in the camp below, when the sun is about to set, the Sons and Daughters of Truth chant their prayer and hope: "she shall bring forth a man-child . . . a marvelous Mighty Counselor. . . . When he is conceived all wombs shall quicken. . . . For Thou wilt bring Thy glorious [salvation] to all the men of Thy Council. . . . They shall reply according to Thy glorious word. . . . They shall send out a bud [forever] like a flower . . . and shall cause a shoot to grow into the boughs of an everlasting Plant" (1QH).

MARRIAGE RITUAL

The Marriage Ritual (4Q502) consists of 344 fragments, mostly very damaged. The following is an attempt to provide the reader with a flavor of this esoteric text:

Group I

Fragments 1, 2, 3 are badly damaged and contain only a few legible phrases and words; the translation that follows reflects the typical sectarian phraseology:

Man (Adam) knows [   ]
the law of God (El) [   ]
the man (Adam) and his wife [were commanded]

to make seed [   ] those
That which [   ] holies thank God [   ]
to him from being holy [   ] he has a daughter of truth which walks [   ]
and his wife/companion (*raʿayatô*) who has knowledge (*śekel*) and under-
    standing (*bînâ*) in the midst of [   ]
[c]alled father [   ] together being for [   ]
a season that [   ]   God forgives [   ]
to the sons of righteousness [   ] on this day [   ] to [A]aron.

*Fragments 4 and 5 contain even fewer legible words, though it does refer to "his
father"; "a happiness together" or, a Yahad happiness (festival); a "command-
ment to us."*

Fragments 6–10 can be summarized as follows:

Israel?
thanks [   ]
together (*yahad*) [   ] place
[   ] He will bless the God of Israel saying:
Blessed is the God of Israel who [   ] [e]nd (fixed time?) of happiness to
    glorify his name
[   ] their elder (*ʾašîšîm*) and young boys (*nĕʿārîm*)
[   ] [c]attle and sheep [   ] our flocks
[   ] and the fowl flying in our heavens and our earth (soil = *ʾădāmâ*) and
    all its bounty [   ] and all the fruit trees [   ] and the waters of the
    deep.
All of us blessing the name of the God of Israel who gave us a fixed time
    (*môʿēd*) for our rejoicing and also [   ]
the blessings [   ] in the midst of the elders (*ʾašîšîm*) of righteousness [   ]
in peace [   ] and he thanks God and praises [   ]
I have elder (*ʾašîšîm*) brothers [   ]
blessed amongst us
holy [   ] elders holy of holies [   ]
today I [   ] bless the God of Israel [   ]
the elders (*ʾašîšîm*) of knowledge [   ]
we are rejoicing [   ]

*Fragments 11, 12, 13 have a few choice words, such as "Israel," "elders of righ-
teousness" (*ʾašîšê ṣedeq*), and "say thanks."*

Fragment 14 is also heavily damaged and contains the following phrases:

The God of Israel who commanded my son
[   ] your honor [   ] and loving kindness [   ]
sons and daughters
and Israel [   ] his father

Group II

] a deed [   ]
] pieties on (about) [   ]
humility in cunning (nakedness) [   ]
world (*tēbēl*) and the right time (for) all

Fragment 18 contains one legible word: "His (his) grace" (*kĕbôdô*)

Fragment 19

And he sat with him in the company (*sôd*) of the holy
a blessed seed old men and women (*zĕkēnîm ûzĕkēnôt*) [   ]
youths
and virgin boys and girls
with all of us together and I, my tongue, will sing
and then the people of [   ] will speak (say)
[and he answered] and said blessed is the God of Israel who [their
      inequities

Fragment 20

The legible words and phrases include: "long life," "fruit of the womb."

Fragment 21 contains the traditional sectarian words "God" *and* "*yaḥad*" = the
community, *and* "in the midst of Israel in his inheritance

Group III

Fragment 22 repeats the idea of a communal festival and joy.

Fragment 23 mentions once again the ʾašîšîm *who sat in the* sôd (congregation
      and secret).

Fragment 24

all the festivals [   ]
blessed is the God of Israel who assisted [   ]
long life for you in the midst of an eternal people
and you will stand in the community of old men and women (*zĕkēnîm
      ûzĕkēnôt*) [   ]
you days in peace and [   ]
in the midst of old people.

Other fragments that are somewhat legible include the following:

Fragment 27

evening and morning
with all the flags of the months (moons)

with the stars of the heavens
your inheritance (your planting)

Fragment 28

"daughter"; "tiny ones" = babies; and possibly "Adam and Eve"
"in seed"

Fragments 30, 31, 32 mention "Leah."

Fragments 33, 34, 35 refer again to "a communal happy occasion" *with* "older men" (ʾašîšîm) and women blessing."

Fragments 36–93 combine isolated words and phrases–all mentioned before and mostly illegible.

Fragments 94–99

He will bless them for sisters [   ]
palm branches before all [   ] seven days [   ] blessed is God
[   ] and they pronounce his greatness [   ] peace [   ]
and happiness [   ] holy of holies [   ]
get up [   ] happiness [   ]
and he answered
[   ]

Fragments 100–103

Emphasis is on the "right time" (môʿēd) *and* "holy of holies."

Fragments 104–107

Old people will bless the God of Israel [   ]
and the joy of the congregation
[   ]

Fragments 108–111

"the father of the girl" *is introduced in this part.*

From this point, the manuscript is even more damaged and less coherent; we point to the more intelligible parts:

Fragment 163 mentions the good and the honest (straight = yāšār) *and* "the fruit of the womb."

Fragment 308: "their sons."

Fragment 309: "his wife."

Notes

INTRODUCTION

1. The association between the Dead Sea sectarians and the Essenes is now being tested seriously. The meaning of the word "essene" is still being debated as well. For a detailed discussion of ancient sources of the Essenes, see Emil Schürer, *The History of the Jewish People in the Age of Jesus Christ* (Edinburgh: Clark, 1979) 2:555–90. See also David Flusser, *The Spiritual History of the Dead Sea Sect* (Tel Aviv: MOD, 1989) 9–14. It is also interesting to note that, according to Josephus, the Essenes link the soul with immortality and suggest that they "come out of the most subtile air" (*Jewish War* 2.8.2); this concept places them within a long, gnostic tradition adherents of which still exist in Iraq. For a more detailed, fascinating study of this group of people and their beliefs and history, see Ethel S. Drower, *The Secret Adam: A Study of Nasoraean Gnosis* (Oxford: Clarendon, 1960). The Essenes have also been associated with medicine (from the Aramaic *asa* = doctor), and one of the more obscure Qumran fragments designated 4QTherapeia (in Allegro, *Dead Sea Scrolls and the Christian Myth*, 235–49) is purported to be a medical document.

2. There are various studies that indeed attempt to show influences, relationships, and similarities between the Scrolls and the New Testament; the most recent is a collection of essays edited by James H. Charlesworth, *Jesus and the Dead Sea Scrolls* (New York: Doubleday, 1992). By the same token, there are many scholars who attempted to link the sect with later Jewish developments; chief among these scholars is Lawrence H. Schiffman, *Law, Custom and Messianism in the Dead Sea Sect* (Israel: Zalman Shazar, 1993) 13–44, 312–17.

3. See *Qumran Cave 4*, ed. John M. Allegro (DJD 5; Oxford: Clarendon, 1968).

4. We will be using Avraham M. Habermann, *Megilloth Midbar Yehuda: The Scrolls from the Judean Desert* (Tel Aviv: Machbaroth Lesifruth, 1959). In addition, we use Geza Vermes's translation of the Scrolls wherever possible because he has synthesized various other translations with his own: *The Dead Sea Scrolls in English* (New York: Penguin, 1987).

5. Specifically in the Pseudo-Daniel fragments, e.g., 4QpsDan A[a] (4Q246): "He shall be called son of God, and they shall designate him son of the Most High"

(2:1–2) (Milik, *Revue Biblique* 1956, pp. 411–15). In a more recent publication: "And the Lord said to me, 'Son of [man . . .]" 4Q385, frag. 3, 1:4 (*Dead Sea Scrolls Uncovered*, 58. There are also various references to "son of your handmaid" in 1QH 16:18; 1QS 11:16.

    6. We will be using the following texts: (a) The Apocrypha, presumably "hidden" writings meant only for initiates. The apocryphal books can be found in Roman Catholic Bibles but not in the Jewish biblical canon even though all of them have Jewish origins. Ironically, all of these books were preserved mostly in Greek and by Christians; their basic text can be found in the Greek translation of the Bible (the Septuagint). The discoveries of the Dead Sea Scrolls brought to light some of the original Hebrew and Aramaic apocryphal texts. (b) The Pseudepigrapha (literally, "a writing with false superscription or title"), which are extra-canonical writings linked with biblical books, characters, and themes. A pseudepigraphical story may have ramifications that shed light on the history, customs, habits, and social conventions of the time. These writings also serve as vehicles to transmit to new generations of Jews (and, later on, Christians) ancient ideals and hopes. "The essence of pseudepigrapha is . . . the keen awareness of . . . ongoing revelation and . . . continuous reinterpretation of the truth and wisdom transmitted in God's history with his people" (M. de Jonge, *Outside the Old Testament* [Cambridge: Cambridge University Press, 1985] 2). In *The Truth about the Virgin* we analyze major portions of *Joseph and Aseneth,* a pseudepigraphical text that we believe is closely linked to the sectarian Dead Sea movement. Numerous fragments of pseudepigrapha have been found at Qumran, for example, the book of *Jubilees,* portions of the *Testaments of the Twelve Patriarchs,* etc. (c) Gnostic literature, which purports to represent a special kind of secret "knowledge." One of the Gnostic teachers, Theodotus (wrote in Asia Minor, 140–160) explained that the Gnostics are those who fully understand "who we were and what we have become; where we were . . . whither we are hastening; from what we are being released; what birth is, and what is rebirth" (cited in Clement of Alexandria, *Excerpta ex Theodoto* 78.2). Gnosticism strives to deliver people from the constraints of earthly existence and to offer them instead a relationship "with a supramundane realm of freedom and of rest" (Kurt Rudolph, *Gnosis,* trans. and ed. Robert M. Wilson [San Francisco: Harper, 1987] 2). Gnosticism spread far and wide, and even today there is a remnant of Mandeans in Iraq and Iran. There is no question that the origins of Gnosticism are Jewish, though it is the Christian forms of the Gnostic religion which are the most well known and whose materials are the most abundant" (Michael E. Stone, *Jewish Writings of the Second Temple Period* [Philadelphia: Fortress, 1984] 444). The most extensive Gnostic "library" is associated with the famous archaeological findings in 1945 near the town of Nag Hammadi at the Jabal al-Tarif (a mountain) in Upper Egypt. We contend that the Gnostics are closely tied to their sectarian brethren in Judea. We quote from some of the Gnostic materials that are readily available in the edition by James M. Robinson, *The Nag Hammadi Library* (San Francisco: Harper & Row, 1977).

    7. We use the word "Qumran" throughout this book to indicate geography as well as sectarianism; this is not to say that every single sectarian word was uttered at Qumran. Certainly, the evidence is now mounting that these sectarians were popular and settled in places other than Qumran. But the core, holy (if not "holiest") group of sectarians did indeed inhabit that part of the country. Even though we do not claim that the sectarians were at Qumran all the time, or even most of

the time, since the majority of texts are associated with that vicinity, we designate them as Qumranites, or the people at Qumran, and so on. There are still some difficult issues that need to be resolved about the origins, continuity, and general availability of the Dead Sea Scrolls. Some of the sectarians probably had their beginnings in the Maccabean rebellion. For a more detailed discussion of various arguments about the above, see the works by Eisenman, Vermes, and others. Another point of view is that of Michael Wise, who maintains that the zealous priesthood took over the Jerusalem Temple with its foreign polluting practices for a few years, but were then forced out (*Thunder in Gemini: And Other Essays on the History, Language, and Literature of the Second Temple Palestine* [Sheffield: JSOT Press, 1994]). It is entirely possible that before and after that "cleansing of the Temple" they could have been at Qumran. In that sense, Qumran was the cult's exilic center (self-imposed or otherwise), where their mysterious rituals took place and where we can find the baths and the tower, and so on.

8. There are many questions about the Bible's unity; see David Noel Freedman, *The Unity of the Hebrew Bible* (Ann Arbor: University of Michigan Press, 1991).

9. There is a growing scholarly chorus that points to the sect's involvement with women. A cautious article by Elisha Qimron points to the presence of at least one group of sectarians who were situated outside of Jerusalem/Qumran and the core of holiness, who were married and had children ("Celibacy in the Dead Sea Scrolls and the Two Kinds of Sectarians," in *The Madrid Qumran Congress: Proceedings of the International Congress on the Dead Sea Scrolls Madrid 18–21 March, 1991,* ed. Julio T. Barrera and Luis V. Montaner [Leiden: Brill, 1992] 287–94). This essay refers to other appropriate scholarship on this topic and pays special tribute to Joseph M. Baumgarten, "The Qumran-Essene Restraints on Marriage," in *Archaeology and History of the Dead Sea Scrolls,* ed. Lawrence H. Schiffman (Sheffield: JSOT Press, 1990).

10. This particular connection has been overtly claimed (and criticized very severely by more traditional proponents and scholars of the Scrolls) by Robert Eisenman in all three of his major books: *Maccabees, Zadokites, Christians and Qumran* (Leiden: Brill, 1983); *James the Just in the Habakkuk Pesher* (Leiden: Brill, 1986); and with Michael Wise, *The Dead Sea Scrolls Uncovered* (Rockport, Mass.: Element Books, 1992). We should also remember that John Allegro, who was one of the original scholars working on publication of the Scrolls, made a similar claim about the very close links between the sectarians (whom he identified as Essenes) and primitive Christianity; see particularly *The Dead Sea Scrolls and the Christian Myth* (Newton Abbot: Westridge, 1979). Barbara E. Thiering's early work deserves some attention, especially *The Qumran Origins of the Christian Church* (Australian and New Zealand Studies in Theology and Religion 1; Sydney: Sydney Theological Explorations, 1979). Roland E. Murphy initially compiled a list of parallels between the New Testament and Qumran scrolls in "The Dead Sea Scrolls and New Testament Comparisons," *Catholic Biblical Quarterly* 18 (1956) 263–72. Donald Juel, *Messianic Exegesis: Christological Interpretation of the Old Testament in Early Christianity* (Philadelphia: Fortress, 1988). For a more extensive bibliography, see *Jesus and the Dead Sea Scrolls,* ed. Charlesworth.

11. Amihai Mazar, *Archaeology of the Land of the Bible 10000–586 B.C.E.* (New York: Doubleday, 1990) 72–74.

12. Ibid., 88.

13. Amos Kloner and Yigal Tepper, *The Hiding Complexes in the Judean Shephelah* (in Hebrew; Tel Aviv: Hakibbutz Hameuchad Pub. House, Israel Exploration Society, 1987).

14. There were three uprisings against Rome in the space of twenty years (from 115 to 136 C.E.): the diaspora rebellion, the Kittos controversy, and Bar Kochba. See Haim H. Ben Sasson, ed., *History of the Jewish People* (in Hebrew; Tel Aviv: Dvir, 1969) 1:318–58.

15. For a discussion of the origins of the Hebrews, see George E. Mendenhall, *The Tenth Generation* (Baltimore: Johns Hopkins University Press, 1973) 19–20; even more concretely, N. Naʿaman, "Habiru and Hebrews: The Transfer of a Social Term to the Literary Sphere," *Journal of Near Eastern Studies* 45 (1986): 271–88. There is some consensus among biblical scholars today that the term Habiru/Hapiru is from the Akkadian meaning "fugitive." Egyptian documents that mention these groups suggest that the Egyptians used them as an unskilled labor force to work on public building projects. See *Ancient Near Eastern Texts,* ed. James B. Pritchard (Princeton: Princeton University Press, 1969) 247 and 255).

16. Judges figure prominently in the books of Joshua and Judges, which report the conflicts, wars, and negotiations for the land.

17. The only stories associated with a united kingdom were those of David and Solomon, which indeed emerged as the two most mythically appealing kings; all the other kings were rulers of a divided (South and North; Samaria and Israel; Judah and Jerusalem) country. Ironically, the rabbis in the first and second centuries commented on the destruction of the Second Commonwealth as due to division and rancor between the various power factions in Judea.

18. In an attempt to clarify the distinction between the North and the South, David Noel Freedman (in an oral communication) drew our attention to the fact that Benjamin (the tenth tribe) remained attached to Judah (the eleventh tribe). Simeon was the twelfth tribe—never one of the northern tribes.

19. See particularly some of the more poetic chapters describing this second return; e.g., Isaiah 40.

20. Most of the information about the Jews of Elephantine can be found in Bezalel Porten, *Archives from Elephantine* (Los Angeles: University of California Press, 1968).

21. On the state of Qumran apocalyptic studies, see I. Frohlich, "Pesher, Apocalyptical Literature and Qumran," in *The Madrid Qumran Congress: Proceedings of the International Congress on the Dead Sea Scrolls, Madrid 18–21 March, 1991,* ed. Julio T. Barrera and Luis V. Montaner (Leiden: Brill, 1992) 1:295–305.

22. Even though the Scrolls never mention this particular war, there is no question that because of the political climate of the time as well as militant activities undertaken by Sicarii and other zealots, the sectarians might as well have alluded to the final confrontation with the Romans. Moreover, an increasing number of scholars tend to agree now that many of the sectarians (if not all of them) were fully sympathetic to the last stand undertaken in Masada. See Michael Wise, "The Dead Sea Scrolls, Masada and Josephus" (lecture delivered at the University of Judaism, May 1993).

23. Scholars believe that the Shephelah hideaways were the actual underground locations of three revolutions and particularly Bar Kochba's. See Amos Kloner, "Hideout-Complexes from the Period of Bar-Kokhva in the Judean Plain"

(in Hebrew), in *The Bar-Kokhva Revolt: A New Approach,* ed. Aharon Oppenheimer and Uriel Rappaport (Jerusalem: Yad Yitshak Ben Tsevi, 1984) 153–71.

24. The best source about the reign of the Goddess is still Marija Gimbutas, *The Language of the Goddess* (San Francisco: Harper & Row, 1989).

25. See below, chapter 1, n. 2.

26. According to Diane Wolkstein and Samuel N. Kramer, "This royal holy marriage ceremony was but one of a number of more mystical cult practices," which helped explain the idea of a "dying god" and his resurrection (*Inanna, Queen of Heaven and Earth: Her Stories and Hymns from Sumer* [San Francisco: Harper & Row, 1983] 124). This ceremony thus helped explain the notion that all "vegetable and animal life languished to the point of death in the hot, parched summer months." The god returned at the autumnal equinox, "the time of the Sumerian New Year, when his sexual union with his wife made fields and farms . . . bloom and blossom once again." The king of the land, too, was resurrected. "Every New Year . . . the Sumerians celebrated with pomp and ceremony, with music and song, the sacred marriage between the king as the risen god and the goddess who was his wife" (ibid.). See also Samuel N. Kramer, *The Sacred Marriage Rite* (Bloomington: Indiana University Press, 1969) 49–66.

27. Eliezer Berkovitz deals with the concept of "righteous women" (*nāšîm ṣadqāniyôt*) and their significant role in Jewish redemptive history (*Jewish Women in Time and Torah* [Hoboken, N.J.: Ktav, 1990]). Of particular interest is the role that Judith and Esther played in their own time (ibid., 20). Rebekah is described by the rabbis as wise and just.

28. See further some of the conclusions of A. Mazar, *Archaeology,* 517.

29. But these demands were different from the roles of virgins in other temples and shrines, for example, the vestal virgins or the naditu virgins who served the Babylonian sun-god, Shamash. For a detailed discussion of the naditus, see Ulla Jeyes, "The Naditu Women of Sippar," in *Images of Women in Antiquity,* ed. Averil Cameron and Amelie Kuhrt (Detroit: Wayne State University Press, 1985) 260–72.

30. Compare the original usage of this term by Ezekiel; the Dead Sea Scrolls use it in a more mystical context, as does the New Testament.

31. The story of the garden and the concepts of covenant, betrayal of covenant, punishment, and ultimately a return via the merciful God (as well as a host of water associations and tree images) are similar to Mesopotamian myths. There is thus good reason to believe that the origins of the myth of the Garden of Eden are Mesopotamian. The myth's redaction was finally accomplished by a Babylonian Jew (or, Jews) who was haunted by the destruction of the first Temple and who attempted to place that catastrophe within a more universal framework.

32. The bulk of the final redaction of the biblical canon was accomplished by scribes and writers who were profoundly influenced by the sixth-century B.C.E. Babylonian exile.

33. See Gimbutas, *Language of the Goddess,* 122–36.

34. Cain's special status is expressed not only as the triumph of patriarchal and patrilineal values but also as an attempt to preserve his mother's tradition. He is thus offering Yahweh "from the fruit of the earth" (4:3b), an offering that is rejected by the male God, who prefers "firstborn cattle" (v. 4). Abel's strong challenge of Cain, who is favored by Yahweh, is a challenge from whoever interpreted this version of the story, who prefers the male deity. But because of the close links

of Genesis with a larger (and mostly lost) oral tradition, a strong presence of a feminine principle that insists on the special circumstance of Cain's birth and affords him singular protection is maintained.

35. See particularly Gershom Scholem's discussion of Enoch in *Major Trends in Jewish Mysticism* (New York: Schocken, 1963) 43–46, as well as the same author's *Jewish Gnosticism, Merkabah Mysticism, and Talmudic Tradition* (New York: Jewish Theological Seminary, 1960) 12, 44, 48.

36. We discuss the role of Sophia and Wisdom in the Scrolls as well as in the more open Jewish tradition in chapters 1 and 3.

37. Specifically in the *Genesis Apocryphon*, which was initially titled the *Lamech Scroll*. See also Shemaryahu Talmon's argument about the sectarians' attitude toward the biblical books, which they saw "as constituent parts of an open-ended, expandable collection of sanctified writings." Moreover, "like the Chronicler had done before them, they injected their personalities into the materials which they transmitted, expanding and contracting . . . within a legitimate latitude of variation which . . . needs yet to be defined" ("The 'Dead Sea Scrolls' or 'the Community of the Renewed Covenant'" [The Albert T. Bilgay Lecture, April 1993; Tucson, Arizona] 16).

38. Indeed, when the Bible suggests that the birth of Seth as a substitute for the slain Abel (Gen. 4:26) is accompanied by the birth of Yahwism, it actually acknowledges the importance of a strong ideological tool that will hold the tribe together. Even so, while the focus of the ideology slowly shifted from the accommodating Goddess to the stricter male God, the command to multiply stayed the same—though obeying God was becoming much more important.

39. Babylonia and Assyria particularly were two of the great empires of the fertile crescent; both were slave societies. Assyria was the first group that used the horse as a weapon of war.

40. Certainly one must account for the antiquity of the institution. The focus on males is attested in other Near Eastern (and Egyptian) cultures that influenced the Hebrews directly or indirectly. Nor is it surprising that much of the book of Leviticus and its P source is fairly ancient. See Jacob Milgrom, *Leviticus* (Anchor Bible; New York: Doubleday, 1992). Further, it is clear from Josephus's works that there was a separate "zealot" party made up of an overwhelming number of priests, who were concentrated in the Temple building (*Jewish War* 4.570). For a more complete linguistic and ideological discussion of the concept "zeal," see Martin Hengel, *The Zealots*, trans. David Smith (Edinburgh: Clark, 1989) 59–73, 171–76, 206–28.

41. It is clear that the Goddess demanded a totally different mental accommodation as well as a different set of values, some of which were indeed more kind and forgiving. But it is often glossed over that some priestesses in some religions were associated with human and animal sacrifice, eunuch-making and bestiality. The existence of human sacrifices is well documented in some ancient cultures (the archaeological evidence comes largely from Carthage, a Phoenician-Canaanite colony), the practice of castration, or eunuch formation, of both younger and older boys, was also undertaken in an attempt to show devotion to the Goddess and her attributes of fertility. See Walter Burkert, *Structure and History in Greek Mythology and Ritual* (Berkeley: University of California Press, 1979) 110, 120. The sacrificed penis served as a symbol of surrendering one's own personal fertility to the Goddess for the good of society. Even in the highly emotional

mythical drama involving the death of Osiris and his resurrection by Isis, Osiris's organ of fertility is never found by the Goddess and she proceeds to shape one for him. The various ceremonies involving castration focused on self-mutilation accompanied by self-flagellation, dancing, singing, and shedding one's organs to the ground. In the circumcision ceremony, which is still practiced today by Jews all over the world, a tradition-minded mohel will throw the foreskin–a substitute penis–into a heap of sand or soil. This particular custom seems to be an echo of the original castration ritual. In fact, the Hebrew Bible (especially Genesis) refers again and again to Yahweh's blessing of his people thus: "and your seed will be like the soil (ʿāphār) of the land and like the sand of the sea" (Gen. 13:16; 28:14; Num. 23:10).

42. See especially the Holiness Code in Leviticus (chaps. 17–26).

43. Norman K. Gottwald claims that the immediate point of origin of the Israelites was Canaan and that even the very prominent myth of the exodus from Egypt acknowledges a former origin in Canaan ("The Israelite Settlement as a Social Revolutionary Movement," in *Biblical Archaeology Today* [Jerusalem: Israel Exploration Society, 1985] 34–46).

44. The patriarchal sagas in Genesis emphasize, by and large, the peaceful attempts to settle in Canaan made by the three major patriarchs. Abraham's efforts are narrated particularly in the story of the purchase of the cave of Machpelah as an elaborate family burial ground (chapter 23). Isaac's dilemmas can be found in the story about the competition for wells and water, which points to his elaborate efforts to satisfy the hostile attitudes of "Philistines" (Gen. 26:13–34). Jacob's settlement in Canaan after his return from Haran is also described as an avoidance of direct confrontations with the local population; in fact, the one very violent episode associated with land and property acquisition is that of Simeon and Levi, who wipe out the tribe of the Hivites in the story of the rape of Dinah (chapter 34). But even in that story Jacob is rather upset with the sons' violent reaction. See Ita Sheres, *Dinah's Rebellion: A Biblical Parable for Our Time* (New York: Crossroad, 1990).

45. The centrality of ritual in worship is even more pronounced when connected with an abstract monotheistic concept of God as a provider of fertility. Indeed, how can a person be convinced that an unseen, incomprehensible deity who demands strict adherence to his rules can deliver abundance to his people? Furthermore, how can there be a connection between moral behavior and soil fertility? The attraction of the Goddess, and specifically the Asherah (who has been found to be popularly worshiped all over Israel), was the rituals associated with fertility; the direct link that was thus established between people and Goddess was invaluable and enduring.

46. Various biblical passages deal with the prominent status of the Asherah, e.g., Deut. 16:21 (an outright prohibition against "planting an Asherah"), 2 Kgs 17:16; 21:3; 23:15 (elaborate references to making, worshiping, and destroying the Asherah). It is interesting that 2 Kgs 23:7 describes women "weaving homes for the Asherah." Is this an analogue to the Torah curtain (*pargôd*)? Further, see Mordechai Cogan and Hayim Tadmor's commentary *II Kings* (New York: Doubleday, 1988) 286.

47. Amos and Hosea preceded the event; Isaiah, both before and after.

48. "As a title which designates a peculiar relationship . . . it [the servant] des-

ignates one who has a peculiar commission from Yahweh" (John L. McKenzie, *Second Isaiah* [Anchor Bible; New York: Doubleday, 1967] xxxviii).

49. The process of political diminution started from the very beginning when Cyrus issued the edict that allowed the Jews to return to Judea. The Second Commonwealth, although enjoying some form of political independence at some times (specifically during the Maccabean period), did collapse with the help of Rome and its dissatisfaction with the various Judean renegades (and legitimate heirs), who appeared to be hungry for power but could not very well sustain it. The most detailed source for this time is still Josephus's *History of the Jewish War* and his *Jewish Antiquities.* We use the translation of William Whiston, *The Works of Flavius Josephus* (Philadelphia: J. B. Lippincott, 1864) as well as that of H. St. J. Thackeray in the Loeb Classical Library (Cambridge, Mass.: Harvard University Press, 1976).

50. Hengel, *Zealots,* 75.

51. Ibid., 266. Hengel has already drawn attention to the appropriate sources describing "the martyrdom of the wise" (see Dan. 11:33–35; *Ethiopian Enoch* 90; *Assumption of Moses* 8, 9; Rev. 6:9–11; 7:9–17; etc.

52. The Gnostics elaborated on the myth of Sophia, the primal virgin mother, the personification of wisdom and light. She gave birth to a daughter who was the image of herself and who lost contact with the heavens; she is described as wandering in the world, entangled in darkness, desperately looking for a way back to her origins. This particular myth uses the image of the curtain to describe the rift between the spiritual and the material. Only when the mother decides to rescue her daughter will the curtain be removed.

CHAPTER ONE: "PAGAN" WORLD SURROUNDINGS

1. On the Goddess religion, see Gimbutas, *Language of the Goddess,* 20–22. Mixed-gender pantheons existed in Sumer and Akkad, Egypt, India, Assyria, Babylonia, Anatolia, Mycenea/Greece, and the Balkan/Etruscan civilizations.

2. There are at least two significant articles dealing with goddess worship issues in *Biblical Archaeology Review* 20/3 (May/June 1994): Beth A. Nakhai, "What's a Bamah? How Sacred Space Functioned in Ancient Israel" (pp. 18–29); and J. Glen Taylor, "Was Yahweh Worshiped As the Sun?" (pp. 52–60). Both pieces deal extensively with the special reverence toward the Asherah. See Introduction, n. 25.

3. The 15th of August, now the feast of the Assumption of Mary into heaven, is a feast of herbs, flowers, and corn; these are brought to church to be blessed by the Goddess. See Anne Baring and Jules Cashford, *The Myth of the Goddess: Evolution of an Image* (New York: Viking, 1991) 556.

4. See Thomas J. Abercrombie, "Arab's Frankincense Trail," *National Geographic* (Oct. 1985): 484–87. There are in the Dead Sea Scrolls also various references to "pleasing odors" in the context of atonement and perfection. For example, 1QS 8:5–12 describes the Community Council as being the "holy of holies Aaron community" who is doing penance for the sake of the whole land and who also offers "a pleasant smelling sacrifice" (8:9). A repetition of this description can be found in the newly published fragment (4Q251) where the rules of the Sabbath are invoked and those who fulfill them, namely, the holy community, "founded on truth for an eternal planting and true witnesses at the

Judgement, and the elect of (God) favor, and a pleasing fragrance to make atonement for the land, from a[ll Evil . . .]" (frag. 3, lines 8–9). Appropriately, the last lines deal with unclean women. See Eisenman and Wise, *Dead Sea Scrolls Uncovered*, 202.

5. Eisenman and Wise, *Dead Sea Scrolls Uncovered*, 266.

6. By the millennium there were perhaps more Jews who lived outside of Judea itself; see *History of the Jewish People*, ed. Haim H. Ben Sasson (Tel Aviv: Devir, 1969) 1:268–70.

7. Trude Dothan, "Lost Outpost of the Egyptian Empire" [Deir el-Balah in the Gaza strip], *National Geographic* (Dec. 1982): 739–68. Further, Hathor's cult place was a cave, in accordance with Canaanite habits and different from the Egyptians. Accordingly, there is a Cave of Sopdu (a cult niche) in the temple of Serabit el-Khadim. See Raphael Giveon, *The Impact of Egypt on Canaan-Palestine* (Freiburg: Biblical Institute, University of Freiburg, Schweiz, 1978) 63. Hathor, according to Giveon, is the goddess of dance and music in Sinai (p. 68).

8. For a discussion of some of the more enduring symbols of the Goddess, see Gimbutas, *Language of the Goddess;* Miriam R. Dexter, *Whence the Goddesses: A Source Book* (New York: Macmillan, 1990); Riane T. Eisler, *The Chalice and the Blade* (San Francisco: Harper & Row, 1987); and Joscelyn Godwin, *Mystery Religions in the Ancient World* (London: Thames & Hudson, 1981).

9. 11QPs^a 26:5 related to Psalm 149 in the Hebrew Bible.

10. Gimbutas attempts to link the Goddess with the actual invention of music (*Language of the Goddess,* 71). Also Sophie Drinker, "The Origins of Music: Women's Goddess Worship," in *The Politics of Women's Spirituality,* ed. Charlene Spretnak (New York: Doubleday, 1982) 39–48.

11. See Philip Aries and George Duby, eds., *A History of Private Life: From Pagan Rome to Byzantium* (Cambridge, Mass: Belknap Press of Harvard University, 1987) 183–233.

12. David Ulansey, *The Origins of the Mithraic Mysteries* (New York: Oxford University Press, 1989). The author argues very persuasively that members of these mystery cults, which demanded total loyalty to the group as well as absolute secrecy, were committed to an astrological worldview. He further points out that the main event of that cult, the slaying of the bull by Mithras (tauroctomy), provided a star map, thus symbolizing the importance of the sky (stars, etc.) rather than the earth and its association with stable, local populations. The participants in the cult of Mithras were indeed fairly well scattered and many of them were soldiers and Roman state officials. See also Ulansey's recent article in *BAR* 20/5 (Sept.-Oct. 1994): 41–53.

13. Among the rich and famous throughout the Roman Empire (and in Judea too), civic obligations were taken so seriously that they yielded up ostentatious gifts, such as public works in their own names. See Aries and Duby, eds., *A History of Private Life,* 1:161–80.

14. Ibid., 1:183–233.

15. See photo of Aphrodite with her son in Kenan T. Ermin (photos by David Brill), "Ancient Aphrodisias Lives Through Its Art," *National Geographic* (Oct. 1981): 529.

16. Raphael Patai, *The Hebrew Goddess* (New York: Ktav, 1967) 137–54. It is worthwhile quoting the last statement on the subject of the Shekinah: "in spite of the masculine predominance on the highest level of the Talmudic God concept,

popular belief and imagination dwelt in a world peopled and haunted by feminine numina" (p. 156).

17. "In every city you shall set aside areas . . . for menstruating women, and women after childbirth, so that they may not cause defilement in their midst by their impure uncleanness" (11QTemple 48:16–17).

18. Lois W. Banner, *In Full Flower: Aging Women, Power, and Sexuality* (New York: Alfred A. Knopf, 1992) 118. There is a very elaborate sibylline literature associated with apocalyptic and sectarian writings of the turn of the millennium, some of which echoes the Dead Sea Scrolls. The three Greek fates also were females of the same knowing nature.

19. *Sibylline Oracles* 5:211–12: "There will be a great heavenly conflagration on earth and from the battling stars a new nature will emerge." There are various overt connections between the imagery used by the Dead Sea sectarians and the *Sibylline Oracles* that point to a sectarian link; the concept of a total destruction, the choice of a singularly important "remnant" at the end, and the battle on earth which reflects that of the stars.

20. In Robinson, *Nag Hammadi Library*, 143.

21. In Robinson, *Nag Hammadi Library*, 101. See also Elaine Pagels, *The Gnostic Gospels* (New York: Random House, 1979) 51–53.

22. First published by John M. Allegro, ed., *Qumran Cave 4* (DJD 5; Oxford: Clarendon, 1968) 85–87. Though the word "wisdom" (*ḥokmâ*) is missing in this fragment, there is a general sense of context and subject that indeed is associated with wisdom or the wise (from the root *śkl*) thing to do.

23. The well-traveled road from Egypt to Canaan was known as the Ways of Horus.

24. The opening of the mouth signified the bounty of the Goddess, from whose mouth flowed nourishing liquids (see Gimbutas, *Language of the Goddess,* 63–65). At Qumran, fertility and "open" imagery have to do with the status of the community and are invariably related to birth and the womb (1QH 8:5–8, 16–17).

25. Aries and Duby, *History of Private Life*, 24.

26. In Egypt we find the trio as the *ba,* the personal soul, the birdlike "determining individualizing force" that can be reincarnated; the abstract *ka* with its vital energy related to the cow goddess's suckling, the "moral appetite" signified by two upraised arms; and the *akh,* also associated with a bird, the creative force or "preexisting light." See Lucie Lamy, *Egyptian Mysteries: New Light on Ancient Knowledge* (New York: Thames & Hudson, 1989) 24–25.

27. "O Re . . . I am you and you are I . . . I will shine in you . . . make me flourish and I will make you flourish, for I am that eye of yours which is on the horns of Hathor . . . I spend the night and am conceived and born every day" (Raymond Oliver Faulkner, *The Ancient Egyptian Pyramid Texts* [Oxford: Clarendon, 1969]) ##703-5, p. 132). Also: "The King takes possession of the sky . . . . The King shines anew in the East. . . . Rejoice at the King, for he has taken possession of the horizon" (ibid., ##304–7; p. 67).

28. Lamy, *Egyptian Mysteries*, 32.

29. Donald B. Redford, "The Monotheism of the Heretic Pharaoh Precursor of Mosaic Monotheism or Egyptian Anomaly?" *Biblical Archaeology Review* 13 (May/June 1987): 16–26. The author comments briefly on the extraordinary beauty of Nefertity, Akhenaton's wife, and contrasts it "with her husband's ugliness." Redford speculates that "perhaps he . . . had a congenital deformity." This

led "some scholars to identify him as a disguised female or a eunuch. Of late the experts have tended to identify his problem with some sort of endocrine disorder in which secondary sex characteristics failed to develop, and eunuchoidism resulted" (pp. 30–31). See also Cyril Aldred, *Akhenaten, Pharaoh of Egypt: A New Study* (New York: McGraw-Hill, 1968) 133.

30. See E. A. Wallis Budge, *The Gods of the Egyptians* (New York: Dover, 1969) vols. 1 and 2.

31. Wolkstein and Kramer, *Inanna Queen of Heaven,* 52–73.

32. Of particular interest is the story of Isis (the magician) fashioning a golden phallus for Osiris. This event was celebrated in a festival that ultimately honored Osiris. See Patricia Springborg, *Royal Persons: Patriarchal Monarchy and the Feminine Principle* (London: Unwin Hymen, 1990) 174.

33. Lamy claims December 25th (*Egyptian Mysteries*, 23).

34. Ibid., 50.

35. These gods are extremely important for the Greeks because their journey of discovery is signified "by divine mental effort, or wits, of something new. . . . The thing discovered is, in its way, a kind of miracle and it causes a succession of good things to happen for man." Prometheus is a cosmic deviser and savior of men; Plato refers to Thoth as the discoverer of the alphabet and writing. Euripides calls Demeter and Dionysus "discoverers" of cereals and wine, etc. See Vera Frederika Vanderlip, "The Four Greek Hymns of Isidorus and the Cult of Isis," *American Studies in Papyrology* 12 (Toronto: A. M. Hakkert, 1972). The references to Isis's hymns will be from this edition.

36. Gimbutas already noted the importance of snakes (*Language of the Goddess,* 45); and there is also an obvious link here with Hathor. See also Barbara Watterson, *The Gods of Ancient Egypt* (New York: Facts on File Publications, 1984) 36.

37. Gimbutas, *Language of the Goddess,* 46.

38. Quoted in Lamy, *Egyptian Mysteries,* 82.

39. The temple at Dendera, which was dedicated to Hathor and still stands today, dates from the Roman period. "Most of it was built between 116BC and AD 34." On the roof of this temple are a few shrines, one of which "has been left open to the sky. It was here that the New Year ceremony was performed, the culminating point of which occurred when the sun shone upon the face of the statue of Hathor which had been carried up from her sanctuary within the temple . . . for this purpose of 'Uniting with the Sun's Disk'" (Barbara Watterson, *The Gods of Ancient Egypt* [London: B. T. Batsford, 1984] 131). See also a third-century B.C.E. inscription of Petosiris: "I constructed the house of Hathor, goddess of the sycamore-tree . . ." and ". . . I eat bread under the foliage which is on the palm tree of Hathor, my goddess . . ." (E. A. Wallis Budge, *The Egyptian Book of the Dead* [New York: Dover, 1967] lxxxii.7 [1550–1080 B.C.E.]).

Hathor was a goddess of fate, and the seven Hathors of Dendera (who could foresee every newborn's fortunes) were seen as young women wearing tunics and headdresses (see Budge, *Gods of the Egyptians,* 1:434).

40. Budge, *Gods of the Egyptians,* 1:30, 78, 92.

41. Robert Thomas Rundle Clark, *Myth and Symbol in Ancient Egypt* (London: Thames & Hudson, 1978) 88.

42. The unifying movement around 100 C.E. coincided with a growing consciousness of an incipient free class that found strength in solidarity via the institution of charity toward each other (Aries and Duby, *History of Private Life,* 262).

43. Hathor was associated with the turquoise mines of Sinai (Claas J. Bleeker, *Hathor and Thoth: Two Key Figures of the Ancient Egyptian Religion* [Leiden: Brill, 1973] 76).

44. A birth shrine "at Catal Huyuk [Anatolia] . . . called the Red Shrine . . . differed from all found so far in being provided with a red-burnished lime-plaster floor. All the walls were painted red as well as platforms and benches. . . . Long red plastered runnels ran along the edge of the later platforms" (Gimbutas, *Language of the Goddess,* 107) Additionally, the furniture of this shrine was painted in red. This shrine is dated to the seventh millennium B.C.E. Between that period and more modern times, there were many other birth shrines devoted to childbirth. "On Malta . . . the temple of Mnajdra yielded clay models of low couches, terra-cotta figurines, and twists of clay. The latter were replicas of two to three months old fetuses . . ." (ibid., 109). The Roman Diana presided over childbirth and was called "the opener of the womb." The Mesopotamian Ninhursaga, Nintur means Lady birth hut, also called "The Lady of the womb." Her emblem, like the Greek omega, was interpreted to mean the representation of a cow's uterus. See Gimbutas, *Language of the Goddess,* 106–8.

45. Springborg, *Royal Persons,* 78.

46. Ibid., 78.

47. Ibid., 104.

48. Particularly in the Genesis accounts but also in the so-called history books of Samuel and Kings.

CHAPTER TWO: OF WOMAN BORN

1. See Elaine Pagels, *Adam, Eve, and the Serpent* (New York: Vintage, 1989).

2. M. Baillet, ed., *Discoveries in the Judaean Desert VII* (Oxford: Clarendon Press, 1982) 176. This particular quotation is from a badly worn manuscript from Cave 4 (4Q507); it is related to a series of other fragments of the same kind that seem to deal with prayers for festivals such as the Day of Atonement and the Day of the First Fruits. The phrase "iniquity (or, sin) from the womb" is repeated in 1QH 4:29–30.

3. We should remember that the prophets already painted women as more prone to sexual wrongdoing especially because of their association with various goddess "cults" and religions. Even within the biblical text the notion of women's uncleanness and corruption is strongly present. We should remember also that there was a literary process involved in creating the metaphor of "original sin" in the aftermath of the first major act of disobedience.

4. See especially the Samson and Delilah story in Judges 16.

5. From the desert experience associated with the exodus from Egypt to the various sectarians and rebels (including the early Maccabees) during the days of the Second Commonwealth, Jews used the desert, mountains, and fields as real and symbolic places of refuge. For the Qumranites, the desert was a new Garden of Eden.

6. In the story of the exodus, there is an echo of the same concept, where Egypt, the land of Isis and Hathor and a host of other goddesses, is ultimately referred to by the fleeing Israelites as the land where they had "pots of flesh" at their disposal (see Exod 16:3).

7. There are various Enochic manuscripts found at Qumran. See J. T. Milik,

The Books of Enoch, Aramaic Fragments of Qumran Cave 4 (Oxford: Oxford University Press, 1976).

8. We speculate that these "giants" are connected with "all the stars with genitals like horses" (Enoch), that is, extended, large genitals (like giant genitals in an erection?).

9. See the detailed discussion in Alexander A. Di Lella, *The Hebrew Text of Sirach* (The Hague: Mouton, 1966). See also Yigael Yadin, *The Scroll of Ben Sira from Masada* (in Hebrew; Jerusalem: Israel Antiquities Exploration Society, 1975) 38, 43.

10. On the face of it, Ben Sira repeats for his audience a message that is embodied in the story of Esther. There too the king asks Vashti, his first wife, "to come before him" (1:11) so that he could show her off "since she was good looking." The command is clearly demeaning and possessive. Vashti refuses the king, thus announcing her independence as well as her disgust with his overt chauvinism. This action is interpreted by the males in the court as rebellious, dangerous, and threatening to the power of all males anywhere in the country. The courtiers contend: "It is not just the king who is being distorted by queen Vashti, but all of the princes and all of the people everywhere in King Ahasuerus' kingdom" (1:16). Moreover, "When the queen's word will be heard, all the women will despise their husbands saying that King Ahasuerus asked queen Vashti to appear before him and she did not come" (1:17). Indeed, as far as these male advisors were concerned, the whole affair would cause "anguish and shame" (1:18b). Therefore, Vashti's voice had to be muted.

But the difference between the point of view of Esther and that of Ben Sira is quite significant. In Esther, the rebellion of Vashti led to her loss of political power, but, ironically, Esther, the woman who took her place, gained the kind of prestige that the Bible rarely accords to women. Esther was the heroine of her time as much as Moses and other saviors were heroes of their time. In fact, Esther's heroism and dedication to her people are still celebrated, viewed by Jewish tradition as an extraordinary feat which brought Haman's plot to destroy the Jews to naught. Appropriately, though, there is good reason to suppose that the sectarians at Qumran did not celebrate Purim, probably because it was difficult for them to accept the notion of a sexual woman being directly related to a redeeming moment in time. For a long time, Esther was the only canonical biblical book not found in Qumran; scholars speculated that perhaps it had to do with the relationship of Esther to the foreign, non-Jewish king or, in line with our approach to the text, because of Esther's clear association with "Ishtar" and the ritual of the *hieros gamos,* which is symbolically described in the two "feasts" that the queen presides over. Now, J. T. Milik's presentation of the Aramaic Esther might lead the scholarly world in new directions. Even though the fragments that he translated do not seem to relate directly to the biblical Esther, it is obvious that the sectarians did have access to that book and that they were aware of Esther's role in the Bible (see J. T. Milik, "Les modèles araméens du livre D'Esther dans la Grotte 4 de Qumran," *Revue de Qumran* [June 1992]: 321–99; referenced as 4Q550 [4QprotEsth[a-f]]). Whereas Esther is portrayed as a virgin in the Bible, and in that sense could have potentially served the sectarians' purpose of "holiness," the association of her name with a female deity, Ishtar, probably made it difficult for them to accept her. Finally, Esther did not commune with a Jewish man and hence potentially "tainted" her blood with that of "foreigners," whom the sectarians abhorred.

11. Even Di Lella, the principal author of *The Wisdom of Ben Sira* (together with Patrick W. Skehan, from whom he took over after the latter's death), who seems to want to place everything within its historical context and defends Ben Sira against claims of misogynism, agrees that "Ben Sira (like other authors of that society and age) writes a great deal more about the evil woman or wife . . . than about the good one" (*Wisdom of Ben Sira,* 347).

12. Di Lella says about this particular verse: "a similar idea is expressed in 2 Cor 11:3 and 1 Tim 2:14. . . . later Jewish theology generally taught that Adam was the real cause for the entrance of sin and death into the world. . . . St. Paul says the same thing in Rom 5:12, 14–19; 1 Cor 15:22" (*Wisdom of Ben Sira,* 348).

13. Warren C. Trenchard, *Ben Sira's View of Women: A Literary Analysis* (Chico, Calif.: Scholars Press, 1982). Trenchard agrees with the general scholarly dating of the text—around 180 B.C.E. (p. 3)—though we assume that it is a later text. He also maintains that "Ben Sira wrote about women as he did, because he was motivated by a personal, negative bias against them" (p. 7).

14. For example, the author of the later pseudepigraphic *Life of Adam and Eve* assigns to Eve a variety of statements that further the notion of the woman's responsibility for human corruption and specifically the original fall: "And Eve said to Adam, 'My lord, would you kill me? O that I would die! Then perhaps the Lord God will bring you again into Paradise, for it is because of me that the Lord God is angry with you'" (3:1–2). And: "I have brought toil and tribulation on you" (5:2). Similarly, we find in *2 Enoch:* "And I created for him a wife, so that death might come . . . by his wife" (30:17b). There are more references to the same concept in texts such as the pseudepigraphic *Apocalypse of Moses* 24:1–3; in the New Testament 1 Tim. 2:14 as well as 2 Cor. 11:3. All of these stem from the earlier texts we have just examined and are all fairly close in time (first century C.E. and later).

15. The sectarians clearly knew of its contents; in fact, the Hebrew fragments alerted the scholarly community to the existence of a Hebrew version of this fairly popular book.

16. Indeed, there may be a negative reference here to the Greeks' gymnasia, which involved baths, nude bodies, short tunics, and no beards. The gymnasia were very popular in the ancient world and many Jews frequented them.

17. Names and the act of naming are important functions in the Bible, denoting power and identity.

18. Of particular interest is a woman such as Alexandra who had some spiritual as well as political impact. Queen Salome Alexandra (d. 67 B.C.E.) successfully saved innocent sages from their deaths (see in *Megillat Taʿanit* 11). See Joseph Sievers, "The Role of Women in the Hasmonean Dynasty," in *Josephus, the Bible, and History,* ed. Louis H. Feldman and Gohei Hata (Detroit: Wayne State University Press, 1989) 132–46. Alexandra was the daughter of Hyrcanus II and the mother of Mariamme, who became Herod's wife. She was accused, among other things, of a plot to overthrow Herod. Alexandra was executed in 28 B.C.E. on charges of having tried to seize control of the garrisons in Jerusalem when Herod was ill (Josephus, *Antiquities* 15.183–86).

19. The absence of Rachel is especially significant because she evolves into

the great compassionate mother figure who is pleading with God for the plight of her exiled children (see Jeremiah 31). Rachel is a wise/righteous woman as well.

20. Miriam is indeed assigned (by the sectarians) to sing the Song of Moses (Exodus 15), which is rather curious and certainly out of character for the sectarians. It points to a very strong oral tradition that reported Miriam as the originator of the song. We should remember that the Song of Moses/Miriam is the oldest reported in the Torah and is closely linked with the Song of Deborah in Judges 5.

21. See Milik, "Les modèles araméens." For Esther allegories and interpretations, see Carey A. Moore, *Daniel, Esther, and Jeremiah: The Additions* (New York: Doubleday, 1981) 159. Moore notes, among other things, the literary and historical controversy surrounding the biblical Esther and shows quite clearly that from very early on Esther had been allegorized rather than treated as a real woman.

22. From the very beginning there were questions about Esther's historicity and canonicity; see Moore, *Esther*, xxi–xxx, xxxiv–xlv.

23. See chapter 3 below for a more complete analysis of this episode.

24. See 4Q274 1 i 7; this text deals with women's menstrual cycles, a record of which is to be kept by either men or women scribes. See Eisenman and Wise, *Dead Sea Scrolls Uncovered*, 207. See further chapter 7 below.

25. They maintain that if a baby is dead in the mother's womb, "the mother remains clean until the child comes forth" (Mishnah Ḥullin 4:3).

26. There is also a rule about pregnant animals in relation to the sacrificial cult whereby the sectarians ban such animals from being offered and declare them to be "an abomination." They are totally "unclean" and undeserving because they signify the loss of virginity and thus wholeness and holiness. For a fuller discussion of the *Temple Scroll* laws of purity, see Yigael Yadin, *The Temple Scroll: The Hidden Law of the Dead Sea Sect* (London: Weidenfeld & Nicolson, 1985) 170–91.

27. Philo of Alexandria, who was influential in establishing an allegorical school of interpretation of Scripture, was also a child of his environment: his comments on sexuality and gender interrelations are instructive and very much in line with the other first-century patterns:

> We children of the Hebrews follow laws and customs which are especially our own. Other people are permitted after the fourteenth year to deal without interference with harlots and strumpets and all those who make a traffic of their bodies. Before the lawful union we know no mating with other women, but come as virgin men to virgin maidens. The end we seek in wedlock is not pleasure but the begetting of lawful children. (*Jos.* 42–43)

For Philo, the procreative goal regulates sexuality even within marriage, so much so that he sharply condemns those who have sexual relations during the infertile periods of the woman's menstrual cycle . . . or those who marry women known to be sterile (see *De specialibus legibus* 3.34–36).

> . . . do not run after rapes and adulteries and other unhallowed forms of intercourse, but only those which are lawful means of propagating the human race . . . . So let us make it our earnest endeavor to bind up [our faculties] with the adamantine chains of self-control. (*Quod deterius potiori insidiari solet* 102–3)

(Discipline is a favorite word with the Qumran sectarians as well.)

Philo's discussion of virginity is illuminating, especially in view of how it was treated in the Dead Sea Scrolls:

It is meet that God should converse with the truly virgin nature; but it is the opposite with us. For the union of human beings that is made for the procreation of children, turns virgins into women. But when God begins to consort with the soul, He makes what before was a woman into a virgin again, for he takes away the degenerate and emasculate desires which unmanned it and plants instead the native growth of unpolluted virtues. (*De Cherubim* 50)

We use the Loeb Classical Library edition of Philo (translated by Francis H. Colson). There are also rabbinic stories of weddings that were attended by the Angel of Death, as if to signify the "deadly" nature of matrimonial union.

28. In Habermann's edition the reading is *ădāmâ*, "earth," rather than "water."

29. Jacob Licht states: "In these and other words, the recognition in the basic weakness of man has turned into an extraordinarily strong feeling—to a total loathing, indeed, to a disgust and repulsion" (*The Hodayot Scroll from the Scrolls of the Judean Desert* [in Hebrew; Jerusalem: Bialik, 1957] 34).

30. Similarly, there is a revulsion expressed by the author of CD concerning "the whorish practice of taking two wives at the same time" (4:20–21). Above all, "they defile the Sanctuary inasmuch as they do not distinguish in accordance with the Law, and lie with her who sees the blood of her flux" (5:6–7). In other words, they lie with women in their periods. Additionally, there is a concerted attack on those who commit incest, alluding perhaps to some of the practices of Herod's house. Sexual purity, especially as practiced by those of special distinction—kings and priests—is at the top of the Qumranites' spiritual agenda, and they are convinced that it leads to the only life worth living, that is, a holy life. By the same token, sexual and other physical impurities must be eradicated from the midst of the community before a holy life can be fully accomplished. The sectarians' strong conviction was that their community and way of being could serve not only as an example for others but, more broadly, could enable them as a chosen covenantal *yaḥad* to start living the life of holiness in the present. See Eisenman, *James the Just, 87–94,* which attempts to link many of the references to "fornication" and "sexual perversion" to the house of Herod.

31. Since the community had a larger purpose and perceived of itself as fulfilling a distinct function, the language of the following attack must be very closely examined for other intentions as well. 4QWiles, first published by John Allegro, was summarized by him thus: "it seems the Covenanters had none too high an opinion of the fair sex" (*The Dead Sea Scrolls, A Reappraisal* [New York: Penguin] 115). He then goes on to suggest, though, that the woman represented "the dangerous philosophies of the pagan world." Similarly, Theodor H. Gaster, in his introduction to the poem, maintains that "this ingenious little sermon . . . is obviously to be understood allegorically, for there would be no point in warning desert ascetics against the ploys of real live urban streetwalkers. The harlot is evidently Apostasy or the like, in line with the Biblical characterization of it as 'whoredom'" (*The Dead Sea Scriptures* [New York: Anchor Books, 1976] 495). Although the approach that objectifies women in the most debasing fashion is dubious, if not wrong (we know now that not all of these covenanters were desert ascetics), it is interesting to focus on some of the key images used in the poem in order to draw attention to the concept of the fundamental defilement of humanity and, even more, to its clear association with women.

32. DJD 5:82.

33. The same phrase, "the elect of righteousness," is used in 1QH 2:13.

34. "Corruption" in this context is expressed as the synonym for *šaḥat*, which is alluded to in the story of Daniel, who was so blameless that, even though some of the king's counselors tried to find fault (from the above root, *šḥt*) with him, they could not (Dan. 6:5).

35. It is quite possible that a segment of the sectarian population stemmed from Egypt and the Temple in Leontopolis, which, we believe, is coded for security reasons in the opposite direction from "Damascus."

36. Richard A. Baer, Jr., *Philo's Use of the Categories Male and Female* (Leiden: Brill, 1970) 50–51.

37. Ibid.

38. We do not rule out the possibility that there was a sect (or an order) within Qumran that was celibate. There is still strong support within the scholarly community for the identification of the Dead Sea sectarians with the Essenes, who are believed to have been celibate. Joseph A. Fitzmyer speculates that the Essenes could be equated with eunuchs (lecture "The Dead Sea Scrolls and Early Christianity," University of Judaism, May 24, 1993). Further, Josephus says that some Essenes were celibate and some were not. We wish to draw attention to the levels of purity observed by the sectarians at Qumran, levels that were translated into certain orders.

CHAPTER THREE: BIRTH NARRATIVES: A FORGOTTEN RITUAL

1. The *Blessings* were originally attached to the *Community Rule* (1QS); they have been pieced together by J. T. Milik (DJD 1; Oxford: Clarendon, 1955) 118–29; we refer to Habermann, *Megillot Midbar Yehuda,* 160–63.

2. See Eisenman, *Maccabees, Zadokites, Christians and Qumran,* especially chapter 2 ("The Zadokite Priesthood"), pp. 4–6.

3. On the differences in the views of the Torah and the Law expressed in the Dead Sea Scrolls from so-called mainstream Jewish beliefs, see Yadin, *Temple Scroll;* Ben Zion Wacholder, *The Dawn of Qumran: The Sectarian Torah and the Teacher of Righteousness* (Cincinnati: Hebrew Union College Press, 1983); Schiffman, *Law, Custom and Messianism in the Dead Sea Sect.* In the most recent publication dealing with the issue of law (halakah) of the sectarians (*Qumran Cave 4 V Miqsat Maʿaśe Ha-torah,* ed. Elisha Qimron and John Strugnell [DJD 10; Oxford: Clarendon, 1994) there is a complete section "The Halakah" (pp. 123–78) and an appendix:"The History of the Halakah and the Dead Sea Scrolls" by Yaʿakov Sussman (pp. 1769–200) focusing on similarities and differences between the sectarians and the rabbis.

4. Matthew Black, *The Scrolls and Christian Origins: Studies in the Jewish Background of the New Testament* (New York: Scribner, 1961) 165. Additionally, Black made the connection to the "so-called sect of the Nazarenes of Acts 24:5" (p. 167) as well as the Jewish Nazarenes of Transjordan. "There is certainly a Nazirite element in Christian origins, as is witnessed, for instance, by Matthew 2:23" (p. 167).

5. Recall that Mary refers to herself as "handmaid" when confronted by Gabriel and his message.

6. In the Qumran *Psalms Scroll* there are previously unknown psalms that purport to be composed by the sectarians' favorite figure, "David." Reading the

scroll and focusing on the main concepts and words expressed there, one can detect the hand of the sectarians who emphasized the seed of David as well as the Nazirite tradition. ". . . they were tall of stature with beautiful hair . . ." 11QPs 151A. See the discussion by Shemaryahu Talmon, *The World of Qumran from Within* (Jerusalem: Magnes Press, 1989) 244–72; he finds it surprising that in a major deviation from the original text of 1 Samuel (where the prophet anoints David), the sectarians mention the beautiful hair of the brothers.

7. There has been much scholarly discussion about millenarian expectations at Qumran. We find Talmon's contributions in *The World of Qumran from Within* (pp. 273–300) very illuminating as well as his discussions of calendrical issues (pp. 147–85). Talmon deals with the various numbers important to the sectarians, for example, "twenty years," when they were "groping for their way" as guilty people, and the period of the next "twenty years," which included the Teacher of Righteousness "to guide them in the way of the heart" (CD 1:8–11). Talmon links the split number forty (a crucial redemptive Israelite number) with the appointment of Samson, who judged Israel twenty years in two separate verses: Judg. 15:20 and 16:31.

8. Using images of cleansing by way of water and wine, Pseudo-Philo wrote about the sons of Aaron in whose line we later find the high priest Zadok: "For they [Phineas and Jabin, sons of Eleazar the priest] prophesied about the vineyard, *the planting of the Lord's delight* (Isa. 5:7) which did not know its planter and would not recognize its cultivator, and the vineyard was corrupted, and its fruit was not good" (Daniel J. Harrington, *The Hebrew Fragments of Pseudo-Philo* [SBL Texts and Translations 3, Pseudepigrapha Series 3; Missoula, Mont.: Scholars Press, 1974] 28.3–4, p. 55).

9. See Drower, *Secret Adam,* 18.

10. Vermes maintains: "More likely than not, the 'wine' drunk by the sectaries, 'the drink of the Congregation,' was unfermented grape-juice" (*Dead Sea Scrolls in English,* 7).

11. Noah plays a special role in the sectarian Nazirite tradition. Noah's activities after the flood are portrayed in Genesis as related to a vineyard: "Noah, a tiller of the soil, was the first to plant the vine" (9:20). Then follows the difficult story about Ham "uncovering his father's nakedness." The language and imagery of the story are explicitly sexual, and whatever evil deed was committed by Ham (incest or otherwise) is viewed as directly associated with Noah's curse of Canaan (Ham's son).

12. *Qumran Cave 4,* ed. Allegro, DJD 5:44. A variation of this passage can be found in Habermann, (4QpPs[a] 3:19–20).

13. It is interesting that Manoah refers to an unborn child as "youth"; maybe to indicate that the life of a baby does not really count for much. Life expectancy in the ancient world as well as the usefulness of children in an agricultural society may come into play here. Possibly also consciousness is important and accounts for an adult's responsibility.

14. This is similar to the "awesome" revelation to Moses in the "burning bush," and its anonymity (both place and name are lacking).

15. Isis asked the god for his name before acquiring her power; the man named his woman Eve; various matriarchs named their children in Genesis.

16. See Savina J. Teubal's main thesis about barren women in *Sarah the Priestess: The First Matriarch of Genesis* (Athens, Oh.: Swallow Press, 1984).

17. See Sheres, *Dinah's Rebellion*. Note also the terrifying events in Judges 11 and 19, where the women who go out of their homes end up dead or tortured or both. Manoah's wife defies the tradition of women staying in the tent; she is found in the field without a man and survives to tell her story. The narrator of the text seems to be saying to Manoah that, by all accounts, the story belongs to his wife. In that sense, too, it seems less important to name the woman; her actions and words speak for themselves and for her. Indeed, this is one of the few times in the Bible where the lack of a woman's name is almost irrelevant because of the strength of her character and actions. She might as well be "Manoah's wife" since he is so inept. While she is initially designated "barren," she certainly does not act like someone who is desperate to have a child and who feels that motherhood is a key to keeping her husband and her position in society.

18. Although the Genesis matriarchs had very deep links with spiritual sources, the overt stories about them tend to trivialize their concerns and narrowly focus on their motherly pursuits (see Savina J. Teubal, *Hagar the Egyptian: The Lost Tradition of the Matriarchs* [San Francisco: Harper & Row, 1990] 20–21).

19. In their early years, the sectarians may have been associated with the Galilee and Galileans, the "freedom fighters" of Judea. It is also significant that the tribe of Dan is associated with a serpent: "May Dan be a serpent by the roadside, a horned snake by the path, that bites the horse's heel" (Gen. 49:17). In a way, we are suggesting that the sectarians' imagery hinted at an assault against the pagan serpent and its relation to the Goddess.

20. The longevity of a worship related to the sun is attested by Epiphanius (fourth-century Christian writer), who talks about an unorthodox Christian sect called Sampsaens, "whose name is certainly connected with the semitic root sh-m-sh (and so has been hitherto thought to indicate 'sun [shemesh]-worshippers'). Epiphanius . . . links these people with the Essenes. . . . Apparently . . . they dwelt in Transjordan . . . on the borders of ancient Moab, and by the eastern shores of the Dead Sea" (John M. Allegro, *The Sacred Mushroom and the Cross* [New York: Doubleday, 1970] 61). Allegro goes on to suggest that there is a clear link between these people and other sects focusing on "healing," "life-giving," "therapy" (Therapeutae) and the Christians. We view these sects as divisions or orders within a larger movement.

21. The bet, which is associated with the riddle about honey in Judges 13, starts out with Samson in complete command of the events and ends up with the loss of some of his possessions and particularly the woman that he married.

22. See the analysis of Mieke Bal, *Lethal Love: Feminist Readings of Biblical Love Stories* (Bloomington, Ind.: Indiana University Press, 1987). Bal presents Samson's misadventures with women as an attempt to be "released" from strong maternal ties; she claims that he finally manages to do it when he tears down the "pillars," but in the process he is killed (pp. 40–62).

23. See Yair Zakovitch, *The Life of Samson* (in Hebrew; Jerusalem: Magnes Press, 1982) 166–213. Also William G. Dever, "What Samson Pulled Down," *Biblical Archaeology Review* (March/April 1991): 65

24. In *Midrash Rabbah,* Numbers, the rabbis point out that Samson was warned by his parents not to take a woman from Timnah for a wife because "the vineyards of Timnah were sown with mixed seed," as were the daughters of that place. See H. Friedman and Maurice Simon, eds. *Genesis Rabbah* (New York: Soncino, 1983) 284–85. In *Genesis Rabbah* 98.13; 99.11, the rabbis emphasize Sam-

son's strength and prowess. There is also an effort to flesh out the personalities of Manoah and his wife and to suggest that at least on one level Manoah was concerned that the angel told his wife some secrets (ritual or otherwise?) which she, in turn, did not tell him.

25. Shaye J. D. Cohen argues that "there is no evidence at all for the common view that Bannous was an Essene" (*Josephus in Galilee and Rome* [Leiden: Brill, 1979] 106). Neither does Cohen believe that he was a "baptizer" as some other scholars tried to argue. Some scholars are now inclined to accept the notion that Bannous could be identified with John the Baptist. It is also possible to connect the name to a Greek bather.

Cohen finally concludes that the three years that Josephus spent with Bannous indicate that the comment about having to make a choice among the three philosophies was completely imaginary (*Josephus in Galilee and Rome,* 107). However, we believe that Cohen is in error and that Josephus had a "mystery" reason that prohibited him from fully explaining who Bannous was. It is also possible that Bannous prepared Josephus for some mysterious initiation about which the author tells us nothing except that he "became a devoted disciple." Who was Bannous? What discipline did he represent? Josephus is hiding more than he reveals about this mystery man, but what is revealed fits the Qumran framework quite well. There may have been a politically sensitive reason for the cover-up. In the version of the *Life* that we have (a later, edited one), Josephus leaves out most of the information about Bannous out, but he does use images that assist in comparisons by conjecture. It is also entirely possible, as Eisenman suggested in *Maccabees, Zadokites, Christians and Qumran,* that the reference to Bannous indicates a desert training period undergone by some priests before taking on their priestly duties in Jerusalem.

26. For the most recent treatment of this particular topic, see Eisenman and Wise, *Dead Sea Scrolls Uncovered,* 230, where the authors analyze the "Baptismal Hymn" (4Q414).

27. An argument for the sect's popularity is put forth by Michael Wise, *Thunder in Gemini;* see also Norman Golb, *Who Wrote the Dead Sea Scrolls? The Search for the Secret of Qumran* (New York: Simon & Schuster, 1995) 104.

28. Sarah and/or Rebekah as well as Rachel, who pleads with Jacob "Let me have children!" seem to be concerned about the continuity of their own line (compared with that of their respective husbands, who could potentially sire children with any woman), thus denoting their independence and separate status. See Teubal's poignant analysis of this particular problem in *Hagar the Egyptian,* 60–62.

29. For example, 1QpHab 6:4–8: "They sacrifice to their standard and worship their weapons of war . . . . they divide their yoke and their tribute over all the peoples year by year, ravaging many lands." And in the Commentary on Nahum (4QpNah 3–4 iv 4): his wives, his children, and his little ones shall go into captivity. His mighty men and honorable men [shall perish] by the sword."

30. In the biblical story, Delilah is not a harlot; she is simply a woman, albeit crafty and resourceful, from Nahal Sorek (Judg. 16:4).

31. The Dead Sea Scrolls sternly warn the adherents, especially the priests, against engaging in sexual activity with nonvirgins and foreign women. Delilah presents double jeopardy for Samson, and he is bound to fall. Of course, it is not clear from the biblical account that Samson actually had sex with Delilah; she

finally is said to "cause him to sleep on her knees" (Judg. 16:19). He finally succumbs "because his soul wished to die" (16:16). Again, we see the theme of sex equated with death. The hero's ultimate redemption is an exoneration of the sectarians as well because "this man deserves to be admired for his courage and strength, and magnanimity at his death, and that his wrath against his enemies went so far as to die himself with them" (Josephus, *Antiquities* 5.8.12). The glorification of suicide for the right cause and ideology is a favorite theme of Josephus and the sectarians, whose influence is now thought to have been the reason behind the mass suicide at Masada, the last stand of the remnant from Jerusalem (and perhaps other cities) and the defender "camps" in the desert. See specifically 1QM 1:12; 13:16–17; 17:1.

32. This text is of the same genre as Qumran's *Genesis Apocryphon*. The author is not at all related to Philo of Alexandria; in fact, there is good reason to believe that he was Palestinian. The name Pseudo-Philo was established because of the title link of his book (*Antiquities*) with Josephus; the assumption was that if the author of this *Antiquities* was not Josephus, then he must have been Philo. See Harrington, *The Hebrew Fragments of Pseudo-Philo,* 3–20.

33. A variation on the name might imply "hiddenness" and a mystery Eluma=Aluma in the context of secrets and hidden meanings.

34. The power of naming a son was maintained by women throughout the tradition. It is therefore significant that Rachel names this son rather than Bilhah.

35. This motif is reminiscent of the biblical encounter between Rachel and Jacob, where Rachel asks Jacob for sons and he, in anger, claims that he is not God.

36. *Qumran Cave 4,* ed. Allegro, DJD 5:52.

37. See also 2 Sam. 14:25–26. Similarly, Absalom (the rebellious son of David who was popular with the people), who seemed to have been a lifelong Nazirite, proud of his hair and sexually promiscuous; "he was hung by his hair" (*Sotah* 1:8).

38. The name the rabbis ascribe to Manoah's wife is indicative of an appeal to God even though there is none recorded by the woman. See Louis H. Feldman, "Josephus' version of Samson," *Journal for the Study of Judaism* 19 (1988): 171–214.

39. Compare the sect of the Nazarenes in Acts 24:24–25. See also n. 20 above.

40. It should be noted that today Jews who are of a Hasidic persuasion leave their sidelocks uncut as a sign of their dedication to God.

41. The biblical redactors describe Moses, the greatest of all prophets, as a hero who was removed from his home and natural surroundings early in his life; so also Samuel and similarly Jeremiah, the prophet who witnessed the destruction of the first Temple. Moses is probably the greatest mythical savior of the Hebrews, who interceded with God twice on behalf of the people. Samuel anoints the first two kings, particularly David. And Jeremiah bears witness to the end of the first cycle of Hebraic history. All three are associated with priestly families and special births: Moses is the son of Levites; Samuel is dedicated to temple service, and Jeremiah is of the family of priests "exiled" to Anathoth by Solomon. The priesthood of the temple at Shiloh dates from premonarchic times and had charge of the ark of Yahweh (1 Sam. 3:3; 4:3). Ultimately, the ark found its way into the Temple of Solomon, who banished Abiathar, the heir to the line of Eli, from the high priesthood. The line of Eleazar (and hence Jerusalem priests) takes over. Some scholars believe that Shiloh was crucial in shaping and articulating the final Deuterono-

mistic program that formed the whole Hebrew Bible. See Baruch Halpern, "Shiloh," *The Anchor Bible Dictionary* (New York: Doubleday, 1992) 5:214–15.

42. Neither Sarah nor Rachel designates her firstborn as a son of the Yahwistic covenant. Samuel's father has no say in his son's affairs and he remains a marginal figure. Accordingly, the text narrates, "and after a period of time" (*litqûfôt hayyāmîm*, "at the turning of the days," a general indication of the passage of a significant amount of time, e.g., a year; it may also be related to the nine months of pregnancy). Hannah became pregnant and gave birth to a son and named him Samuel, because "'I have borrowed [the root of the verb, *š'l*, is also related to the verb "to ask"] him from Yahweh'" (1 Sam. 1:20). Hannah thus asks as much as she "borrows" her special son, who is characterized as directly connected to Yahweh's "remembrance." Elkanah is portrayed as actively associated with Samuel only at the point in the narrative where he "goes up to offer the sacrifice and his vow" (v. 21). There is no recorded "vow" of Elkanah; the only vow the narrative mentions is that of Hannah. The sacrificial offering made by Hannah is reminiscent of the sacrifice offered by Manoah and his wife in the previous narrative; here, though, the woman uses a "bull," whereas in Judges a "kid" was sacrificed.

43. *Qumran Cave 4,* ed. Allegro, DJD 5:9–11.

44. The description of Hannah's "gladness," similar to Sarah's "laughter" in Genesis, should be compared to a state of beatitude.

45. The author focuses on the taunting of Peninah, Elkanah's fertile wife.

46. This differs from the more elaborate Sibylline literature, which was quite popular for a very long period of time. The earliest Sibyls date from the fifth century B.C.E., and the word may refer to the name of a prophetess. See "Sibylline Oracles," in *Old Testament Pseudepigrapha,* ed. Charlesworth, 1:317–24. The so-called "historical" apocalypses date from the period of the Maccabean revolt. See John J. Collins, *The Apocalyptic Imagination* (New York: Crossroad, 1984) 93.

47. See C. A. Brown, *No Longer Be Silent: First Century Jewish Portraits of Biblical Women* (Louisville: Westminster John Knox, 1992) 140–80. Brown emphasizes Hannah's newly found voice, which Brown felt was the most significant aspect of Pseudo-Philo's version of the story. Although we agree, we contend also that the images of barrenness, milk, and wisdom have far-reaching ramifications. In the context of the times, Pseudo-Philo's Hannah should alsao be compared with the sibyls.

48. David N. Freedman drew our attention to the biblical Hannah's song, which is even more astounding than the one expressed here; in it, there is a clear reference to "king" and "messiah" (1 Sam. 2:10).

49. Scholars agree in placing Pseudo-Philo in Judea in the first century C.E.

50. In the introduction to his translation and commentary, David Winston assumes that "there is a close affinity between Wisd's eschatology and that of I Enoch . . . and the Dead Sea Scrolls" (*The Wisdom of Solomon* [New York: Doubleday, 1979] 63).

51. Cited in Winston, *Wisdom of Solomon,* 131.

52. The context of the Wisdom of Solomon is quite similar to that of the Hannah story; the author thus continues: "It is better to be childless, provided one is virtuous / for in virtue's remembrance there is immortality, / since it wins recognition both from God and from men" (4:1). The superiority of "virtue," or "righteousness," is depicted by the author in conjunction with "the root of wisdom." He

claims that true posterity is associated with all of the positive concepts described above, which, in turn, are related to the virgin.

53. See *Old Testament Pseudepigrapha*, ed. Charlesworth, 1:86.

54. In orthodox Jewish marriage rituals, the groom is supposed to wear white in remembrance of death. Further, both bride and groom are supposed to fast before the actual wedding ceremony.

55. It is entirely possible that the first white wedding dress originated at Qumran.

56. On another level, Lamech's concern about his "strange" son was connected to the story of the "sons of God" who "visited" the daughters of men in a mythical encounter that produced evil. The text seems to suggest that Noah is so extraordinary that Lamech cannot see himself as a partner in his conception. While the "evil" echoes of the story recorded in Genesis are missing from Lamech's overt statements, it is clear that this story is in the background because it preoccupied Enochic literature and, as we will see further on, the sectarians themselves.

57. The writer of the *Genesis Apocryphon* (1QapGen) seems to echo overtly Isaiah's "new heaven and new earth" (Isa. 66:22) as well as the more obscurely articulated phrase by Jeremiah: "God has created something new in the land; a female will compass (woo, surround, court) a man" (31:21). Traditionally, this phrase was taken to mean that the new age would bring about a new relationship between Israel and Yahweh, namely, she (Israel) would now court him (Yahweh). But this explanation is not fully satisfactory because it is vague and general. Stanley Brice Frost suggests that in one of the possible translations, the verb (*šwb*) should be read as "turned into" (*tišob*) producing a radical text which claims that women will become men (*The Interpreter's One Volume Commentary on the Bible* [New York: Abingdon, 1989] 392). John Bright is befuddled and says: "Quite possibly we have here a proverbial saying indicating something that is surprising and difficult to believe, the force of which escapes us" (*Jeremiah* [New York: Doubleday, 1979] 282). Bright may be right, and it is therefore possible that the sectarians (closer to the time of the redaction) might have still known that meaning. Possibly, too, their own search for "new things" may have led them in the direction of this "new birth, new conception." Some Gnostic texts speak of the potential for women to become like men, once past their childbearing years.

58. There is, though, a J story about Lamech, who had two wives (Adah and Zillah, Gen. 4:19–24), but none by the name of Bathenosh.

59. The assumption is based on the biblical text, where he is described as the son born to Lamech (Gen. 5:28); after some time more children are born to him (5:30).

60. The sectarians manifest an obsession with "truth" as well as "lying" (the Spouter of Lies). All of these linguistic usages highlight the *Genesis Apocryphon*'s (and particularly Lamech's) concern with the "truth" about Bathenosh. Moreover, that "truth" seems to be reduced to sexual matters. Similarly, if a *sôṭâ* (a woman who sexually digressed) is telling the "truth," the bitter water that she drinks will ultimately redeem her.

61. Philo's description of the virginal number seven comes to mind too: "the essentially motherless . . . begotten by the father of the universe alone" (see Baer, *Philo's Use of the Categories Male and Female*, 50). We show again and again that the sectarians, in a sense, co-opted from the Goddess the holy number seven.

62. This particular idea is even more pressing if one accepts the notion, as the Christian polemicist Tertullian (100 C.E.) did in his *Veil of the Virgins*, that the sperm was already a child immediately after ejaculation. See our more complete discussion of this issue in chapter 6.

63. *Qumran Cave 4*, ed. Allegro, DJD 5:11.

64. The common approach to this psalm is that the speaker discusses a very turbulent period in Jewish and/or sectarian history. See Licht, *The Hodayot Scroll*.

65. Compare Cain and Abel and the twins, Esau and Jacob.

66. The commentary on this hymn is fairly extensive and "violent." For example, scholars such as Sigmund Mowinckel, Lou H. Silberman, Frank M. Cross, and John M. Oesterreicher reject a messianic interpretation. See S. Mowinckel, "Some Remarks on Hodayot 39:5–20," *Journal of Biblical Literature* 75 (1956): 276ff. See also Oesterreicher, "The Community of Qumran," *The Bridge* 2 (1956): 131. By contrast, John Allegro, Matthew Black, Krister Stendahl, J. Dupont-Sommer, John V. Chamberlain, etc. are of the opinion that this is a messianic text. The latter (Chamberlain) refers to the sect as the mother of the Messiah ("Another Qumran Thanksgiving Psalm," *Journal of Near Eastern Studies* 14 [1955]: 37. Jean Daniélou says: "it is definitely a question of the messiah" (*The Dead Sea Scrolls and Primitive Christianity* [Baltimore: Helicon Press, 1958] 78).

67. J. A. Sanders, *The Psalms Scroll of Qumran Cave 11* (DJD 4; Oxford: Clarendon, 1965) 96–97 (Psalm 151A).

68. Incidentally, David/the Teacher of Righteousness is a poet/psalmist who associates himself with some/Goddess accouterments: "musical instruments and a lyre." See Sanders, *Psalms Scroll*, 86–87 (Psalm 140, xxvii:2).

CHAPTER FOUR: SPEAKING IN TONGUES

1. Gunnar Berenfelt, *A Study on the Winged Angel* (Stockholm: Almqvist & Wiksell, 1968) 18.

2. Ibid., 11–16.

3. While biblical "angels" as such do not have names, the sometimes monstrous "cherubim" and "seraphim" do.

4. Gabriel is the angel who appeared to both Elizabeth and Mary in the miraculous annunciation scenes in Luke. Therefore, it has been suggested that Gabriel is rooted in female myths. A folk story tells of "how *she* [our emphasis] takes the invariably protesting soul from paradise, and instructs it for the nine months while it remains in the womb of its mother" (Malcolm Godwin, *Angels, An Endangered Species* [New York: Simon & Schuster, 1990] 44).

5. "Whoever has murmured against the foundations of the community shall be expelled and shall not return" (1QS 7:17). See also other reasons for expulsion, which, by and large, relate to a member's behavior contrary (to the community):1QS 8:21–24; 6:27–7:2; 7:22–23.

6. In that testament, the birth of Solomon is also associated with a virgin.

7. The story recorded in *Hagigah* 14b is about the four rabbis who entered the Pardes (orchard = paradise); three of them were hurt in one manner or another (in fact, one became "another" = *ʾaḥēr* = abandoned Judaism), and only R. Akiba (the great mystic of the age of Bar Kochba) entered the "orchard" and returned safely. The legend's purpose is to highlight the difficulties of mystical journeys and to warn those who do wish to undertake such endeavors to be fully

prepared. See Joseph M. Baumgarten, "The Qumran Sabbath Shirot and Rabbinic Merkabah Traditions," *Revue de Qumran* 49–52 (Oct. 1988): 208–13. See also the chapter entitled "Hymns and Mysteries" in Dead Sea Scrolls Uncovered, 227–28.

8. See Scholem, *Jewish Gnosticism.*

9. Cherubim in later thought were considered an order of angels.

10. Baumgarten, "Qumran Sabbath Shirot," 206–7.

11. These clear images, though, are also related to the world of the Goddess and particularly to fertility and birth. Brick stools, for example, were used for the birthing process itself.

12. Carol Newsom, *Songs of the Sabbath Sacrifice: A Critical Edition* (Atlanta: Scholars Press, 1985).

13. Ibid., 17.

14. The "seasonal" order (*mớēd*) is associated both with a festival celebrated in its time and with a woman's "due time" to give birth (see the confrontation between Sarah and the angel about the birth of Isaac). Qumran literature attests to the sectarians' interest in both of these "due times."

15. Newsom, *Songs,* 17–18.

16. For example, Lev. 19:2: "You should be holy because I, Yahweh your God, am holy." Further, Exod. 9:6: "And you shall be to me a kingdom of priests and a holy nation." See also Deut. 4:2.

17. Newsom makes the point about the form of the *Songs,* which is heavily focused on the number seven and the Sabbath (*Songs,* 13).

18. Newsom observes that in the book of *Jubilees* "the two highest angel classes, the angels of the Presence and the angels of Sanctification, share with Israel two marks of distinction—Sabbath observance and circumcision (*Jub.* 2:18)" (*Songs,* 20).

19. On the role of Melchizedek in the Dead Sea Scrolls, see Paul J. Kobelski, *Melchi-ṣedeq and Melchi-reša<* (Washington, DC: Catholic Biblical Association, 1981) 49–74. Melchizedek is presented in 11QMelch as the heavenly redeemer of the sons of light.

20. See Newsom, *Songs,* 97.

21. Ibid., 19.

22. See Carol Meyers, "Cherubim," in *Anchor Bible Dictionary,* 1:899–900. Though the Bible refers to cherubim in various complex contexts (sometimes as being the closest guards of Yahweh), they do finally develop in the West as baby winged creatures.

23. Column 8 of the *Damascus Document* describes in some detail the fate of those who ultimately betray them.

24. Newsom, *Songs,* 19.

25. See Scholem, *Major Trends,* 49–51.

26. Newsom, *Songs,* 63.

27. It is possible that the sign of the zodiac assigned to this time was Gemini, the twins. See Wise, *Thunder in Gemini.*

28. Newsom, 213–14.

29. In Exodus, the anointment is that of the ark of the covenant.

30. Newsom tentatively suggests that it is possible to read this word (she translates it as "perfect light") in line with a similar one in 1QH 18:29 and 4:6 as "double light" (*ôrātîm*) which means "daybreak" (*Songs,* 231). 'Ôrātayim would be "double light": the sun and the morning star.

31. See William Hugh Brownlee, *Interpreter's One Volume Commentary on the Bible,* 427. Further: "Trade in purple dye and purple-dyed clothing . . . aided Tyre during the Greco-Roman period, as remains of abundant shells located near the city indicate. In addition, the murex snail shell, from which purple dye was made, is found on the reverse imperial coins of Tyre. The trade was lucrative, although (according to Pliny) the dying process was smelly" (Douglas R. Edwards, "Tyre," in *Anchor Bible Dictionary,* 6:691).

32. The word *riqmâ* is used also in the context of the fall of Sisera (Judg. 5:30). Priestesses were always associated with spectacular dress.

33. There are similar fire images in Ezekiel and Psalms.

34. Elsewhere the Dead Sea Scrolls utilize this image in CD 2:5 as well as in 4Q487 in DJD 7:5.

35. See Newsom's discussion of the word *badan,* which appears sixteen times in the *Šîrôt.* In one context at least, it could mean "short sleeveless coat"; in other contexts it is fairly clear that the meaning is indeed related to some kind of clothing (*Songs,* 283–84).

36. Newsom, *Songs,* 67.

37. Newsom had already observed that this passage should not be read as being associated with "priestly garments" because not all four colors are mentioned (*Songs,* 337).

38. Allegro, *Sacred Mushroom,* 69; see also the use of the "hour of incense" in Luke 1:10.

39. Interestingly, the Egyptians, who are thought to have originated the Hebrews' practice of circumcision, probably used drugs for that surgery, as suggested by two reliefs in the "tomb of Ankh-ma-Hor at Saqqara (VIth dynasty). In one of the drawings . . . a man is standing and in front of him is a kneeling person called the 'circumcising priest,' holding an oblong object applied vertically to the organ to be operated on. . . . The face of the patient shows no pain. The operator says: 'This ointment is to make it acceptable,' from which it has been concluded that the drawing represents a form of anesthesia" (Daral-Al-Maaref, *Health and Healing In Ancient Egypt* [Cairo: Zeinab el Dawakhly, 1963] 96).

40. Dale C. Allison, "The Silence of Angels: Reflections on the Songs of the Sabbath Sacrifice," *Revue de Qumran* 49–52 (Oct. 1988). Allison draws attention to the following texts in order to demonstrate the point about "angel language": 1 Cor. 3:1 and 2 Cor. 12:4; see also his p. 190 n. 6, as well as *Testament of Job* 48:2 and 50:2, the last statement of which reads: "And she spoke in the dialect of the cherubim, glorifying the master of virtues by exhibiting their splendor" (p. 191).

41. Ibid.

42. Ibid., 191–92. Allison enumerates the various references to ecstatic language in the Apocrypha, Pseudepigrapha, and the Dead Sea Scrolls.

43. Ibid., 192.

44. Ibid. Allison cites various references to silence in heaven in the *Šîrôt* (p. 193). "God reveals himself in silence" and humble silence is the appropriate response to God's self-revelation or theophany (p. 194). Silence is also a vehicle of praise, as is particularly manifested in *Sefer Harazim* (the Book of Mysteries) (p. 195). Finally, "silence is the language of the kingdom of Heaven" (pp. 196–97).

45. See Carol A. Newsom, "Merkabah Exegesis in the Qumran Sabbath Shirot," *Journal of Jewish Studies* 38 (1987): 11–30; the author suggests that the text was deliberately interested in heavenly sounds.

46. See *Jub.* 2:18, referred to by Newsom (*Songs,* 20).

47. The Rechabites make their first appearance in the time of Jeremiah (2 Kgs 10:15); they reappear during the time of the millennium committed to purity of a very special kind: "Remove clothes from your body, do not drink a carafe of wine, and do not eat bread from fire, and do not drink liquor and honey until the Lord hears your petition" (*The History of the Rechabites, Vol I: The Greek Recension,* trans. and ed. James H. Charlesworth [Atlanta: Scholars Press, 1982] 51). Presumably, this type of extreme behavior will cause God to have mercy on Jerusalem (p. 53). The Rechabites lived in caves, nude, in a quasi-animalistic state: "with us there is no vine, nor cultivated field, nor is there a house" (p. 67).

48. Newsom already made that observation (*Songs,* 30).

49. See also 4Q403 1 i 24; 1 i 30-31; 4Q404 frag. 5, line 4; 4Q405 frag. 13, line 5; frag. 17, line 3; 11QŠirŠabb frags. 2, 1, 9, line 5.

50. This is the seventh psalm, where there are numerous references to "tongues."

51. See Newsom, *Songs,* 69; as well as 4Q213–214, which uses a similar terminology in imploring God to remove "evil and fornication" from the speaker (see Eisenman and Wise, *Dead Sea Scrolls Uncovered,* 137).

52. This phrase may be compared with the godly revelation to Elijah, described as a mystery, in 1 Kgs. 19:12. There, after the noise and the fire, there was "a voice of thin stillness."

53. In line with other sectarian pronouncements about extraordinary, secret revelations that have been bestowed on them.

54. In John 3:29–32 we read: "The bride is only for the bridegroom and yet the bridegroom's friend, who stands there and listens, is glad when he hears the bridegroom's voice. The same joy I feel, and now it is complete . . . he who is born of the earth is earthly himself and speaks in an earthly way. He who comes from heaven [i.e., Jesus] bears witness to the things he has seen and heard." We will see that there is a "friend" in a similar context in Qumran's Marriage Ritual.

55. The rabbis assign Psalm 91 to be thus recited. A recension of this psalm from Qumran Cave 11 has been published in *Revue Biblique* 72 (1965): 210–17. See also Sanders, *Psalms Scroll of Qumran,* 86.

56. Newson, *Songs,* 64; see also Newsom's comments on p. 46 and the various Ezekiel references about the same.

57. A similar event is narrated in Luke 1:42, where Elizabeth, the mother of John the Baptist, gives a "loud cry" when she is filled and made fertile by the Holy Spirit.

58. Newsom suggests an interesting scenario related to the story in Zechariah (*Songs,* 67).

59. The Hijras, "impotent and emasculated men, have this traditional role of conferring blessings of fertility on newborn males and on newlyweds. . . . As ritual performers, they are viewed as vehicles of the divine power of the Mother Goddess, which transforms their impotence into the power of generativity" (Serena Nanda, *Neither Man Nor Woman: The Hijras of India* [Belmont, Calif.: Wadsworth, 1990] 5). A full description of the operation and its attendant ideology follows: "The client's penis and scrotum are tightly tied with a string, so that a clean cut can be made. The client looks at the picture of Bahuchara and constantly repeats her name. . . . This apparently produces a trance-like state during which the dai ma [midwife] takes the knife from her sari and makes two quick opposite diagonal

cuts. The organs—both penis and testicles—are completely separated from the body. A small stick is put into the urethra to keep it open. None of the hijras . . . felt any pain . . . ; it was variously described as 'a small pinch' or 'like an ant bite.' . . . No stitches are made in the wound after the surgery, and the wound is healed through repeated applications of hot *gingili* (sesame seed) oil and heat to prevent infection" (pp. 27–28).

60. See Carlo Ginsburg, *Ecstasies: Deciphering the Witches' Sabbath,* trans. R. Rosenthal (New York: Penguin, 1991) 226–95.

61. In 1 Chr. 15:17–24; 16:4–7; 25; there were singers among the Levites in David's time. W. F. Albright suggests that David originated musical guilds ("The List of Levitic Cities," in *Louis Ginzberg Jubilee Volume,* ed. Saul Lieberman [New York: American Academy of Jewish Research, 1945] 49–73).

62. The priests, in addition to supervising slaughter and the raising of animals—and gelding was a well-known technique in the ancient world—are also the healers of the ancient world. Undoubtedly, Aaron's magical knowledge helps in the brothers' performance in front of the pharaoh. Not by accident, Zipporah, Moses' wife, performs a circumcision on him and/or their son or both, an act which saves the life of the Israelite/Egyptian savior (Exod. 4:24–26).

63. Nehemiah, who is portrayed in the Masoretic Text as "the king's cupbearer" (1:11b), is referred to in the Septuagint as "the king's eunuch." Jacob Myers's new translation, introduction, and commentary on *Ezra Nehemiah* (New York: Doubleday, 1981) harmonizes the Hebrew and Greek traditions by suggesting that the cupbearer was an important official in the Persian royal household and that he was a eunuch because he served in the queen's presence (p. 96). There is, of course, the fairly intriguing story in Acts 8:26–40 about the so-called Ethiopian eunuch, who was converted to Christianity through the deacon Philip. Eusebius claims that this Ethiopian "was the first of the Gentiles . . . the first fruits of the faithful . . . the first to return to his native land and preach the Gospel" (*Church History* 2.1.13). Origen, the most important theologian of the Greek church (d. 254), castrated himself in looking for Christian perfection. Ambrosius, Origen's patron and disciple, was a strict ascetic who never touched meat, wine, or women. Origen influenced Gregory of Nyssa (d. 395) who claimed that "Prelapsarian life was like that of the angels, who multiply without marriage and sexual reproduction" (*De hominis opificio* 17). See Uta Ranke-Heinemann, *Eunuchs for the Kingdom of Heaven* (New York: Doubleday, 1988). Heinemann recounts a story associated with Justin Martyr (p. 150), who "tells . . . about a young Christian man who had applied to the Roman governor for permission to be castrated. Back in the first century the Emperor Domitian (d. 96) had made castration subject to criminal punishment" (p. 46). This prohibition (close to the time of the sectarians) perhaps indicates the popularity and commonness of the phenomenon. John Chrysostom (d. 407) of the Eastern Church wrote: "In keeping with God's will man and woman dwelt in Paradise like angels, enflamed by no sensual lustfulness" (*In Genesin Homiliae* 15.3.4). As Heinemann aptly summarizes, "virginity and immortality, marriage and death belong together" (p. 55). In the fourth century as well, according to Ambrose (d. 397), virginity was the Christian virtue (p. 57).

64. The Yazidis of Sheik Adi, Iraq, are a vanishing sect that seems to carry many of the Qumranites symbols and rituals. Specifically, they are forbidden to disclose their secret rituals; they are involved in cleansing; they venerate fire and sun; and their "priest," Baba Shaweesh, became a eunuch "to resist the temptation

of the flesh." In fact, he carried out the operation himself with a knife and juice from some medicinal plants (C. Hedges, *New York Times,* 31 May 1993, p. 2).

65. See Newsom, *Songs,* 237. Clement of Alexandria (150–215) talks about psalms sung by virgins, the chorus of the just, and the hymn to the God of the universe. He suggests that "the union of many voices . . . constitutes . . . a single symphony, with the chorus obeying a single leader and instructor, the Logos, and finding its repose in truth itself" (quoted in *The Eucharist of the Early Christians,* ed. Willy Rordort et al. [New York: Pueblo, 1978] 107). Interestingly, Gregorian chants too attempt a monotone in unison rejecting any rhythmic elements that may be too "bodily."

66. Newsom, *Songs,* 163.

67. About bodily emissions, see CD cols. 12–15 as well as 1QS col. 7 and 11QTemple.

68. St. Augustine's (354–430) claim about human nature is in line with the sectarian legacy: "for by them [Adam and Eve] so great a sin was committed, that by it the human nature was altered for the worse, and was transmitted also to their posterity. . . . Is not this proved by the profound and dreadful ignorance which produces all the errors that enfold the children of Adam, and from which no man can be delivered without toil, pain, and fear?" Augustine goes on to list a variety of "sins" and "shortcomings" culminating thus: "shamelessness, fornications, adulteries, incests, and the numberless uncleannesses and unnatural acts of both sexes. . . . These are indeed the crimes of wicked men, yet they spring from that root of error and misplaced love which is born with every son of Adam" (*The City of God,* trans. M. Dods, J. J. Smith, and G. Wilson [Edinburgh, 1872] 22.22). In a very extreme statement about the hopelessness of people, Augustine emphasizes the uncontrollable aspect of sin, which therefore must be checked in a repressive fashion, as he advocates.

69. Eisenman and Wise, *Dead Sea Scrolls Uncovered,* 4Q477.

70. Water purification in 1QS and CD includes everyone.

71. See 11QMelch, which portrays Melchizedek as a judge "who will return them there and will proclaim to them liberty, forgiving them [the wrong doings] of all their iniquities."

72. Newsom, *Songs,* 203.

CHAPTER FIVE: THE VIRGIN OF THE DEAD SEA SCROLLS

1. About the matriarchs and their handmaids as priestesses, see Teubal, *Sarah the Priestess;* idem, *Hagar the Egyptian.*

2. Scholars now begin to study the possible connections between other pseudepigraphic works and the Dead Sea Scrolls. Of particular interest is Devorah Dimant, "New Light from Qumran on the Jewish Pseudepigrapha–4Q390," in *The Madrid Qumran Congress,* ed. Barrera and Montaner, 405–47. Of more immediate interest is a consistent scholarly claim that *Joseph and Aseneth* is an Essene work. See Mathias Delcor, "The Apocrypha and Pseudepigrapha of the Hellenistic Period," in *The Cambridge History of Judaism,* ed. W. D. Davies and Louis Finkelstein (Cambridge: Cambridge University Press, 1989) 2:502. The *Testament of Levi* in its Aramaic form has been found at Qumran as well as a curious Joseph fragment to which we refer farther on.

4. Eisenman and Wise, *Dead Sea Scrolls Uncovered,* 36. This specific passage

is considered by some to belong to a presumed Book of Noah that may have originated at Qumran. Although some of the characteristics of the birth of Noah story are present here (e.g., the special marks), we believe that the thrust and emphasis (especially the eternal secrets which imply an apocalyptic end) are more current and more in line with the sectarians' own life and environment. Moreover, we have already seen that the fragments of the birth story of Noah were important for the Qumranites in the context of a "special birth and a special conception." See the discussion about "the lost Book of Noah" in F. García Martínez, *Qumran and Apocalyptic* (Leiden: Brill, 1992) 1–44.

5. The lunar calendar is undoubtedly the older one, but it was overshadowed (and overtaken) with the rise of popular gods such as Re and Osiris. Plutarch (46–120 C.E.) in his classical work on Isis and Osiris (chapter 12) tries to synthesize both calendars telling about a game of checkers between Hermes (Greek god of commerce, invention, cunning, and theft) and Selene (Greek goddess of the moon) in which he won one-seventieth of each day from her. He combined these fractions to create five whole days, which he added to the 360 days of the lunar year. Rea's children were born on these days: On the first, Osiris; on the second, Horus; Seth on the third; Isis on the fourth; and Nephthys on the fifth (*Plutarch's On Isis and Osiris,* ed. with an introduction, translation, and commentary by J. Gwyn Griffiths (Cardiff: University of Wales Press, 1970) 134–37.

6. Aseneth's "foreignness" was always a problem for classical commentators and rabbis, who had to justify her marriage to one of the greatest and most righteous of patriarchs. See Robert Graves and Raphael Patai, *Hebrew Myths: The Book of Genesis* (New York: McGraw-Hill, 1966) 261–62.

7. Recall the importance of the stars and astrological signs for the Qumran sectarians.

8. Priests, holiness, purity, and righteousness—to name just a few of the main concepts in the Scrolls—are essential to *Joseph and Aseneth* as well.

9. The talmudic rabbis particularly use this adjective when describing Joseph. In the *Testaments of the Twelve Patriarchs* (specifically the one devoted to Joseph), he is portrayed as the model of righteousness, humility, and chastity; indeed, the patriarch emphasizes in his own words that he did not have an affair with his benefactor's wife. Some of the testaments found at Qumran (Levi, Kohath) probably were used because they deal with the priesthood, but it is likely that most of the testaments were known to the sectarians. In a recently published fragment (4Q213–214) Joseph is recognized as a "teacher" and "interpreter" of the Torah. The sectarians too (particularly the Teacher) interpreted the Torah. As for Joseph's chastity, it is a recognized theme throughout classical Jewish literature because of the unsuccessful attempts by the wife of Potiphar to seduce him.

10. See also James H. Charlesworth, *The Old Testament Pseudepigrapha and the New Testament* (Cambridge: Cambridge University Press, 1985) 85; and particularly the earlier work done by Leonhard Rost, *Judaism Outside the Hebrew Canon* (trans. David E. Green; Nashville: Abingdon, 1976). Rost leans toward the hypothesis of A. Dupont-Sommer, who sees the *Testaments* originating around 100 B.C.E. within the Qumran community. He claims that "it would be more accurate to say that the Damascus Document and the Testaments draw on the same tradition" (pp. 144–45). Harm W. Hollander mentions the possibility of links between Qumran and the *Testaments,* though he does not reach any final conclusions (*Joseph As An Ethical Model in the Testaments of the Twelve Patriarchs* [Leiden: Brill, 1981] 9).

11. Eileen Schuller, "4Q372 1: A Text About Joseph," *Revue de Qumran* 55 (Jan. 1990): 349–76. Schuller points to the "puzzling" aspect of this text and suggests that it be read as a polemic against the Samaritans, another sect that left its legacy within and without Judaism. We are not questioning Schuller's interpretation; rather, we wish to point to this fairly elaborate manuscript in order to make the point about Joseph's importance to the sectarians.

12. In Genesis, the pharaoh names Joseph *Zofnat Pa'neach* (41:45), which in Egyptian means "God speaks: he lives."

13. "Discipline" and "disciple" are associated both in the Bible and in the pseudepigrapha.

14. If a male child is born, the woman is required to separate from her spouse/man for seven days; if it is a girl, she must cleanse for two weeks.

15. The use of hormonal drugs to enhance beauty, maturity, and fertility was well known to the Egyptians. See Maaref, *Health and Healing,* 125–26; compare also the elaborate descriptions of the woman's physical beauty in the Song of Songs.

16. See our discussion of the number seven in the preceding chapter. Also pertinent is the importance of the Sabbath.

17. In Genesis, the woman is approached by the serpent presumably on his initiative. Here, Aseneth falls in love with Joseph and beseeches the God of the Hebrews, who responds by sending the angel to her.

18. Interestingly, women who wish to convert perform the ritual of immersion in the *mikva* too.

19. DJD 7, text 502, pp. 81–105.

20. We have already seen the use of the color white, and there are various other verses describing the white linen interwoven with violet and gold (e.g., 2:8; 3:6; 10:10; 14:14; 18:5).

21. In deference to the "conversion" version, but perhaps engraved with new signs at Qumran.

22. The "pomegranates" may very well be associated with worship of an Asherah and her promise of fecundity. See Marvin Pope, *Song of Songs* (Anchor Bible 7C; New York: Doubleday, 1977) 659–60.

23. Charles Burchard points out that doves may be related to the Hebrew *gôzālîm,* possibly stemming from *ʾĕgôzîm* (nuts) or may be a corrupt form of the Greek *tais persikais* (peaches) (*Old Testament Pseudepigrapha,* ed. Charlesworth, 2:206).

24. See particularly Marvin Pope's discussion of pomegranates in *Song of Songs* (New York: Doubleday, 1977). Further, the reference to "nuts" rather than "doves" lends more credence to the associations with the Garden of Eden, where the first humans were not allowed to eat meat.

25. "The pomegranate was in general use as a cultic object and was not unique to the worship of Yahweh in Jerusalem." Editorial, "The Pomegranate Scepter Head: From the Temple of the Cord or from a Temple of Asherah?" *Biblical Archaeology Review* 18:3 (May/June 1992): 43.

26. Horses were of utmost importance to the Egyptian power structure because of their rarity and therefore the price the pharaohs had to pay in order to have access to them (see discussion in the following chapter).

27. In the *Testament of Levi,* the various colorful vestments and the oil are related to priestly chosenness and glory: "To you and your posterity will be every-

thing desired in Israel, and you shall eat everything attractive to behold, and your posterity will share among themselves the Lord's table" (*T. Levi* 8:16).

28. We should remember that there are various legends that place Joseph in the pharaoh's court even as the next in line for succession to the throne. See Louis Ginzberg, *The Legends of the Jews,* trans. Henrietta Szold (5 vols.; Philadelphia: Jewish Publication Society, 1969) 2:74. See also the *Gospel of Thomas,* where a woman from the crowd said to him, "Blessed are the womb which bore you and the breasts which nourished you" (II. 2:79, in Robinson, 127).

29. The aggadah maintains that "God gives every man the wife he deserves, and so Asenath was worthy of being the helpmeet of Joseph and pious . . . [she] was slender like unto Sarah, beautiful like Rebekah, and radiant in appearance like Rachel" (Ginzberg, *Legends,* 2:170). Note that the rabbis place Aseneth in the company of three "barren" matriarchs.

30. We have to account for the presence of ʾaḥim ʾāšišim, which is translated as "older brothers." The concept ʾāšiš, though, is not necessarily always "old"; in fact, in its biblical manifestation, it is almost always related to raisins and/or some kind of aphrodisiac (Song of Songs). Raisins are dried up grapes—no longer succulent, bursting with seed. We therefore find that the language of "holy," "seed," "Adam," and ʾāšiš hints at a special communal ritual which may have involved a priest (holy) attempting to perpetuate his "seed." The ritual must have included ʾāšiš in either food or drink form, which might have enhanced the spirits of the participants and/or enhanced the possibility of conception. If ʾāšiš is to be read as "old," then the text might refer to a certain class of sectarians who were "old" in the sense of wise and experienced and, therefore, more trustworthy, where secrets (like conception rituals) came into play.

31. Married priests in the early church often became celibate after the age of thirty. See Aries and Duby, *History of Private Life,* 269.

32. Hagar, for example, stepped in for Sarah, who could not (or, maybe, would not) have children (see Teubal, *Hagar the Egyptian*). Hagar's status in the text is far from insignificant, and, as Teubal has shown, there is enough evidence to suggest that she was, in her own right, a great matriarch, and of the "family" of Sarah (Teubal, *Hagar the Egyptian,* 50–70).

33. The role of the Teacher and specifically references to stars and the end of days abound in the Scrolls and their companion texts. See CD; 1QM; 4QFlorilegium. Also, a recently published fragment about "the Son of God" (4Q246) says: "He will be called the son of God. . . . Like the shooting stars that you saw . . ." (Eisenman and Wise, *Dead Sea Scrolls Uncovered,* 68). We should also include the "War Prayer" which "evokes despair at the overwhelming losses of destruction . . ." which states: "[your gl]orification of one born of woman is certain, but see the destruction of the sons . . ." 1.5. Published as an isolated fragment in *Biblical Archaeology Review* (Nov./Dec. 1991): 65. Commentary and translation by Robert H. Eisenman.

Josephus narrates a "star" phenomenon in *Jewish War* as follows: "Thus there was a star resembling a sword which stood over the city, and a comet that continued a whole year . . . and at the ninth hour of the night so great a light shone round the altar and the holy house, that it appeared to be bright daytime; which light lasted for half an hour" (6.5.3). Interestingly, this sign occurred, according to Josephus, during the Passover holiday and it was commented on by various "prophets" who interpreted the events one way or the other. When the author of

Joseph and Aseneth introduces the "star" into his romance, he is clearly using a heavenly sign/symbol that must have stirred quite a few people who may have been able to relate to it on a concretely historical level.

34. In *Testament of Levi* 21 the priests are commanded to take "a wife in her virginity . . . a virgin of his own people" (vv. 13–14).

35. ". . . and he sent to call Uzziel his youngest brother, and [gave] to him [in marr]iage [Miri]am [his] daughter. [For he said] 'You (Miriam) are thirty years old'" (4Q543, 545–548 manuscript C i 5–6).

36. The rabbis tested for adultery by making the woman drink "waters of bitterness"; see the fifth tractate, *Sota,* in *Nashim.*

37. The oral tradition's stories about Miriam focus particularly on the well and its medicinal properties; in one of those stories, a leper who bathed in that well (placed at the Sea of Tiberias) was instantly cured. See Ginzberg, *Legends,* 3:50–54.

38. The question that is asked by scholars attempting to analyze this passage hinges on issues of ritual. John Collins summarizes that analysis by saying that "attempts to elucidate the references [to bread, wine, and oil] by analogies with the Christian eucharist, the Qumran meal, or the meal of the Therapeutae have been unsuccessful." The general conclusion reached by critics who analyzed this highly descriptive passage is somewhat murky and suggests both ritual and a more general characterization of the Jewish way of life. In other words, some commentators claim that if the text indeed describes an elaborate ritual, then it can be understood only within a more mystical framework. If this is the case, then "Joseph and Aseneth does not provide adequate reason for positing a mystic ritual which is otherwise unknown, since the formulaic language can be referred to the everyday rituals of Jewish life." See the introduction to *Joseph and Aseneth in Old Testament Pseudepigrapha,* ed. Charlesworth, 2:177–201 and 212. However, this solution is rather weak because it fails to account for the atmosphere as well as some of the other "mysterious" symbols and possible rituals present in the text.

39. There is also no question about the social, communal impact of foods. "The Lipit-Ishtar law code, for example, stipulates that a man with a childless wife who secures offspring from a common harlot must provide the harlot with grain, oil, and clothing" (*Ancient Near Eastern Texts,* 160). This ritualized practice as well places the food (and clothing) within an unmistaken fertility context.

40. In the *Genesis Apocryphon* (1QapGen) Abram performs a ritual of laying on of hands.

41. E.g., Song of Songs 5:4: "My loved one thrust his hand into the hole, and my inwards seethed for him."

42. In a very telling comparison, Paul's letter to the Romans deals with a similar issue using the same discourse: "While we were living in the flesh, our sinful passions, aroused by the law, were at work in our members to bear fruit for death. But now we are discharged from the law, dead to that which held us captive, so that we serve not under the old written code but in the new life of the spirit" (Rom. 7:5–6 RSV; see also 2 Cor. 3:6). Paul may be using the terms "law" and "spirit" in a polemical fashion, but he too points to the new environment that is created as a result of the work of the spirit of God. Indeed, that "spirit" is the justification for the basic antinomianism which permeates Paul's approach to the "new covenant." At all times, when new prophets and mystics arise, they challenge not only social conditions and customs but above all their underlying ideol-

ogy; and while sometimes these new prophets/mystics remain within the realm of current ideology, more often than not they boldly rewrite, revise, and interpret so as to clearly manifest that a totally new reality is about to dawn (or has already dawned) and therefore the old rules do not apply. In an even more relevant comparison with *Joseph and Aseneth,* the above Pauline texts suggest a transformation which is so radical and new that the "flesh" gives way to the "spirit." In the romance, too, Joseph sets up the framework for a new beginning for Aseneth, who is to be governed by the "spirit." Aseneth is about to be "fruitful" but not in the old way.

43. A most instructive example (from a contemporary text) is the role of Mary, who has a voice, comparable to the disciples, in the *Gospel of Thomas* (II. 2:21, Robinson, 120. So does Salome (II. 2:61), who claims that she is a disciple too. But their comments seem to get lost in the general male discourse of the Gospel.

44. In the book of Esther, for example, the combination of *nĕʿārâ bĕtûlâ* (girl/virgin) was used to denote very young teen-aged girls who were brought to the king's harem to first be properly pampered and then offered to the king (Esth. 2:2–3). In fact, in that text, the virgin/girls were carefully "oiled" (2:12).

45. One of the translators and commentators on this text argues that, while the wording of this quote is clearly reliant on various passages in Job (e.g., 36:6; 4:19; 10:9) and Genesis (2:7), it ultimately belongs to the milieu of the Wisdom of Solomon and the talmudic rabbis who claim: "I was modelled in flesh inside a mother's womb, / where, for ten months, in blood I acquired substance—the result of virile seed and pleasure, sleep's companion" (Wisd. Sol. 7:1–2). The elements of this quotation that are missing in the biblical view are the "virile seed" and the "blood"—one associated with the male and the other with the female. In rabbinic literature, the relationship between people and mortality is highlighted by the classical metaphor in the *Sayings of the Fathers:* "Know from where you come: from a stinking drop" (*Abot* 3:1). The sectarians agree with this general portrayal of people as "aspiring to the dust" and eating the "bread of worms." Furthermore, in other Qumran literature, the "I" refers to himself as being "made out of clay and kneaded with water" (1QH 1:22b); the clay is obviously part of the red soil imagery, and the water is associated here with semen. This is especially poignant because the next line comments on the "secret of nakedness and the source of a woman's blood (*niddâ*)."

46. Inanna talks about the death of the Goddess and her journey to the underworld. See Samuel N. Kramer, *The Sacred Marriage Rite* (Bloomington, Ind.: University of Indiana Press, 1969) 133.

47. In addition, God's might is expressed in the traditional recognition of his creative powers; he is thus described as creating "also the heavens and the stars" (1QH 1:15). Stars are also related to angels and saints who die and become stars. Indeed, in *Joseph and Aseneth* the star "rose as a messenger" (Greek *aggelos*) (v. 1); namely, as a sign. Also see reference to shooting stars in Eisenman and Wise, *Dead Sea Scrolls Uncovered,* 70.

48. The scene is somewhat reminiscent of the angel's appearance to Hagar in Genesis, when she is forlorn in the desert and ready to give in to despair. It should be remembered that in the Hagar incident the main governing image was a well and water, which signified the handmaid's spiritual independence from Sarah her mistress (Gen. 16:11–15).

49. The "lightning" related to the face is reminiscent of the god of lightning (Baal), who was also a god of fertility.

50. Eisenman and Wise, *Dead Sea Scrolls Uncovered,* 89. Also, the god Ra, who epitomized the sun.

51. Ibid., 141.

52. In a "motif analysis" essay, Michael Fishbane provides some more insights into the use of the phrase "living water" though he extends it to include the "well" too. Fishbane maintains that the Bible uses the phrase in the context of "life and nourishment"; later on in the Jewish tradition it is used as a metaphor for wisdom (Michael Fishbane, "The Well of Living Water: A Biblical Motif and its Ancient Transformations," in *"Sha'arei Talmon": Studies in the Bible, Qumran, and the Ancient Near East Presented to Shemaryahu Talmon,* ed. Michael Fishbane and Emanuel Tov [Winona Lake, Ind.: Eisenbrauns, 1992] 3–16). Fishbane's chapter is divided into four sections dealing with the various literary strata and sources that make use of the phrase "well of living water": the Bible, Qumran literature, Pseudepigrapha and ancient Christian and Gnostic sources, and ancient and early medieval rabbinic sources. He further points to a certain progression from the "well" as a symbol of physical and spiritual nourishment in the Bible to "the well" in CD 6:3–10, which "transform[s] the biblical passage into a religious history of the sect" (p. 7). The emphasis in the *Damascus Document,* according to Fishbane, is ultimately on the importance of Torah interpretation and understanding. The Torah becomes "a source of living instructions," and it provides "sustenance from mysterious depths" (p. 8). The author then proceeds to comment on two more quotations from the *Community Rule* (1QS 3:17–19) and the *Hodayot* scroll; he summarizes the function of the well motif in the Dead Sea Scrolls by saying: that "the well motif occurs on three distinct . . . levels . . . : the cosmic, the earthly, and the personal. The Torah is the dynamic link between these realms" (p. 9). The heavenly source of wisdom is ultimately transmitted to inspired "teachers" below and thus transforms them. Similarly, in 4 Ezra (4:38–41), where there is "pneumatic testimony" (p. 12) and in Ben Sira, who testifies that "through contact with divine wisdom, I . . . became a stream from a river" and "will pour out instruction like prophecy" (Sir. 24:31, 35) (pp. 12–13). Interestingly, the rabbinic sources point to "'the well which the patriarchs of the world, Abraham, Isaac, and Jacob, dug from olden times . . . Moses and Aaron . . . drew (it) forth . . . .' The history of this well is thus a genealogy of leadership and instruction" (p. 13). In one of the most interesting quotations from the rabbinic tradition (*Abot R. Nathan* B/37, in *Talmud Minor Tractates: Abot de-Rabbi Nathan,* ed. Solomon Schechter [New York: Feldheim, 1945]), the well of Miriam which disappeared from the desert after her death, "is given the status of one of the special things created by God prior to the first sabbath" (p. 13). We add the idea that Miriam's well is associated with Goddess fertility and thereby, a clan, a tribe, or a nation's immortality. Fishbane summarizes his fine essay by reflecting: "One may wonder . . . at the sensibility which nurtured the biblical figure . . . and which continued to sustain it as an active metaphor of the religious imagination" (p. 16). We suggest that this metaphor's power, in part, stemmed from the reality of procreation and insemination.

53. A major and quite typical polemic of early rabbinic Judaism deals with the problem of a *mamzēr,* or bastard. See Fred Rosner, "Artificial Insemination in Jewish Law," in *Jewish Bioethics,* ed. Fred Rosner and J. David Bleich (New York: Sanhedrin, 1979) 105–17.

54. Eisenman and Wise, *Dead Sea Scrolls Uncovered,* 62.

55. It is possible that the origin of all the sexually oriented water images and symbols can be found in the poem to Inanna, the great Sumerian epic (closely tied to Ur, Abraham's hometown); there, the Goddess "plucked the tree from the river; / I brought it to my holy garden. / I tended the tree, waiting for my shining throne and bed" (Wolkstein and Kramer, *Inanna,* 8). But because of various unkind (maybe even evil) forces that settle in the tree, the process of fertility comes to a halt. When the hero Gilgamesh enters the picture he attempts to remove the powers of distraction and provide his "sister" (Inanna) with the throne and the bed. In the guise of a warrior, Gilgamesh then "entered Inanna's holy garden" (p. 9). Interestingly, even the talmudic rabbis, in a later pronouncement, used the combination of "well" and "closed" to describe a virgin; and in the "blessing over virginity" the rabbis say: "a stranger shall not rule over (or on) a closed (intact) well." The Law (which contains all wisdom) is also inviolable.

56. "Hand" that "opens" in a "measured" way "according to the . . . sun" are sexual/fertility images; they are all sectarian symbols as well, particularly the allusion to the "sun" as a yardstick and "the season of heat" which can be read externally and internally—that is, the heat of the summer, which is sometimes treacherous (after all, these are desert communities) as well as the "heat" of the womb which indeed provides "strength" for the fetus.

57. Roman decency required nonharlots to have sex with their brassieres on. The act of intercourse was to be performed in the dark, and decent males were supposed to only touch, not caress, and only with their left hand (*A History of Private Life from Pagan Rome to Byzantium,* ed. Philippe Aries and Georges Duby [Cambridge, Mass.: Belknap Press of Harvard University, 1987] 203). We wonder if the left hand represents uncleanness, which is appropriate for this activity!

58. George Robert Stow Mean, *Thrice Greatest Hermes* (London: Theosophical Publishing Company, 1906) 1:273.

59. The whole image of a person who assumes redemptive, metaphorical meaning is very close to the Qumran sectarians, who also viewed themselves as refugees from corruption, who founded a "city of refuge" for themselves and others who wished to join "behind walls" and in the afterlife. There, indeed, they "repented" for their own sins as well as those of others; there too they formed a secretive, closed community that practiced purification and shunned the rest of the evil world.

60. Also, the sectarians are reluctant to articulate their more "secret" activities for fear of misunderstandings as well as retaliation by the established political order in Jerusalem. Their penchant for secrets was probably also a recognition on their own part that some of their rituals would have been questioned and looked upon as heretical. Ironically, the "veil" of secrecy that they voluntarily placed over their own deeds was never lifted and their ideology and practices remained "covered" for a significant period of time.

61. Aseneth tries to inquire about the "man" who is now communicating with her, thus imitating two other biblical heroes: Jacob/Israel and Manoah and his wife. In the Samson story, which is more directly relevant to Aseneth, the parents-to-be deal with the matter of the man/angel's name after he appears to them for the second time. While Manoah inquires of him outright about his name (13:17), Manoah's wife points out that she did not ask the angel for his name

(13:6). In a way, the answer that the man/angel gives Manoah (and his wife) in Judges is echoed in *Joseph and Aseneth.*

62. Abraham sets the table for the men/angels who come to tell him about Sarah's miraculous conception; in fact, she prepares the "cakes" while Abraham is busy with the lamb (Genesis 18). Manoah and his wife in Judges also prepare a meal which consists of a lamb that is ultimately consumed by fire (Judges 13). Further, in a most curious episode related to Saul and Samuel, after Saul's famous consultation with the necromancer (loosely translated as "witch," with all the negative connotations the Bible gives to powerful, spiritual women) in En Dor, she offers him a meal that she prepares herself in order to lift his spirits as well as ritually acknowledge that indeed the end is near and that he, like the lamb she prepares, will be offered as a communal sacrifice to the God of Samuel, who anoints David of the family of Jesse (1 Samuel 28).

63. In the story of the necromancer from En Dor, she, as both priestess and seer (not unlike the sibyls by millennium parlance), prepares the meal for Saul. Naturally, he resists quite strongly. The woman from En Dor not only sacrifices a calf (fatted for the occasion) but, like Sarah, bakes cakes.

64. "His [Belial's] rule shall not come to pass, but he will cause a multitude to be defiled (and) there will be no seed left. The mulberry bush will not produce wine, nor the bee honey" (4Q385–389 3 ii 4–6).

65. From very early on (Neolithic age), it was believed that bees arose out of the carcass of a bull (Baring and Cashford, *Myth of the Goddess,* 74). In addition, one of the most important functions of honey was embalming and preservation; the Egyptians used honey to preserve their dead bodies. "The Cretan New Year began at the summer solstice . . . and 20 July was the day when . . . Sirius rose in conjunction with the sun, as it did also in Sumeria and Egypt" (ibid., 119). Appropriately, Sirius was the star of both Inanna and Isis. Sirius's rising in the sky signaled the climax of the forty-day ritual celebration of the New Year at which time fermented mead (made of honey) was drunk by the participants; it was clearly an intoxicating drink which led to further celebration and ecstasy. The humming of the bees must also be taken into account because they are thus perceived as representing the voice of the Goddess, or the sound of creation (Virgil, *Georgics* 4.63). One of the greatest of Hebrew prophets is Deborah (the bee). She is not only a holy woman who carries the word of God but she sings (the Song of Deborah, which is strongly linked with the Song of Moses); she is also referred to as a mother in Israel (Judges 5).

66. Scholars invariably focus on the honey and honeycomb as harking back to the wilderness manna episodes, where the manna is described as having a variety of tastes, most predominantly, the taste of honey. In a more esoteric context, though not too far removed from *Joseph and Aseneth,* the Gnostics talk about ". . . a pure seed is kept in storehouses that are secure" ("Authoritative Teaching," VI. 3.25; in Robinson, 279).

67. Similar practices mixing sperm, blood, and mother's milk were spelled out in later Gnostic texts. Stephen Gero, "Encartitite Orthodoxy and Libertine Heresy," in *Nag Hammadi and Early Christianity,* ed. Charles W. Hedrick and Robert Hodgson (Peabody, Mass.: Hendrickson, 1986) 294–95. There are references to "planting" in Drower, *The Secret Adam,* 18, 20, 31, 65.

68. Ignatius of Antioch, in his *Epistle to the Smyrnaeans,* asserts quite adamantly that Christ "truly was of the race of David according to the flesh; . . .

truly born of the virgin . . ." (1.4). In the apocryphal *Gospel of the Birth of Mary,* the angel tells Joachim (the prospective "father") that his future daughter will be born "in a more wonderful manner . . . and that which is born will appear to be not the product of lust, but the gift of God" (2.5). Appropriately, in the same text, the author associates the pregnancy of Mary's mother (Anna) with "the first mother of your nation Sarah . . . in whom the promise was made a blessing to all nations." Further, "Rachel . . . was mother of Joseph who . . . delivered many nations from perishing with hunger." And, as if delivering a thesis on special birth narratives, the *Gospel of the Birth of Mary* goes on to instruct us: "Who among the judges was more valiant than Samson, or more holy than Samuel? And yet both their mothers were barren" (2.6–8). But in a "feminist" twist, detailing the miraculous birth of a woman, the narrator, using the voice of the angel, tells Joachim that "Anna your wife shall bring you a daughter, and you shall call her name Mary" (v. 9b). The angel continues to instruct Joachim, as the angel in the annunciation to the wife of Manoah did in Judges—namely, "She shall . . . be devoted to the Lord from her infancy . . . . She shall neither eat nor drink anything which is unclean . . ." and shall become a resident of the temple (priestess) "so she may not fall under any slander or suspicion of what is bad" (v. 11). When the same angel appears to Anna, he announces that he is not "a spirit" (3.1) and that he was sent to "inform" her that her future daughter "shall be blessed above all women . . . shall there [in the temple] serve the Lord . . . shall abstain from every unclean thing, and never know any man. But, being an unparalleled instance without any pollution or defilement, and a virgin not knowing any man, shall bring forth a son . . . who shall be the Saviour of the world" (2.2–5). The same concerns that were uppermost in the minds of the sectarians persist in this text as well: virginity, pollution, corruption, genealogy, and perfection. Additionally, the *Gospel of the Birth of Mary* is very close in spirit and outcome to *Joseph and Aseneth;* indeed, Mary is described in terms that are reminiscent of Aseneth, though we are fully prepared for her "miraculous" conception from the very start.

In the *Protevangelion of James* there is a very similar story about Joachim and Anna; it is instructive to observe that the initial emphasis of that Gospel is on Anna (rather than Joachim), who, before the angel appears to her, puts on her wedding garment ("cleansed her head and put on her bridal garments") and proceeds to "her garden" where she prays to God. The main concept of a barren/virgin/woman preparing for a special ritual of conception which is attended by an angel (in the *Protevangelion of James,* there are two angels) is repeated once again. Justin Martyr (110–166) says that he was "born of God in a peculiar manner, different from ordinary generation" (*Apology* 1.22). Further, that Mary's conception was "like Adam and Eve" (*Dialogue* 84), see *Saint Justin Martyr: The First Apology, the Second Apology, Dialogue with Trypho, Exhortations to the Greeks, Discourse to the Greeks, the Monarchy or the Rule of God,* ed. Thomas B. Falls (Washington, D.C.: Catholic University Press, 1965).

69. Quoted in J. Gwyn Griffiths, *The Conflict of Horus and Seth* (Liverpool: Liverpool University Press, 1960) 104. Griffiths's main source for this legend is Pierret's *Etudes egyptologiques,* 1:22. The author goes on to suggest that Isis, "since she revived the dead Osiris, was in a way responsible for both aspects of the sexual act" (p. 105).

70. Quoted in Lamy, *Egyptian Mysteries,* 15.

71. *Gospel of Philip* II, 3.59, in Robinson, *Nag Hammadi Library,* 135.

72. The symbolism of the "right hand" is important in Kabbalistic lore as well.

73. All of them were associated with "rings" of power: Joseph was given the ring of the pharaoh; Daniel, the ring of the Babylonian emperor; and Tamar, the ring of Judah.

74. There is also a strong ring association in the story of Esther, another Jewish woman who gained power in a foreign court and brought about communal redemption.

75. We have commented on Joseph's presence in Qumran literature; certainly Daniel was a major source of inspiration, and Tamar is the "righteous" woman in Genesis who is the direct matriarch of the Davidic line.

76. All quotes from the Sacrament of Marriage in the Byzantine Rite were taken from John Meyendorff, *Marriage: An Orthodox Perspective* (New York: St. Vladimir's Seminary Press, 1975).

CHAPTER SIX: HORSE POWER

1. There are two significant hypotheses related to the Indo-European invasions: first, the Gimbutas model of the Kurgan invasion "pictured the original Indo-Europeans as mounted warriors ranging out from a homeland north of the Black Sea beginning in about 4000 B.C." (*Language of the Goddess*). According to this model, "the first wave of invasions brought the warriors to Greece by about 3500 B.C.E. thence they spread north and south." They moved into Anatolia (Turkey) and the Levant around 2500 B.C.E. The other model, that of Gamkrelidze-Ivanov, proposes their origins south of the Black Sea in the Caucasus Mountains and Anatolia itself. In either case, remains are documented in the ancient Anatolian city of Hattusas close to the Black Sea. (Lecture with maps by Dr. Mark Stefanovich, UCLA Symposium on language origins: "Echoes of Ancient Voices: Early Indo-Europeans and their world," 6.6.92).

2. The word "Hyksos" derives from the Egyptian *heka-khasut* (rulers of foreign lands).

3. Francis L. Griffith, *The Leyden Papyrus: An Egyptian Magical Book* (New York: Dover, 1974) 203.

4. This is not to say that there was not sporadic use of horses for war at other times in Jewish history. It is possible, for example, that during the Bar Kochba rebellion horses were used.

5. Edward Yoxen, *Unnatural Selection? Coming to Terms With the New Genetics* (London: Heinemann, 1986).

6. Quoted in Wilfred J. Feingold, *Artificial Insemination* (Springfield, Ill.: Charles C. Thomas, 1964) 5.

7. *Science News,* June 1990, 340.

8. *Science News,* June 1993, 22.

9. Ibid.

10. Arthur Vernon, *The History and Romance of the Horse* (New York: Dover, 1946) 39–58.

11. In Indian myth for example, Indra, the sun-god, rode across the heavens with a flaming chariot drawn by almighty steeds that glistened and added to the brilliance of the sun. In Celtic mythology too the horse is connected to a fertility goddess, Epona, who actually penetrated the Roman world as well. Epona became the protective goddess of horses and was adopted by Roman cavalry units. The

cult of Epona spread from Spain to eastern Europe and northern Italy to Britain. The horse goddess is a mother goddess who protects the living and the dead. See Carlo Ginzburg, *Ecstasies: Deciphering the Witches' Sabbath,* trans. Raymond Rosenthal (New York: Penguin, 1991) 104–5 and 116–17.

12. The horse is also a mother symbol, as in the mythical report about Boreas, who assumed the form of a stallion and mated with the mares of Erichthonius (the king of Athens who introduced the worship of Athene), who "turned their vulvae" to him, the god of the North Wind, to be fertilized without real stallions. "And from this union were born twelve young mares so light of step that 'they ran across fields of standing corn without bruising an ear of grain and over the crests of the sea without wetting their feet'" (*New Larousse Encyclopedia of Mythology* [Middlesex: Hamlyn, 1968] 144). This particular legend humanizes the horses to an extraordinary degree and places them within a framework that reverberates with ideas like fertility as it is related to "cornfields" and "grain" as well as the immaculate conception, which assumes the form of the hidden god Boreas impregnating mares who give birth to remarkable horses or, quasi horse/spirits ("light of step").

13. Eusebius, *Ecclesiastical History,* trans. Christian Frederick Cruse (Grand Rapids: Baker, 1987) 184.

14. Isaiah's vision of the end of days, which articulates a time when swords will be converted into plowshares, points to "a land filled with horses" as an image of idolatry and total self-reliance (2:7–8).

15. Robert E. Boling and G. Ernest Wright, *Joshua* (New York: Doubleday, 1982); they comment on the "light war chariot . . . introduced to western Asia by the Aryans, near the beginning of the eighteenth century B.C." Boling and Wright go on to say: "Such military efficiency reflects a feudal system in which the charioteers . . . belong to a class enjoying special privileges and performing special services for the king" (p. 307).

16. The word "multiply" used in the text, derives from the verb *rbh* (literally, "multiply") and has sexual connotations.

17. Scholars generally agree that the dates offered by Ezekiel are accurate and that the book's contents fall between 593 and 571. In 598 Nebuchadnezzar arrived in Jerusalem to quell a rebellion against Babylon undertaken by King Jehoiakim and his heir Jehoiachin. The entire royal establishment in Jerusalem surrendered to Nebuchadnezzar, who then proceeded to appoint Zedekiah, Jehoiachin's uncle, as the new king; see 2 Kings 23 and 24 for more details of the rebellion as well as Josephus's rendition of the same in *Antiquities* 10.7.1.

18. There have been various attempts to reconstruct the history of the sectarians from their key document, CD (*Damascus Document*). Ben Zion Wacholder claims that the Qumran sectarians headed by the Teacher of Righteousness indeed duplicated the action of King Josiah during the First Commonwealth (*The Dawn of Qumran: The Sectarian Torah and the Teacher of Righteousness* [Cincinnati: Hebrew Union College, 1983]). The Torah found in the Temple by Hilkiah the priest and endorsed by the king led to major reforms in the religion of Israel. One of the outcomes of this reform was the banishment of the Asherah and her worshipers from the Temple in Jerusalem. The leader of the Qumranites, another son of Zadok, claims that he found a hidden Torah, which the sect then followed very strictly and which clearly maintains that various customs and behaviors accepted by the majority of Jews in Judea, were anathema. Moreover, according to

that "hidden Torah" the Teacher assumed prophetic as well as priestly stature and was charged with conveying the word of God to his disciples; those who joined and accepted his words eventually became holy, whereas those who did not would be destroyed in the coming apocalyptic war (see specifically pp. 101–40).

Another attempt to relate history to the texts of Qumran suggests that the major antagonistic concepts of the sectarians originating with the Teacher reflect a deep-seated dislike (if not hatred) of the Herodian court and the Temple associated with it. Accordingly, the sectarians' emphasis on incest and other excessive or forbidden sexual practices hint at practices of the Herodian court.

19. "Indeed, the emergence of the extensive imperial states of the ancient world, such as the New Kingdom in Egypt and the Hittite and the later Assyrian empires, was possible in part because of the extensive use of horse-drawn chariots" (Carol L. Meyers and Eric M. Meyers, *Haggai, Zechariah 1-8* [New York: Doubleday, 1987] 317).

20. There is an equation here of warrior energies with sexual energies.

21. Yigael Yadin, in his discussion of this particular reference to horses, speculates about the issue of sexual purity but finally decides against it (see *The Scroll of the War of the Sons of Light against the Sons of Darkness*, trans. Batya and Chaim Rabin [London: Oxford University Press, 1962]).

22. Solomon H. Steckoll, "Preliminary Excavation Report in the Qumran Cemetery," *Revue de Qumran* 23/6 (Feb. 1968): 323–44. It was actually determined that the man (horseman) was around forty years old and that he sustained lower limb bone changes.

23. E.g., Elephantine and Egypt (Leontopolis) were known for their financial support of Jerusalem even though they had their own temples to which they contributed as well.

24. Hershel Shanks, "The Qumran Settlement," *Biblical Archaeology Review* 19/3 (May/June 1993): 62–65.

25. Ibid. Shanks, though, finally concludes that there is not strong enough evidence to assert flatly that indeed the "settlement" was a villa; he tends to agree with Roland de Vaux's earlier statements that the place was more "monastic" in nature.

26. Norman Golb agrees that Qumran led a popular movement but disagrees with our view (and most scholars) that the Dead Sea Scrolls are a sectarian library (*Who Wrote the Dead Sea Scrolls?*) 3–150.

27. See Michael Wise's lecture, "About *Dead Sea Scrolls Uncovered*," April 3, 1993, University of Judaism. Wise also added that an ostracon from Masada reads "sons of light."

28. See See E. Isaac's introduction to *1 Enoch* (*Old Testament Pseudepigrapha* 1:7); as well as Matthew Black, *The Book of Enoch or I Enoch* (Leiden: Brill, 1985).

29. For a full discussion of the history of horses in Egypt, see George Posener, *Dictionary of Egyptian Civilization* (New York: Tudor, 1959) 128–29.

30. Josephus describes his family as being "not ignoble" and as having "a connection with the priesthood [which] is the hallmark of an illustrious line. . . . Moreover, on my mother's side I am of royal blood" (*Life* 1.1–2).

31. The whole of column 47 is dominated by the word *ṭāhôr*. See Yigael Yadin, *Megilat Hamikdash* (*The Temple Scroll*) (in Hebrew; 3 vols.; Jerusalem: Israel Exploration Society, 1977) 2:142–44.

32. *Midrash Rabbah Lamentations*, ed. H. Friedman and Maurice Simon (New York: Soncino, 1983) I.13:41.

33 "Authoritative Teaching," in Robinson, *Nag Hammadi Library,* 279.

34. Julius Prease, *Biblical and Talmudic Medicine,* ed. Fred Rosner (New York: Sanhedrin Press, 1978) 378. Soranus reports in 100 C.E. in Galatia that pigs became fatter following removal of their uterus. Galen asserts the same thing about "female testicles" (i.e., ovaries). Other reports suggest that the excision of the testicles in the Orient was for the purpose of youthful beauty (ibid., p. 377).

35. Adolf Erman, *Life in Ancient Egypt,* trans. H. M. Tirard (New York: Dover, 1971) 438.

36. Ibid., 41.

37. Cheri Pies, *Considering Parenthood* (San Francisco: Spinsters/Aunt Lute, 1988) 167–79.

38. Julius Preuss, *Biblical and Talmudic Medicine,* trans. and ed. F. Rosner (New York: Sanhedrin Press, 1987) 41.

39. See Paul Ghalioungui, *Magic and Medical Science in Ancient Egypt* (London: Hodder & Stoughton, 1963) 68.

40. Galen, *On the Natural Faculties* (Loeb Classical Library; London: Heinemann, 1991) 2:229.

41. See Tosaffot, *Ḥullin* 42b; *Zebaḥim* 116a; *Sanhedrin* 78a, where these unavoidable conclusions (from animals to humans) were indeed drawn.

42. Rabbi Ishmael related that Cleopatra brought some of her pregnant slave women who were sentenced to death to the pharaoh, who cut their bellies open and found that a male fetus was formed at forty days and a female at eighty days (*Tosefta Niddah* 4:17).

43. See Ghalioungui, *Magic and Medical Science.* All scholarly books dealing with the topic refer to various Egyptian papyri which describe medical procedures first-hand. Some of the most extensive references are in the Ebers, Edwin Smith, Carlsberg and the Karhoun papyri; the latter is dedicated mainly to gynecology and is similar to the Berlin papyrus.

44. Ghalioungui, *Magic and Medical Science,* 69.

45. This story is similar in overall impact to the story of Isis, who "molded" her son with the help of Osiris's artificial penis. For God "molding" a uterus for Sarah, Rebekah, and Ruth, see *Genesis Rabbah* 47:2 and 63:5; *Ruth Rabbah* 8:14.

46. Preuss, *Biblical and Talmudic Medicine,* 377.

47. See also *Encyclopedia Judaica* on "Medicine."

48. John M. Riddle (*Contraception and Abortion from the Ancient World to the Renaissance* [Cambridge, Mass.: Harvard University Press, 1992] 28).

49. Arthur Caplan, "History Shows birth control nothing new," *L.A. Times,* June 21, 1992. Caplan, who is the director of the Center for Biomedical Ethics at the University of Minnesota, claims: "Mice given daily doses of extract from the squirting cucumber failed to ovulate. And pulegone, a chemical ingredient of pennyroyal (labiate herbaceous plant which yields an aromatic oil), has been shown capable of inducing abortions in animals and human beings . . . [and] women in such disparate places as rural North Carolina and India still chew Queen Anne's lace seeds to reduce their fertility."

50. Galen, vol. 2, p. 19.

51. Ibid., 135.

52. Tertullian, *De Anima,* edited with an introduction and commentary by J. H. Waszink (Amsterdam: J. M. Meulenhoff, 1947) 266–67. See also John Kaye,

The Ecclesiastical History of the Second and Third Centuries: Illustrated from the Writings of Tertullian (Cambridge: J. Smith, 1829).

53. Susan T. Hollis, *The Ancient Egyptian "Tale of Two Brothers": the Oldest Fairy Tale in the World* (Norman: University of Oklahoma Press, 1990) 81.

54. Daniel J. Lasker, "Kabbalah, Halakah, and Modern Medicine: The Case of Artificial Insemination," *Judaism* 8/1 (Fall 1988): 1–11.

55. Ibid., 9.

56. Ibid., 11.

57. Eisenman and Wise, *Dead Sea Scrolls Uncovered,* 245.

58. Onan, who does that, is killed by God (Genesis 38). As far as the Hebrews were concerned, women too had semen, which, of course, was of a lesser quality. Additionally, Jewish law as articulated in the *Shulḥan Aruch* ("A Set [prepared] Table" = summary of Jewish Law), strongly condemns masturbation in order to obtain sperm. Interestingly, the prohibition is based on a prophetic text: "your hands are full of blood" (Isa 1:15), which is interpreted by Rabbi Eleazar as referring to those who commit masturbation with their hands. At the same time, "the use of a mechanical vibrator applied to the anal area to induce erection and ejaculation to procure semen for examination can . . . be approved, if necessary" (Fred Rosner and Rabbi M. D. Tendler, *Practical Medical Halacha* [New York: Feldheim Publishing, 1980] 25).

59. See 4Q477 about the man who "loved his bodily emissions" (ii 8) and the commentary suggesting that the fears expressed here have to do with impurity, which led the sectarians to instruct their adherents to separate from "the majority of the people and go out into the wilderness camps" (Eisenman and Wise, *Dead Sea Scrolls Uncovered,* 272).

60. The Borborites are described by Epiphanius as involved in extreme sensuous rituals which culminate thus: "the woman and the man take the man's emission in their own hands, and stand there looking up towards heaven" (Rudolph, *Gnosis,* 249).

61. Daral-Al-Maaref, *Health and Healing in Ancient Egypt* (Cairo: Zeinab el Dawakhly, 1963) passim.

62. We should note that Herophilus of Chalcedon (300 B.C.E.) was an Alexandrian physician whose book on midwifery was known for centuries. Galen makes numerous references to this source.

63. Ghalioungui, *Magic and Medical Science,* 118.

64. Ibid.

65. Ibid., 119–20.

66. Ibid., 120. More primitive populations who did not have access to these syringes "administered the enema by blowing it in with their mouths . . . the Apache Chiricahuas still pour the fluid into a wooden tube and then inject it by blowing it in with the mouth, and the Liberian aborigines use a gourd in the same way" (ibid., 120).

67. Erman, *Life in Ancient Egypt,* xiv.

68. Allegro based much of his major thesis of *The Sacred Mushroom and the Cross* on that notion.

69. Ibid., 44.

70. Ray Hertz, "The Estrogen Problem: Retrospect and Prospect," in *Estrogen in the Environment, II: Influences on Development,* ed. John A. McLachlau (New York: Elsevier, 1985) 4–5.

71. Ibid., *69*.

72. Estrogen hormonal treatments of poultry and beef ceased a decade ago because of sexual changes (ibid.).

73. See, for example, some of the overt "enhancing" techniques mentioned in Esther, e.g., 1:12.

74. It has already been affirmed by researchers (e.g., Riddle and Estes) that the Egyptians had knowledge of hormones and/or auxins especially as related to pregnancy urine.

75. Eunuchs came into being as part of a fertility ritual where there was self-mutilation (including castration) and flagellation. The "sacrificed" sexual organs of the male participating in the ceremony were offered to the Goddess as a tribute and an assurance of fertility.

76. Rachel asked Leah for her "mandrakes" before she presumably became pregnant with Joseph (Gen. 30:14). The mandrake (mandragora) which was found in Elephantine was used, according to the Ebers papyrus, "in the manufacture of intoxicating and narcotic drinks employed in medicine and magic. Further, it was explicitly associated with the cult of Hathor. See Charles John Samuel Thompson, *The Mystic Mandrake* (London: Rider &Co., 1934) 34–45.

77. "Essenes" could be linguistically related to physicians, from the Aramaic *ʾsʾ*.

CHAPTER SEVEN: THE SIGN

1. Of additional interest is the Gnostic tractate *Zostrianos*, which is ultimately about "the salvation of masculinity" (Robinson, *The Nag Hammadi Library*, 368–93).

2. At the same time, one can point to some Dead Sea Scrolls fragments that deal with activities of a magical/exorcism type that may have been used in their ritual of "new conception and birth." See, as one striking example, 4Q560, which the translators titled "An Amulet Formula against Evil Spirits," where there is an obscure reference to a "new mother" (1 i 2) (Eisenman and Wise, *Dead Sea Scrolls Uncovered,* 266).

3. The forty years may have been calculated by the sectarians to fit the biblical comment about Samson's rule over Israel, which was mentioned in two different places, each one using the number twenty. It also corresponds to the forty years in the wilderness (after the exodus from Egypt) as well as to Ezekiel's adaptation of the same number (forty years) to the Babylonian exile.

4. "The Samuels, Isaiah, and the Psalms contain the great bulk of 'Davidic' literature . . . and those are the books which, along with Deuteronomy, were the most meaningful to the faithful at Qumran (and to the New Testament writers as well)" (Sanders, *Psalms Scroll,* 11).

5. See Sanders's introduction (*Psalms Scroll,* 16). Part of the Jewish mourning ritual includes a "memorial" (from the verb *zkr*) prayer for the dead.

6. *Qumran Cave 4*, ed. Allegro, DJD 5:60-67.

7. This quote is from the combined and compressed Greek translation of two versions of the Psalm as presented in Sanders, Psalm 151B lines 6–7. The Qumran

version is fairly truncated and is reproduced in 28:13–14. In 1 Sam 17:26 and 36, Goliath is referred to as "this uncircumcised Philistine."

8. See P. Kyle McCarter, Jr., *II Samuel* (New York: Doubleday, 1984) 479; he points to some difficulty in fully deciphering the meaning of the psalm but finally settles on the interpretation that points to the "righteousness" of David and the utter destruction of his enemies.

9. Cf. David Rosenberg's translation in *The Book of J,* interpreted by H. Bloom (New York: Grove Weidenfeld, 1990): "Now look: man becomes a creature of flesh."

10. Eisenman and Wise, *Dead Sea Scrolls Uncovered,* 207–9.

11. Even though we know very little of women's initiation ceremonies, we can assume from the record that we do have that they involved a short retreat from the community at large. In that retreat, women who started their menstrual cycles were possibly "taught" by older women.

12. By comparison, churching (the ceremony ending the separation of the "polluted" woman who just gave birth) has been conducted from very early on.

13. The vestal virgins are required to stay in that state because one should "not perceive Vesta/as anything but the living flame/and you see/that no bodies are born of flame/Therefore, she is justly a virgin/who neither sends forth/nor takes seeds . . ." (Ovid, *Fasti* 6.288–92; 43 B.C.E. to ca. 17 C.E.). We should mention also the Mexican Catholic practice of female penitents pinning their hair offering in church at the image of the virgin of Guadalupe.

14. The "redness" of the bones found in the cemetery at Qumran is probably owing to an ingestion of a decoction containing alizarin (the root of the madder plant) (Pessah Bar-Adon, "Another Settlement of the Judean Desert and Sect at En El-Ghuweir," *Bulletin of the American Schools of Oriental Research* 227 [1977]: 1–25; see also Solomon H. Steckoll, "Marginal Notes," *Journal of Medical Science* 7:1219–23).

15. Bar-Adon, "Another Settlement." See also Steckoll, *Journal of Medical Science.* "The burial system of a recess for the body at the bottom of the shaft together with an 'air pocket' over the corpse covered by bricks was particularly prevalent in Egypt" (Steckoll, 333). In traditional Judaism, to this very day, small bricks are placed on the graves of the dead.

16. In the Leyden Papyrus, bricks are used often for curing rituals, e.g., "put three bricks round about the vessel, of new bricks, and place seven clean loaves on the bricks that surround the vessel. . . . You make him sit on a new [brick] and you also sit on another brick" (col. 10.13–14). See *The Leyden Papyrus,* ed. Francis L. Griffith and Herbert Thompson (New York: Dover, 1974).

17. Allegro, *The Sacred Mushroom and the Cross,* 121.

18. See *The World Book Encyclopedia* (1988) s.v. "henna," 187. Henna contains a chemical molecule (lawsone) that by itself is colorless but when exposed to sunlight or to air is converted to a new compound that has the characteristic red color. When imbedded in the vegetable matrix of the henna plant, lawsone is protected from the environment and therefore is colorless. Some people add oily materials to get a more intense color. The henna is also used on manes and hoofs of horses as well as on parts of women's feet, nails, and fingertips. It may also be worthwhile to examine a photo of a Mujahedeen warrior who is said to help the Serbs in their "holy war" (*Newsweek,* October 1992). Is it henna? Indeed, only his beautician knows! Also, we have a hair recipe in the Ebers papurys that combines

"Iron Red-lead Onions Alabaster Honey," in *Ancient Egyptian Medicine: The Papyrus Ebers,* trans. Cyril P. Biyan (New York: Appleton, 1931) 156.

19. See 4QMessAr, which could be read as related to the birth either of the Teacher or of Noah.

20. Charlesworth believes that the Teacher's name might have been Zadok. See Charlesworth, *Jesus and the Dead Sea Scrolls,* 140. While we by and large agree with this speculation, we believe that "Zadok" at this point in history already signified a priestly title.

21. See Jacob Milgrom, "The Paradox of the Red Cow (Num. XIX)," *Vetus Testamentum* 31 (1981): 62–72. Two mishnaic tractates (*Parah* and *Ohalot*) are also devoted to the laws of the "red heifer." J. Bowman ("Did the Qumran Sect Burn the Red Heifer?" *Revue de Qumran* 1 [1958]: 73–84) is more directly related to our topic. John Gray in his commentary on Exod. 32:20 (*The New Interpreter's Bible* [New York: Abingdon, 1989] 64) suggests that "the story of the people drinking water mixed with the ashes of the golden calf may provide a clue and indicate that the Hebrews had taken over some primitive rite connected with a cow-goddess. The redness of the cow may be required in order to match the color of the earth beneath which the dead dwelt; or it may be symbolic of the color of blood . . . life" (p. 64). R. de Vaux maintains that "this rite certainly originated in pagan practices, and it must have been originally a magic rite: many peoples regard red as a protective colour to avert evil and to put demons to flight, and the ashes of animals are often used for lustrations, as running water is used to take away defilement" (*Ancient Israel* [New York: McGraw-Hill, 1965] 2:461). As for the red heifer ceremony that might have taken place at Qumran, it has already been reported by S. H. Steckoll that "one of the unique discoveries at Qumran consisted of burnt or partially burnt animal bones which were buried inside earthen-ware jars" ("The Qumran Sect in Relation to the Temple of Leontopolis," *Revue de Qumran* 21/6 [Feb. 1967]: 55). In another essay he goes on to argue that this particular custom, which is not fully known in Judaism, must have been imported from Leontopolis, where bones of this sort were routinely buried in these jars. Steckoll speculates that although the initial settlement at Qumran might have been of priests from the Temple in Jerusalem, at a later date some prominent priests from Leontopolis may have joined them and brought some of their own practices with them ("Marginal Notes on the Qumran Excavations," *Revue de Qumran* 25/7 [Dec. 1969]: 36). We suggest that these "special" buried bones might have been the remains of the red heifer. We wonder also if there was an actual sacrificial ceremony related to Hathor and Horus as the calf that was offered on the altar of some ritual symbolizing a major mythical confrontation between the forces of good and bad.

22. This pseudepigraphic text dates to the first century and has been fairly popular; see the discussion of its history and impact in Charlesworth, *Old Testament Pseudepigrapha,* 1:487–90.

23. *Apocryphon of Ezekiel,* frag. 3 (Charlesworth, *Old Testament Pseudepigrapha,* 1:494).

24. Edgar Hennecke and Wilhelm Schneemelcher, eds. and trans., *New Testament Apocrypha* (Philadelphia: Westminster Press, 1963) 2:644–63. The *Ascension of Isaiah* is dated to the first century.

25. The association of beards as well as heads in the Nazirite, fundamentalist, zealot tradition is significant because it distinguished them from foreigners, who

were clean-shaven. Even to this day, long hair and beards are associated with various fundamentalist sects in the salvation religions.

26. David is described in the Bible as being "ruddy (*ʾadmônî*)-looking with beautiful eyes" (1 Sam 16:12).

27. They would also add to the external "beauty" of the community; that part of a person's attributes has been traditionally associated with God's grace and inspiration. Thus, Saul's (as well as David's) good looks are not just casual reports about their appearances but about their closeness to God.

28. Charlesworth, *Odes of Solomon,* 8.13–18.

29. The Gnostics, for example, used anointment with oil as an initiation into purity which was more significant than baptism. The anointing was usually done close to the baptismal event. Additionally, the Gnostics believed that anointing oil expelled demons and protected against them; it also "cured and dispelled the 'sickness' of the soul and the body. Hence exorcism . . . was performed by means of anointing. . . . Often the anointing is taken as a 'sealing' . . . it is a protective act and a declaration of property" (Rudolph, *Gnosis,* 228). Ultimately, the Gnostics' anointment was meant to assure them of redemption, and since it was closely bound with the olive tree, which was presumably the paradisal tree of immortality, it became bound up with the sign of life. In the *Gospel of Philip* we find the statement about "the tree of life in the midst of the paradise and the olive tree from which the oil of anointing comes; through it [came] the resurrection" (2/3/73) (Robinson, *Nag Hammadi Library*). The phenomenon of a life-giving tree can be found in a wall painting from the burial chamber of Pharaoh Tuthmosis III, where the ruler is seen suckled by a breast which protrudes from a sycamore tree. See *Biblical Archaeology Review* (Sept./Oct. 1991): 54. That particular painting and tree might allude to an estrogen-producing willow.

30. An Egyptian remedy for hair is full of the color "red" in its relation to the sun:

O Shining One, Thou who hoverest above!
O Xare! O Disc of the Sun!
O Protector of the Divine Neb-apt!
To be spoken over
iron
red-lead
onions
alabaster
honey (Papyrus Ebers, p.156).

31. Others have already remarked that the sectarians' observance of the Mosaic Law was consistent with the sect's perception of itself as "holier" than others and therefore obligated to fulfill the law strictly and "correctly." For a detailed discussion of Qumran's comprehension and observances of the Sabbath, see Schiffman, *Law, Custom and Messianism in the Dead Sea Sect,* 90–135.

Bibliography

Abercrombie, Thomas J. "Arab's Frankincense Trail." *National Geographic* (Oct. 1985): 484–87.

Aldred, Cyril. *Akhenaten, Pharaoh of Egypt: A New Study*. New York: McGraw-Hill, 1968.

Allegro, John M. *The Dead Sea Scrolls: A Reappraisal*. New York: Penguin, 1990.

———. *The Dead Sea Scrolls and The Christian Myth*. Newton Abbot: Westridge, 1979.

———.*The Sacred Mushroom and the Cross*. New York: Doubleday, 1970.

Allison, D. C. "The Silence of Angels: Reflections on the Songs of the Sabbath Sacrifice." *Revue de Qumran* 49-52 (Oct. 1988).

Aries, Philip, and George Duby, eds. *A History of Private Life from Pagan Rome to Byzantium*. Cambridge, Mass.: Belknap Press of Harvard University, 1987.

Augustine. *The City of God*. Translated by M. Dods, J. J. Smith, and G. Wilson. Edinburgh, 1872.

Baer, Richard A., Jr., *Philo's Use of the Categories Male and Female*. Leiden: Brill, 1970.

Baillet, M. *Discoveries in the Judaean Desert VII, Qumran Grotte 4*. Oxford: Clarendon Press, 1982.

Bal, Mieke. *Lethal Love: Feminist Literary Readings of Biblical Love Stories*. Bloomington, Ind.: Indiana University Press, 1987.

Banner, Lois W. *In Full Flower: Aging Women, Power, and Sexuality*. New York: Alfred A. Knopf, 1992.

Baring, Anne, and Jules Cashford. *The Myth of the Goddess: Evolution of an Image*. London: Penguin, 1991.

Barrera, Julio T., and Luis V. Montaner, eds. *The Madrid Qumran Congress: Proceedings of the International Congress on the Dead Sea Scrolls Madrid 18–21 March, 1991*. Leiden: Brill, 1992.

Baumgarten, Joseph M. "The Qumran Sabbath Shirot and Rabbinic Merkabah Traditions." *Revue De Qumran* 49-52 (Oct., 1988): 208–13.

Ben Sasson, Haim H., ed. *History of the Jewish People* (in Hebrew). Volume 1. Tel Aviv: Dvir, 1969.

Berenfelt, Gunar. *A Study on the Winged Angel.* Stockholm: Almqvist & Wiksell, 1968.

Berkovitz, Eliezer. *Jewish Women in Time and Torah.* Hoboken: Ktav, 1990.

Black, Matthew. *The Book of Enoch or I Enoch.* Leiden: Brill, 1985.

———. *The Scrolls and Christian Origins: Studies in the Jewish Background of the New Testament.* New York: Scribner, 1961.

Bleeker, Claas Jouco. *Hathor and Thoth: Two Key Figures of the Ancient Egyptian Religion.* Leiden: Brill, 1973.

Bright, John. *Jeremiah.* Anchor Bible. New York: Doubleday, 1979.

———. "The Qumran-Essene Restraints on Marriage." In *Archaeology and History of the Dead Sea Scrolls.* Edited by Lawrence H. Schiffman. Sheffield: JSOT Press, 1989.

Boling Robert G., and G. Ernest Wright. *Joshua.* Anchor Bible. New York: Doubleday, 1982.

Brown, C. A. *No Longer Be Silent: First Century Jewish Portraits of Biblical Women.* Louisville: John Knox Press, 1992.

Budge, E. A. Wallis. *The Egyptian Book of the Dead.* New York: Dover, 1967.

———. *The Gods of the Egyptians.* 2 volumes. New York: Dover, 1969.

Burkert, Walter. *Structure and History in Greek Mythology and Ritual.* Berkeley: University of California Press, 1979.

Charlesworth, James H., ed. *The Old Testament Pseudepigrapha and the New Testament.* Cambridge: Cambridge University Press, 1985.

———. *The Old Testament Pseudepigrapha.* New York: Doubleday, 1983.

———. *Jesus and the Dead Sea Scrolls.* New York: Doubleday, 1992.

———, trans. and ed. *The History of the Rechabites, Vol I: The Greek Recension.* Atlanta: Scholars Press, 1982.

Clark, Robert Thomas Rundle. *Myth and Symbol in Ancient Egypt.* London: Thames & Hudson, 1978.

Cogan, Mordechai, and Hayim Tadmor. *II Kings.* New York: Doubleday, 1988.

Cohen, Shaye J. D. *Josephus in Galilee and Rome.* Leiden: Brill, 1979.

Collins, John J. *The Apocalyptic Imagination.* New York: Crossroad, 1984.

Daniélou, Jean. *The Dead Sea Scrolls and Primitive Christianity.* Baltimore: Helicon Press, 1958.

Daral-Al-Maaref. *Health and Healing in Ancient Egypt.* Cairo: Zeinab el Dawakhly, 1963.

De Jonge, Marinus. *Outside the Old Testament.* Cambridge: Cambridge University Press, 1985.

Dexter, Miriam R. *Whence the Goddesses: A Source Book.* New York: Macmillan, 1990.

Di Lella, Alexander A. *The Hebrew Text of Sirach.* The Hague: Mouton, 1966.

———, and Patrick W. Skehan. *The Wisdom of Ben Sira.* Anchor Bible. New York: Doubleday, 1987.

Dothan, Trude. "Lost Outpost of the Egyptian Empire. *National Geographic.* Dec.1982, pp. 739-68.

Drower, Ethel S. *The Secret Adam: A Study of Nasoraean Gnosis.* Oxford, 1960.

Eisenman, Robert. *James the Just in the Habakkuk Pesher.* Leiden: Brill, 1986.

———. *Maccabees, Zadokites, Christians and Qumran.* Leiden: Brill, 1983.

————, and Michael Wise. *The Dead Sea Scrolls Uncovered.* Rockport, Mass.: Element Books, 1992.

Eisler, Riane T. *The Chalice and the Blade.* San Francisco: Harper & Row, 1987.

Erman, Adolf. *Life in Ancient Egypt.* Translated by H. M. Tirard. New York: Dover, 1971.

Ermin, Kenan T. "Ancient Aphrodisias Lives Through Its Art." *National Geographic* (Oct. 1981): 529.

Estes, J. Worth. *The Medical Skills of Ancient Egypt.* Canton, Mass.: Science History Publications, 1989.

Eusebius. *Ecclesiastical History.* Translated by Christian F. Cruse. Grand Rapids: Baker Book House, 1987.

Faulkner, Raymond Oliver. *The Ancient Egyptian Pyramid Texts.* Oxford: Clarendon, 1969.

Feingold, Wilfred J. *Artificial Insemination.* Springfield, Ill.: Charles C. Thomas, 1964.

Feldman, Louis H. "Josephus' version of Samson." *Journal for the Study of Judaism* 19 (1988): 171–214.

Fishbane, Michael. "The Well of Living Water: A Biblical Motif and its Ancient Transformations." In *"Sha'arei Talmon": Studies in the Bible, Qumran, and the Ancient Near East Presented to Shemaryahu Talmon.* Edited by Michael Fishbane and Emanuel Tov. Winona Lake, Ind.: Eisenbrauns, 1992.

Flusser, David. *The Spiritual History of the Dead Sea Sect.* Tel Aviv: MOD Books, 1989.

Frankfort, Henri. *Kingship and the Gods.* Chicago: University of Chicago Press, 1948.

Freedman, David N. *The Unity of the Hebrew Bible.* Ann Arbor: University of Michigan Press, 1991.

Frohlich, I. "Pesher, Apocalyptical Literature and Qumran." In *The Madrid Qumran Congress: Proceedings of the International Congress on the Dead Sea Scrolls, Madrid 18–21 March, 1991.* Volume 1. Edited by Julio T. Barrera and Luis V. Montaner. Leiden: Brill, 1992.

Galen. *On the Natural Faculties.* Loeb Classical Library. II, 1991.

García Martínez, F. *Qumran and Apocalyptic.* Leiden: Brill, 1992.

Gaster, Theodor H. *The Dead Sea Scriptures.* New York: Anchor, 1976.

Ghalioungui, Paul. *Magic and Medical Science in Ancient Egypt.* London: Hodder & Stoughton, 1963.

Gimbutas, Marija. *The Language of the Goddess.* San Francisco: Harper & Row, 1989.

Ginzberg, Louis. *The Legends of the Jews.* Translated by Henrietta Szold. 5 vols. Philadelphia: Jewish Publication Society, 1969.

Ginzburg, Carlo. *Ecstasies: Deciphering the Witches' Sabbath.* Translated by Raymond Rosenthal. New York: Penguin, 1991.

Giveon, Raphael. *The Impact of Egypt on Canaan-Palestine.* Freiburg: Biblical Institute University of Freiburg Schweiz, 1978.

Godwin, Joscelyn. *Mystery Religions in the Ancient World.* London: Thames & Hudson, 1981.

Godwin, Malcolm. *Angels, An Endangered Species.* New York: Simon & Schuster, 1990.

Golb, Norman. *Who Wrote the Dead Sea Scrolls? The Search for the Secret of Qumran.* New York: Simon & Schuster, 1995.

Gottwald, Norman K. "The Israelite Settlement as a Social Revolutionary Movement." In *Biblical Archaeology Today.* Jerusalem: Israel Exploration Society, 1985.

Graves, Robert, and Raphael Patai. *Hebrew Myths: The Book of Genesis.* New York: McGraw-Hill, 1966.

Griffith, Francis L. *The Leyden Papyrus: An Egyptian Magical Book.* New York: Dover, 1974.

Griffiths, J. Gwyn. *The Conflict of Horus and Seth.* Liverpool: Liverpool University Press, 1960.

Habermann, Avraham Meir (ed.), *Megilloth Midbar Yehuda: The Scrolls From the Judean Desert.* Hebrew. Tel Aviv: Machbaroth Lesifruth, 1959.

Harrington, Daniel J. *The Hebrew Fragments of Pseudo-Philo.* SBL Texts and Translations 3, Pseudepigrapha Series 3. Missoula, Mont.: Scholars Press, 1974.

Hengel, Martin. *The Zealots.* Translated by David Smith. Edinburgh: T. & T. Clark, 1989.

Hertz, Ray. "The Estrogen Problem: Retrospect and Prospect." In *Estrogen in the Environment, II: Influences on Development.* Edited by John A. McLachlau. New York: Elsevier, 1985.

Hollander, Harm W. *Joseph As An Ethical Model in the Testaments of the Twelve Patriarchs.* Leiden: Brill, 1981.

Hollis, Susan T. *The Ancient Egyptian "Tale of Two Brothers": The Oldest Fairy Tale in the World.* Norman: University of Oklahoma Press, 1990.

The Interpreter's Bible. New York: Abingdon, 1956.

Jeyes, Ulla. "The Naditu Women of Sippar." In *Images of Women in Antiquity.* Edited by Averil Cameron and Amelie Kuhrt, 260–72. Detroit: Wayne University Press, 1985.

Juel, Donald. *Messianic Exegesis: Christological Interpretation of the Old Testament in Early Christianity.* Philadelphia: Fortress, 1988.

Justin Martyr. *The First Apology, the Second Apology, Dialogue with Trypho, Discourse to the Greeks, the Monarchy or the Rule of God.* Edited by Thomas B. Falls. Washington, D.C.: Catholic University of America Press, 1965.

Kaye, John, Bp. of Lincoln. *The Ecclesiastical History of the Second and Third Centuries: Illustrated from the Writings of Tertullian.* Cambridge: J. Smith, 1829.

Kessler, David. *Falashas: The Forgotten Jews of Ethiopia.* (New York: Schocken, 1982.

Kloner, Amos. "Hideout-Complexes From the Period of Bar-Kokhva in the Judean Plain." In *The Bar-Kokhva Revolt: A New Approach* (in Hebrew). Edited by Aharon Oppenheimer and Uriel Rappaport. Jerusalem: Yad Yitshak Ben-Tsevi, 1984.

Kloner, Amos, and Yigal Tepper. *The Hiding Complexes in the Judean Shephelah* (in Hebrew). Tel Aviv: Hakibbutz Hameuchad, Israel Exploration Society, 1987.

Kobelski, Paul J. *Melchi-sedek and Melchi-rešaᶜ.* Washington, DC: Catholic Biblical Association of America, 1981.

Kramer, Samuel Noah. *The Sacred Marriage Rite*. Bloomington: University of Indiana Press, 1969.

Lamy, Lucie. *Egyptian Mysteries: New Light on Ancient Knowledge*. London: Thames & Hudson, 1989.

Lasker, Daniel J. "Kabbalah, Halakah, and Modern Medicine: The Case of Artificial Insemination." *Judaism* 8 (Fall 1988): 1–11.

Licht, Jacob. *The Hodayot Scroll from the Scrolls of the Judean Desert* (in Hebrew). Jerusalem: Bialik, 1957.

Lieberman, Saul, ed. *Louis Ginzberg Jubilee Volume*. New York: American Academy for Jewish Research,1945.

McKenzie, John L. *Second Isaiah*. Anchor Bible. New York: Doubleday, 1967.

Mazar, Amichai. *Archaeology of the Land of the Bible 10,000–586 B.C.E.* New York: Doubleday, 1990.

Mead, George Robert Stow. *Thrice Greatest Hermes*. London: The Theosophical Publication Society, 1906.

Mendenhall, George E. *The Tenth Generation*. Baltimore: Johns Hopkins University Press, 1973.

Meyendorff, John. *Marriage: An Orthodox Perspective*. New York: St. Vladimir's Seminary Press, 1975.

Meyers Carol L., and Eric M. Meyers. *Haggai, Zechariah 1-8*. Anchor Bible. New York: Doubleday, 1987.

Milik, J. T. "Les modèles araméens du livre d'Esther dans la Grotte 4 de Qumran." *Revue de Qumran* (June 1992): 321–99.

Moore, Carey A. *Daniel, Esther, and Jeremiah: The Additions*. Anchor Bible. New York: Doubleday, 1981.

———. *Esther*. Anchor Bible. New York: Doubleday, 1981.

Murphy, Ronald E. "The Dead Sea Scrolls and New Testament Comparisons." *Catholic Biblical Quarterly* 18 (1956): 263–72.

Myers, Jacob M. *Ezra–Nehemia*. Anchor Bible. New York: Doubleday, 1981.

Na'aman, N. "Habiru and Hebrews: The Transfer of a Social Term to the Literary Sphere." *Journal of Near Eastern Studies* 45 (19**): 271–88.

Nakhai, B. A. "What's a Bamah? How Sacred Space Functioned in Ancient Israel." *Biblical Archaeology Review* 20 (May/June 1994): 18–29.

Nanda, Serena. *Neither Man Nor Woman: The Hijras of India*. Belmont, Calif.: Wadsworth Publishing Company, 1990.

Newsom, Carol. "Merkabah Exegesis in the Qumran Sabbath Shirot." *Journal of Jewish Studies* 38 (1987): 11–30.

———. *Songs of the Sabbath Sacrifice: A Critical Edition*. Atlanta: Scholars Press, 1985.

Oesterreicher, John M. "The Community of Qumran." *The Bridge* 2 (1956).

Olyan, Saul. *Asherah and the Cult of Yahweh in Israel*. Society of Biblical Literature Monograph Series 34. Atlanta: Scholars Press, 1988.

Pagels, Elaine. *Adam, Eve, and the Serpent*. New York: Vintage, 1989.

———. *The Gnostic Gospels*. New York: Random House, 1979.

Patai, Raphael. *The Hebrew Goddess*. New York: Ktav, 1967.

Pies, Cheri. *Considering Parenthood*. San Francisco: Spinsters/Aunt Lute, 1988.

Pope, Marvin H. *Song of Songs*. Anchor Bible. New York: Doubleday, 1977.

Porten, Bezalel. *Archives from Elephantine*. Los Angeles: University of California Press, 1968.

Posener, Georges. *Dictionary of Egyptian Civilization*. New York: Tudor, 1959.

Preuss, Julius. *Julius Preuss' Biblical and Talmudic Medicine*. Translated and edited by Fred Rosner. New York: Sanhedrin Press, 1978.

Qimron, Elisha, and John Strugnell. *Qumran Cave 4 V Miqsat Maʿaśe HaTorah*. Oxford: Clarendon, 1994.

Ranke-Heinemann, Uta. *Eunuchs for the Kingdom of Heaven*. New York: Doubleday, 1988.

Redford, Donald B. "The Monotheism of the Heretic Pharaoh Precursor of Mosaic Monotheism or Egyptian Anomaly?" *Biblical Archaeology Review* 13 (May/June 1987).

Riddle, John M. *Contraception and Abortion from the Ancient World to the Renaissance*. Cambridge, Mass.: Harvard University Press, 1992.

Robinson, James M. *The Nag Hammadi Library*. San Francisco: Harper & Row, 1977.

Rordorf, Willy, et al., eds. *The Eucharist of the Early Christians*. New York: Pueblo, 1978.

Rosner, Fred, and Rabbi Tendler, M.D. *Practical Medical Halacha*. New York: Feldheim Publishing, 1980.

Rost, Leonard. *Judaism Outside the Hebrew Canon*. Translated by David E. Green. Nashville: Abingdon, 1976.

Rudolph, Kurt. *Gnosis: The Nature and History of Gnosticism*. Translated by R. M. Wilson. San Francisco: Harper, 1987.

Schiffman, Lawrence H. *Law, Custom and Messianism in the Dead Sea Sect*. Jerusalem: Zalman Shazar Center, 1993.

Scholem, Gerschom. *Jewish Gnosticism, Merkabah Mysticism, and Talmudic Tradition*. New York: Jewish Theological Seminary, 1965.

Schuller, Eileen M. "4Q372 1: A Text About Joseph." *Revue de Qumran* 55 (Jan. 1990): 349–76.

Schürer, Emil. *The History of the Jewish People in the Age of Jesus Christ*. 2 vols. Edinburgh: Clark, 1979.

Shanks, Hershel. "The Qumran Settlement." *Biblical Archaeology Review* 19 (May/June 1993): 62–65.

Sheres, Ita. *Dinah's Rebellion: A Biblical Parable for Our Time*. New York: Crossroad, 1990.

Sievers, Joseph. "The Role of Women in the Hasmonean Dynasty." In *Josephus, the Bible, and History*. Edited by Louis H. Feldman and Gohei Hata. Detroit: Wayne State University Press, 1989.

Springborg, Patricia. *Royal Persons: Patriarchal Monarchy and the Feminine Principle*. London: Unwin Hyman, 1990.

Steckoll, Solomon H. "Preliminary Excavation Report in the Qumran Cemetery." *Revue de Qumran*, 23 (Feb. 1968): 323–44.

Stone, Michael E., ed. *Jewish Writings of the Second Temple Period*. Philadelphia: Fortress Press, 1984.

Talmon, Shemaryahu. *The World of Qumran from Within.* Jerusalem: Magnes Press, 1989.

Taylor, J. G. "Was Yahweh Worshiped As the Sun?" *Biblical Archaeology Review* 20 (May/June 1994): 52–60.

Tertullian. *De Anima.* Edited with introduction and commentary by J. H. Waszink. Amsterdam: J. M. Meulenhoff, 1947.

Teubal, Savina J. *Hagar the Egyptian: The Lost Tradition of the Matriarchs.* San Francisco: Harper & Row, 1990.

———. *Sarah the Priestess: The First Matriarch of Genesis.* Athens, Oh.: Swallow Press, 1984.

Thackeray, H. St. J., trans. *Josephus.* Loeb Classical Library. Cambridge, Mass.: Harvard University Press, 1976.

Thiering, Barbara E. *The Qumran Origins of the Christian Church.* Australian and New Zealand Studies in Theology and Religion 1. Sydney: Sydney Theological Explorations, 1979.

Trenchard, Warren C. *Ben Sira's View of Women: A Literary Analysis.* Chico, Calif.: Scholars Press, 1982.

Ulansey, David. *The Origins of the Mithraic Mysteries.* New York: Oxford University Press, 1989.

Vanderlip, Vera F. *The Four Greek Hymns of Isidorus and the Cult of Isis.* In *American Studies in Papyrology.* Vol. 12. Toronto: A. M. Hakkert, 1972.

Vermes, Geza. *The Dead Sea Scrolls in English.* New York: Penguin, 1987.

Vernon, Arthur. *The History and Romance of the Horse.* New York: Dover, 1946.

Wacholder, Ben Zion. *The Dawn of Qumran: The Sectarian Torah and the Teacher of Righteousness.* Cincinnati: Hebrew Union College, 1983.

Watterson, Barbara. *The Gods of Ancient Egypt.* London: B. T. Batsford Ltd, 1984.

Whiston William, trans. *The Works of Flavius Josephus.* Philadelphia: J. B. Lippincott, 1864.

Wilding, Dietrich. *Egyptian Saints: Deification in Pharaonic Egypt.* New York: New York University Press, 1977.

Winston, David. *The Wisdom of Solomon.* Anchor Bible. New York: Doubleday, 1979.

Wise, Michael. *Thunder in Gemini: And Other Essays on the History, Language and Literature of Second Temple Palestine.* Sheffield: JSOT Press, 1994.

Wolkstein, Diane, and Samuel N. Kramer. *Inanna Queen of Heaven and Earth: Her Stories and Hymns from Sumer.* San Francisco: Harper & Row, 1983.

Yadin, Yigael. *Megilat Hamikdash* (The Temple Scroll; in Hebrew). Jerusalem: Israel Exploration Society, 1977.

———. *The Scroll of the War of the Sons of Light against the Sons of Darkness.* Translated by Batya and Chaim Rabin. London: Oxford University Press, 1962.

———. *The Temple Scroll: The Hidden Law of the Dead Sea Sect.* London: Weidenfeld & Nicolson, 1985.

Index